Filipino
(Tagalog)
PHRASEBOOK & DICTIONARY

Acknowledgments
Publisher Mina Patria
Product Editor Kate Mathews
Series Designer James Hardy
Language Writer Aurora Santos Quinn
Cover Image Researcher Naomi Parker

Thanks
Elizabeth Jones, Chris Love, Wayne Murphy, Branislava Vladisavljevic

Published by Lonely Planet Publications Pty Ltd
ABN 36 005 607 983

5th Edition – August 2014
ISBN 978 1 74321 194 6
Text © Lonely Planet 2014
Cover Image El Nido, Palawan, Christian Aslund/Getty ©
Printed in China   10 9 8 7 6 5 4 3 2 1

Contact lonelyplanet.com/contact

MIX
Paper from
responsible sources
FSC™ C021741

ACKNOWLEDGMENTS

Aurora Santos Quinn is a professional Filipino language translator and maintains her links with the language and culture of the Philippines by making regular visits to the country. She's also a teacher by profession and taught in the Philippines for a short while before moving to Papua New Guinea where she practised in the education industry for ten years. In 1979 she moved to Australia with her husband and three children and they have called Australia home ever since.

Aurora wishes to thank her husband Kevin and her children for their support, her sisters Lina Streimann and Bebs Calderon, her brother Joel Santos, as well as other Filipino friends in Australia for their invaluable advice and assistance.

For the feature on other languages of the Philippines, thanks go to: Nida Mistica and Jay Rose Mistica for the Kapampangan translations; Oscar Nagrampa for Bikolano; Flor Gerona and Pablo Gastar for Ilonggo and numerous others who helped with Cebuano, Ilokano and Pangasinan.

make the most of this phrasebook ...

Anyone can speak another language! It's all about confidence. Don't worry if you can't remember your school language lessons or if you've never learnt a language before. Even if you learn the very basics (on the inside covers of this book), your travel experience will be the better for it. You have nothing to lose and everything to gain when the locals hear you making an effort.

finding things in this book

For easy navigation, this book is in sections. The Basics chapters are the ones you'll thumb through time and again. The Practical section covers basic travel situations like catching transport and finding a bed. The Social section gives you conversational phrases, pick-up lines, the ability to express opinions – so you can get to know people. Food has a section all of its own: gourmets and vegetarians are covered and local dishes feature. Safe Travel equips you with health and police phrases, just in case. Sustainable Travel, finally, completes this book. Remember the colours of each section and you'll find everything easily; or use the comprehensive Index. Otherwise, check the two-way traveller's Dictionary for the word you need.

being understood

Throughout this book you'll see coloured phrases on each page. They're phonetic guides to help you pronounce the language. You don't even need to look at the language itself, but you'll get used to the way we've represented particular sounds. The pronunciation chapter in Basics will explain more, but you can feel confident that if you read the coloured phrase slowly, you'll be understood.

communication tips

Body language, ways of doing things, sense of humour – all have a role to play in every culture. 'Local talk' boxes show you common ways of saying things, or everyday language to drop into conversation. 'Listen for ...' boxes supply the phrases you may hear. They start with the language (so local people can point out what they want to say to you) and then lead in to the pronunciation guide and the English translation.

introduction 8

map 8	introduction 9

basics 11

pronunciation 11	prepositions 28
vowel sounds 11	requests 30
consonant sounds 12	tense & aspect 31
syllables &	there is/are 32
word stress 13	verbs 32
regional variations 13	word order 33
reading & writing 14	glossary 34
a–z phrasebuilder 15	**language difficulties** 35
contents 15	**numbers & amounts** 37
adjectives 17	cardinal numbers 37
adverbs 17	ordinal numbers 39
be 18	fractions 39
demonstratives 18	useful amounts 40
focus 19	**time & dates** 41
have 21	telling the time 41
location 22	the calendar 42
negation 22	present 43
nouns 23	past 43
particles 23	future 44
personal pronouns 25	during the day 44
possession 26	**money** 45

practical 47

transport 47	**border crossing** 61
getting around 47	border crossing 61
tickets 48	at customs 62
luggage 50	**directions** 63
plane 51	**accommodation** 65
bus 51	finding accommodation 65
train 53	booking ahead &
boat 53	checking in 66
taxi & tricycle 54	requests & queries 68
car & motorbike 56	complaints 70
bicycle 59	checking out 71
local transport 60	camping 72
	renting 73
	staying with locals 74

shopping	**75**
looking for	75
making a purchase	75
bargaining	77
clothes	78
repairs	78
hairdressing	79
books & reading	80
music	81
electronic goods	81
photography	82
communications	**83**
post office	83
phone	84
mobile/cell phone	87

the internet	87
banking	**89**
sightseeing	**91**
getting in	93
tours	93
business	**95**
doing business	95
looking for a job	97
senior & disabled travellers	**99**
children	**101**
travelling with children	101
talking with children	103
talking about children	104

social 105

meeting people	**105**
basics	105
greetings & goodbyes	106
addressing people	108
making conversation	109
nationalities	111
age	112
occupations & studies	112
family	114
farewells	116
regional languages	117
interests	**121**
common interests	121
music	122
cinema & theatre	123
feelings & opinions	**125**
feelings	125
opinions	126
political & social issues	127
the environment	129
going out	**131**
where to go	131
invitations	132
responding to invitations	133
arranging to meet	133
drugs	134
romance	**135**

asking someone out	135
pick-up lines	136
rejections	137
getting closer	137
sex	138
love	139
problems	140
leaving	140
beliefs & cultural differences	**141**
religion	141
cultural differences	142
art	**143**
sport	**145**
sporting interests	145
going to a game	146
playing sport	146
basketball	148
cockfighting	148
diving	149
horse racing	151
horse riding	152
outdoors	**153**
hiking	153
beach	155
weather	156
flora & fauna	157

food 159

eating out **159**
  basics 159
  finding a place to eat 159
  at the restaurant 161
  at the table 163
  talking food 164
  methods of
    preparation 165
  nonalcoholic drinks 167
  alcoholic drinks 168
  in the bar 169
  drinking up 170
self-catering **171**
  buying food 171
  cooking utensils 172
vegetarian &
special meals **173**
  ordering food 173
  special diets & allergies 174
menu decoder **175**

safe travel 183

essentials **183**
  emergencies 183
  police 184
health **187**
  doctor 187
  symptoms & conditions 190
  women's health 193
  parts of the body 194
  alternative treatments 195
  allergies 195
  pharmacist 196
  dentist 197

sustainable travel 199

dictionaries 203

english–filipino
  dictionary **203**

filipino–english
  dictionary **231**

index 255

filipino

Luzon Strait

Babuyan Islands

Laoag

PACIFIC
OCEAN

LUZON

Philippine
Sea

San Carlos
Tarlac   Cabanatuan
Angeles   San Fernando
Manila   Quezon City
San Pablo   San Pedro
Batangas   Lucena

Baguio

Catanduanes

South
China
Sea

MINDORO   Sibuyan
Sea

San Jose

Legaspi

MASBATE   SAMAR

PHILIPPINES

PANAY   Tacloban

Iloilo   Bacolod   CEBU   LEYTE

Cebu

Puerto Princesa   BOHOL

PALAWAN   NEGROS   Bohol
Sea   Butuan

Cagayan
Iligan   de Oro

Sulu Sea

MINDANAO

Zamboanga   Moro Gulf   Davao

Basilan

General
Jolo   Santos

Malaysia   Celebes
SABAH   Sea

Tawitawi

- first language
- second language

China   Japan

South
East
Asia   **Philippines**

Malaysia   Indonesia

For more details, see the **introduction**.

So which language exactly is this a phrasebook for – is it Filipino, Pilipino or Tagalog? And what's the difference anyway? This multitude of names causes confusion for Filipinos and foreigners alike, but in the end the naming reflects the political history of one language, the lingua franca of the 7000-island archipelago of the Philippines.

Filipino was first incarnated as 'Tagalog', a local language still spoken in the Manila region. Once Manila was selected as the national capital in 1595, Tagalog became the country's most widely spoken language. Chosen the official language in 1939, it was renamed 'Pilipino' 20 years later to reflect its status as a truly national language – this acknowledged the many elements incorporated from other Philippine languages. The final evolution of the language's name was in 1987, when its initial 'p' was symbolically replaced by an 'f' to make it 'Filipino'. While the islands' local languages have no native 'f' sound, it was introduced into the language through centuries of contact with other languages, particularly Spanish and English, thus acknowledging the diverse background of the modern language.

In a republic with over 165 living languages, Filipino is the archipelago's

at a glance ...

language names:
Filipino, Pilipino, Tagalog

names in language:
Filipino pee·lee·*pee*·no
Pilipino pee·lee·*pee*·no
Tagálog ta·*ga*·log

language family:
Malayo-Polynesian

approximate number of speakers: 45 million

close relatives:
Bikol languages spoken in southeastern Luzon, North Bisayan languages

donations to English:
boondocks (from *bundók* 'mountain')

introduction

9

unifying force. Although not the mother tongue of every Philippine citizen, it's spoken as a second language throughout the country, and is an official language used for university instruction and in most legal, business and governmental transactions (the other official language is English). Continuing migration to other parts of Asia, the Middle East and the USA has made Filipino a language spoken by 45 million people on at least three continents. For more information on major regional languages in the Philippines, see the map and basic phrases in the special section on page 117.

Filipino belongs to the Malayo-Polynesian family of languages, which spreads from Madagascar off the coast of Africa to Tonga in the South Pacific. From these foundations, the Philippine lingua franca has been enriched with vocabulary from many sources, including the islands' other native languages. Seafaring merchants offered words of Chinese and Arabic origin during their many years of trade in the Pacific, and the 300 years of Spaniard rule left a wealth of Spanish vocabulary. Western travellers may find Filipino grammar a challenge, but they'll also find familiar vocabulary in the linguistic tapestry – English influences have been readily assimilated in recent times, so much so that the term 'Taglish' has been used to name today's Filipino.

This book will ensure that you have the words and phrases you need to speak like a true Filipino or Filipina. It's also packed with fun, social phrases to help deepen your travel experience by relating with people in their own language. Local knowledge, new relationships and a sense of satisfaction are on the tip of your tongue, so don't just stand there, say something!

abbreviations

a	adjective	m	masculine
adv	adverb	n	noun
excl	exclusive	pl	plural
f	feminine	pol	polite
incl	inclusive	prep	preposition
inf	informal	sg	singular
lit	literal translation	v	verb

Filipino is relatively easy to pronounce as most sounds are familiar to English speakers. In addition, the relationship between Filipino sounds and its spelling is straightforward and consistent. For example, when, you see an 'e' it's always pronounced the same way.

vowel sounds

Vowels are always pronounced separately even when they're written in sequence. For example, *panauhin* (visitor) is pronounced pa·na·*oo*·heen.

symbol	english equivalent	filipino example	transliteration
a	cart	*katók*	ka·*tok*
ai	aisle	*babay*	ba·*bai*
ay	say	*displéy*	dees·*pley*
e	bed	*kotse*	*kot*·se
ee	bee	*ikáw*	ee·*kow*
ew	like ee with rounded lips	*balíw*	ba·*lew*
o	hot	*súsunód*	soo·soo·*nod*
oh	go	*pos kowd*	pos kohd
oo	moon	*hulíng*	hoo·*leeng*
ow	cow	*ikáw*	ee·*kow*
oy	boy	*kahoy*	ka·*hoy*
ooy	tweak (slowly) or Spanish muy	*arúy*	a·*rooy*

consonant sounds

Filipino consonants are easy to pronounce as most are very close to their English counterparts.

symbol	english equivalent	filipino example	transliteration
'	like the 'tt' in the cockney pronunciation of bottle	*bansâ* (accent over the vowel)	ban·*sa'*
b	**b**ig	**b**abae	ba·*ba*·e
d	**d**in	**d**agdág	dag·*dag*
g	**g**o	**g**agamit	ga·ga·*meet*
h	**h**e	**h**alakhák	ha·lak·*lak*
j	**j**ump	di**dy**ital	dee·jee·*tal*
k	**c**at	**k**atók	ka·*tok*
l	**l**oud	**l**álalà	*la*·la·la'
m	**m**an	**m**alamáng	ma·la·*mang*
n	**n**o	**n**agnanasa	nag·na·*na*·sa
ng	si**ng**	anghá**ng**	ang·*hang*
p	**p**ig	**p**alapág	pa·la·*pag*
r	**r**un, but stronger and rolled	ka**r**era	ka·*re*·ra
s	**s**o	**s**úsunód	soo·soo·*nod*
t	**t**in	is**t**átuwa	ee·*sta*·too·wa
ts	ca**ts**	**ts**ards	tsards
w	**w**in	**w**asiwas	wa·*si*·was
y	**y**es	bi**y**ayà	bee·*ya*·ya'

There are only two consonant sounds which may seem unusual to English speakers, even though both occur in English.

The ng combination, which is found in English at the end or in the middle of words such as 'sing' and 'ringing', also appears at the beginning of words in Filipino. You can practise by saying 'sing along' slowly and then eventually do away with the 'si' at the beginning. With a little practice, it should come easily.

The ' symbol represents a sound called a 'glottal stop', which is found in the cockney accent of East London (eg the 'tt' in bottle). If you're not familiar with this accent, think of it as like the pause between the two syllables of 'uh-oh'.

syllables & word stress

Stressed syllables – the ones that have the emphasis – are indicated in our pronunciation guides in italics. Note that long words can have more than one stressed syllable. In general, stressed vowels are slightly longer and higher pitched than unstressed ones. Stress is usually indicated by the use of accents over vowels in written Filipino. Sometimes an accent over a vowel doesn't indicate stress, but a glottal stop (shown in our pronunciation guides by an apostrophe).

Don't worry about these subtleties in pronunciation as you'll be understood if you simply follow the italicised syllable in the pronunciation guides.

regional variations

Like most languages spread over a wide area, Filipino has many dialectical variations. This phrasebook uses the standard form, which is based on the variety spoken in the capital, Manila. If you venture outside the capital you'll find that pronunciation and some vocabulary may differ a little from what's in this book, but never to the extent that you can't understand what's being said or make yourself understood. Simply follow the words and phrases in this book and you'll be able to get your message across!

reading & writing

Generally the relationship between Filipino sounds and their spelling is straightforward and consistent. A couple of exceptions to the generally phonetic spelling are the words *ng* (of), which is pronounced nang, and *mgá* (used to make nouns plural), which is pronounced ma·nga.

In written Filipino the glottal stop sound is represented, not by a letter, but by a circumflex (ˆ), a grave (ˋ) or acute accent (ˊ) over the vowel that's followed by a glottal stop. The circumflex is used when the following word begins with a vowel, otherwise either an acute or grave accent is used, for example the word *hindî* heen·dee' (no) may also be spelled *hindí*.

The Filipino alphabet, known as *abakada* a·ba·ka·da, has 28 letters that represents all the sounds in Filipino as outlined in the vowel and consonant tables. Note that the double-barrelled letters *ch* and *ng* are considered separate letters, so look up words starting with *ng* or *ch* in the **dictionary** and **menu decoder** under these letter combinations and not under *n* or *c*. For example, the word *ngayon* nga·yon (meaning 'now') can be found under *ng* and not *n*.

alphabet						
A a a	*B b* ba	*C c** ka	*Ch ch* tsa	*K k* ka	*D d* da	*E e* e
F f fa	*G g* ga	*H h* ha	*I i* ee	*J j* dya	*L l* la	*M m* ma
N n na	*Ng ng* nang	*O o* o	*P p* pa	*R r* ra	*Rr rr*** ra	*S s* sa
T t ta	*U u* oo	*V v* va	*W w* wa	*X x* ksa	*Y y* ya	*Z z* za

* Sometimes the English 'c' see is used to spell words out.

** When spelling out double letters use *doble do·ble* before the letter.

contents

The list below shows grammatical structures you can use to say what you want. Look under each function – in alphabetical order – for information on how to build your own phrases. For example, to tell the taxi driver where your hotel is, look for **giving directions/orders** and you'll be directed to information on **location**, **requests** etc. A glossary of grammatical terms is included at the end of this chapter.

asking a question

particles	23	questions	29

describing things

adjectives	17	adverbs	17

doing things

focus	19	tense & aspect	31
verbs	32		

expressing time

particles	23	tense & aspect	31

giving directions/orders

location	22	prepositions	28
requests	30		

giving your opinion

adjectives	17	be	18

making a request

particles	23	requests	30

making a statement

be	18	focus	19
have	21	personal pronouns	25
there is/are	32	word order	33

naming things

focus	19	nouns	23

negating

negation	22	there is/are	32

pointing things out

demonstratives	18	location	22
prepositions	28		

possessing

have	21	possession	26

glossary 34

adjectives

The adjective usually comes after the noun, with the linking word *na* na in between. If the noun ends in a vowel, replace the word *na* with the ending *-ng* ·ng.

a long journey
   paglalakbáy na mahaba   pag·la·lak·*bai* na ma·*ha*·ba
   (lit: journey *na* long)

a clever child
   batang matalino   *ba*·tang ma·ta·*lee*·no
   (lit: child-*ng* clever)

These *na* and *-ng* 'linkers' are also used with numerals, eg 'one child'. See **nouns**.

adverbs

A simple, effective and usually correct way of forming an adverb is to put *nang* nang (roughly meaning 'in the manner of') before an adjective.

fast	mabilis	ma·bee·*lees*
quickly	nang	nang
	mabilis	ma·bee·*lees*

Don't drive quickly.
   Huwag kang magmaneho   hoo·*wag* kang mag·ma·*ne*·ho
   nang mabilis.   nang ma·bee·*lees*
   (lit: don't you-*ng* drive *nang* fast)

a-z phrasebuilder

be

giving your opinion • making a statement

There's no verb 'be' in Filipino. A verb isn't required when you want to say that someone or something is a type of thing.

I'm a tourist.
   Turista ako.   too·*rees*·ta a·*ko*
   (lit: tourist I)

The same holds when you want to describe or give your opinion about something.

My room is dirty.
   Marumi ang kuwarto ko.   ma·roo·*mee* ang koo·*war*·to ko
   (lit: dirty *ang* room my)

See also **word order** and **adjectives**.

demonstratives

pointing things out

Demonstratives (ie words like 'this' and 'that') are used to point things out. They can be used to indicate specific things like 'this chair' or 'that dog', in which case they come after the noun, or used on their own, as in 'I want this' or 'Give me that'.

I want this dress.
   Gústo ko ang baròng ito.   goos·to ko ang *ba*·rong ee·*to*
   (lit: want I *ang* dress this)

I want that.
   Gústo ko iyan.   goos·to ko ee·*yan*
   (lit: want I that)

this	*ito*	ee·to
that (nearby)	*iyan*	ee·yan
that (farther)	*iyon*	ee·yon
these	*mga ito*	ma·nga ee·to
those (nearby	*mga iyan*	ma·nga ee·yan
those (farther)	*mga iyon*	ma·nga ee·yon

focus

doing things • making a statement • naming things

In Filipino there's a complex relationship between the verbs and the markers (discussed below) used to focus on the most important characters in a sentence. While you might find the explanations of verbs and markers somewhat challenging, they'll make more sense to you as you speak with and listen to Filipinos.

actor & patient voice verbs

The example below uses the actor voice (**av**) and patient voice (**pv**) forms of the verb 'buy', which has the basic form *bili* bee·*lee* (to buy). The first sentence is in the patient voice form *binili* bee·nee·*lee* (buy-**pv**), and could be an answer to the question '**What** did your friend buy?' – patient voice verbs automatically focus on the receiver of the action. The second answer uses the actor voice form *bumili* boo·mee·*lee* (buy-**av**), and may be a response to the question '**Who** bought the ticket?' – actor voice verbs concentrate on the doer of the action. Most verbs have both actor and patient voice forms.

My friend bought a ticket.
   Binili ng kaibigan   bee·nee·*lee* nang ka·ee·*bee*·gan
   ko ang tiket.   ko ang *tee*·ket
   (lit: bought-**pv** *ng* friend my *ang* ticket)

   Bumili ang kaibigan   boo·mee·*lee* ang ka·*ee*·*bee*·gan
   ko ng tiket.   ko nang *tee*·ket
   (lit: bought-**av** *ang* friend my *ng* ticket)

In English, this distinction in focus would be shown by stressing either 'my friend' or 'the ticket' with your voice. To do this in Filipino you use *ang* ang and *ng* nang to mark the main characters or objects.

ang & ng markers

The markers *ang* ang and *ng* nang always appear as separate words before the noun. For example *ang anak* ang a·*nak* (child) and *ng babae* nang ba·*ba*·e (woman). The *ang* marker always indicates the most important character in the sentence (according to the speaker), not necessarily the doer of the action – it marks the noun that's the focus of the sentence while *ng* marks the non-focus noun.

The location of *ang* and *ng* in a sentence is determined by whether the verb is in its patient voice form or its actor voice form. With an actor voice verb, the actor must be marked with *ang* and the receiver with *ng*. In the patient voice form, the receiver is marked with *ng* and the actor with *ang* (as shown in the first example where the actor 'the woman' is marked with *ng* nang, and the patient 'the child' with *ang* ang). The sentences which follow are both in the patient voice form; the meaning changes entirely when *ang* and *ng* mark the 'opposite' noun.

The woman took the child to the station.
> *Inihatid ng babae*   ee·nee·ha·*teed* nang ba·*ba*·e
> *ang anak sa istasyon.*   ang a·*nak* sa ees·tas·*yon*
> (lit: take-**pv** *ng* woman *ang* child to station)

The child took the woman to the station.
> *Inihatid ng anak*   ee·nee·ha·*teed* nang a·*nak*
> *ang babae sa istasyon.*   ang ba·*ba*·e sa ees·tas·*yon*
> (lit: take-**pv** *ng* child *ang* woman to station)

These markers have different forms when they're used with proper nouns (the names of people or places), as shown in the next table. Pronouns also need to change their form depending on whether they are *ang* or *ng* pronouns (see **personal pronouns**).

	noun		proper noun sg		proper noun pl	
focus	*ang*	ang	*si*	see	*siná*	see·na
non-focus	*ng*	ng	*ni*	nee	*niná*	nee·na

have

possessing

To say you 'have' something in Filipino use the words *mayroon* mai·ro·on or *may* mai at the beginning of the sentence. See **word order**.

Do you have a credit card?
> *Mayroon ka bang*   *mai·ro·on ka bang*
> *kredit kard?*   *kre·deet kard*
> (lit: have-**av** you *ba-ng* credit card)

To respond negatively to a question with the word 'have' (*mayroon* mai·ro·on or *may* mai), say *wala* wa·*la* (none/without).

Does the room have a fan?
> *May bentiladór ba ang*   mai ben·tee·la·*dor* ba ang
> *kuwarto?*   koo·*war*·to
> (lit: have-**av** fan *ba ang* room)

No.
> *Wala.*   wa·*la*
> (lit: none)

See also **possession**, **question** and **word order**. For an explanation of the question particle *ba* ba see **questions**.

location

Filipino has one word for 'here' and two words for 'there' – one that refers to a place that's close by and the other to a place further away from the speaker.

here	*dito*	dee·to
there (not too far away)	*diyán*	dee·*yan*
there (further away)	*doón*	do·*on*

Put my bags down over there.
> *Ilagay mo ang bagahe*   ee·la·*gai* mo ang ba·*ga*·he
> *ko doón.*   ko do·*on*
> (lit: put-**pv** you *ang* bag my there)

negation

To negate a word or statement, put the word *hindí* heen·*dee* (no/not) before the word or phrase negated.

| **expensive** | *mahal* | ma·*hal* |
| **not expensive** | *hindí mahal* | heen·*dee* ma·*hal* |

When you use *hindí* before a sentence, the word order changes.

I'm hungry. *Gutom ako.*   goo·*tom* a·ko
> (lit: hungry I)
I'm not hungry. *Hindî ako gutom.*   heen·*dee'* a·ko goo·*tom*
> (lit: not I hungry)

To negate a request or command, use *huwág* hoo·*wag*.

Don't drink.
> *Huwag kang uminom.*   hoo·*wag* kang oo·mee·nom
> (lit: do-not you-*ng* drink)

See also **word order**.

nouns

naming things

Filipino nouns have only one form for both singular and plural. Nouns, however, are marked according to focus (see **focus**).

person/people	*tao*	*ta·o*
ticket/tickets	*tiket*	*tee·ket*

If you want to explicitly express plurality you, place *mga* ma·*nga* directly before the noun.

I saw the children.
   Nakita ko ang mga bata.   na·*kee*·ta ko ang ma·*nga ba*·ta
   (lit: saw-**pv** I *ang* plural child)

The number one (*isá* ee·*sa*) can be used to guarantee you're only talking about one thing:

I saw a child.
   Nakita ko ang isáng bata.   na·*kee*·ta ko ang ee·*sang ba*·ta
   (lit: saw-**pv** I *ang* one-*ng* child)

Note that numerals such as 'one' also take the linker *na* na or -*ng* ·ng when following by a noun (see **adjectives**).

particles

asking a question · expressing time · making a request

Filipino has lots of particles – words that don't have a precise translation or meaning but serve specific functions. For example, the following particles express time concepts and normally appear as the second word in the sentence:

particle		function
pa	pa	expresses that an event hasn't yet occurred but is expected to take place (like 'yet')
na	na	expresses that an event/action has taken place or is taking place, and that it was expected to occur (like 'already')

He hasn't fixed my car yet.

Hindí pa niyá nagagawá   heen·*dee* pa nee·*ya* na·ga·ga·*wa'*
ang kotse ko.   ang *kot*·se ko
(lit: not yet he fixed-**pv** *ang* car my)

He's fixed my car already.

Nagawá na niyá ang   na·ga·*wa'* na nee·*ya* ang
kotse ko.   *kot*·se ko
(lit: fixed-**pv** already he *ang* car my)

Particles can also show the speaker's attitude to events:

particle		function
nga	nga	affirms/emphasises a statement
		softens requests or makes a question less invasive
pala	pa·*la*	expresses surprise at unexpected information (like 'apparently')
naman	na·*man*	softens a request
		gives emphasis

This is (so) delicious!

Ang sarap naman nito!   ang sa·*rap* na·*man* nee·*to*
(lit: *ang* delicious *naman* this)

Also see **requests** for how other particles are used. See also **focus**.

personal pronouns

Pronouns have two forms: the 'ang' and 'ng' forms. The form you use depends on the pronoun's role and whether the verb is an actor voice (av) or patient voice (pv) verb (see **focus** and **verbs**).

Filipino also distinguishes between informal (inf) and polite (pol) pronouns. When talking with an adult you're familiar with, it's friendlier to use the informal forms, otherwise use the polite forms.

There's only one word for 'he' and 'she' and none for 'it'. Use 'this' or 'that' as substitute for 'it' (see **demonstratives**).

'ang' pronouns		
I/me	*akó*	a·ko
you sg inf	*ikáw/ka*	ee·kaw/ka
you sg pol	*kayó*	ka·yo
he/she/him/her	*siyá*	see·ya
we/us incl	*tayo*	ta·yo
we/us excl	*kamí*	ka·mee
you pl pol&inf	*kayó*	ka·yo
they/them	*silá*	see·la

To replace a word marked with '*ang*' (as *ang babae* in the example below) with a pronoun, use an '*ang*' pronoun.

The girl is going to my friend's house.
*Pupunta **ang babae** sa*   poo·poon·ta ang ba·ba·e sa
bahay ng kaibigan ko.   ba·hai nang ka·ee·bee·gan ko
(lit: go-av ang girl to house of friend my)

She is going to my friend's house.
*Pupunta **siyá** sa bahay*   poo·poon·ta see·ya sa ba·hai
ng kaibigan ko.   nang ka·ee·bee·gan ko
(lit: go-av she to house of friend my)

a–z phrasebuilder

25

'ng' pronouns		
I/me	*ko*	ko
you sg inf	*mo*	mo
you sg pol	*ninyó*	neen·yo
he/she/him/her	*niyá*	nee·ya
we/us incl	*natin*	na·teen
we/us excl	*namin*	na·meen
you pl pol & inf	*ninyó*	neen·yo
they/them	*nilá*	nee·la

They're visiting my friend.
> *Pupuntahan* **nila** *ang*   poo·poon·ta·han nee·la ang
> *kaibigan ko.*   ka·ee·bee·gan ko
> (lit: go-pv they *ang* friend my)

When *ko* ko and *ikáw* ee·kow are used in the same sentence they're replaced by *kita* kee·ta.

I like you.
> *Gústo ko ikáw.*   goos·to ko ee·kaw
> (lit: like I you)
> *Gústo kitá.*   goos·to kee·ta
> (lit: like I-to-you)

For possessive pronouns, see **possession**.

possession

possessing

A simple way of saying 'my', 'your' etc in Filipino is to use a word from the table after the thing that's owned.

my	*ko*	ko
your sg inf	*mo*	mo
your sg pol	*ninyó*	neen·yo
his/her	*niyá*	nee·ya
our incl	*natin*	na·teen
our excl	*namin*	na·meen
your pl inf&pol	*ninyó*	neen·yo
their	*nilá*	nee·la

That's my wallet.
Ang wallet ko iyán.   ang *wa*·let ko ee·*yan*
(lit: *ang* wallet my that)

The equivalents of 'yours' and 'mine', as in 'This seat is mine', are listed below:

mine	*akin*	a·keen
yours sg inf	*iyó*	ee·yo
yours sg pol	*inyóng*	een·yong
his/hers	*kanyá*	kan·ya
ours incl	*atin*	a·teen
ours excl	*amin*	a·meen
yours pl inf&pol	*inyóng*	een·yong
theirs	*kaniláng*	ka·nee·lang

That's mine.
Akin iyán.   a·keen ee·*yan*
(lit: mine that)

Another way to express ownership is by using *ng* nang, which roughly corresponds to 'of'. This word comes after the owner and before the thing owned.

My friend's train is late.
> *Nahuli ang tren **ng***   na·hoo·*lee* ang tren nang
> *kaibigan ko.*   ka·ee·*bee*·gan ko
> (lit: be-delayed *ang* train of friend my)

For proper names replace *ng* with *ni* nee (singular) or *nina* nee·na (plural).

Tom's train is late.
> *Nahuli ang tren **ni** Tom.*   na·hoo·*lee* ang tren nee tom
> (lit: be-delayed *ang* train *ni* Tom)

See also **have**.

prepositions

giving directions/orders • pointing things out

The word *sa* sa translates as many different English prepositions and is often used in combination with other words.

across	*sa kabilâ ng*	sa ka·bee·*la* nang
at	*sa*	sa
for	*para sa*	*pa*·ra sa
from	*buhat sa mulâ sa*	boo·*hat* sa moo·*la* sa
in	*sa*	sa
in front of	*sa haráp ng*	sa ha·*rap* nang
inside	*sa loób ng*	sa lo·*ob* nang
on	*sa*	sa
towards	*patungò sa*	pa·too·*ngo* sa

My hotel is opposite the bus stop.
> *Sa kabilâ ng hintuán*   sa ka·bee·*la* nang heen·too·*an*
> *ng bus ang otél ko.*   nang boos ang o·tel ko
> (lit: at opposite-side of stopping-place of bus *ang* hotel my)

There's a different set of prepositions used with proper names
The first translation is used for singular proper names and the
second for plural ones.

across	*sa kabilâ ni*	sa ka·bee·*la* nee
	sa kabilâ kiná	sa ka·bee·*la* kee·*na*
for	*para kay*	*pa*·ra kai
	para kiná	*pa*·ra kee·*na*
in front of	*sa harap ni*	sa ha·*rap* nee
	sa harap kiná	sa ha·*rap* kee·*na*

questions

asking a question

To turn a statement into a yes/no question, simply raise the
intonation at the the end of the sentence. You can also add
the word *ba* ba, which usually comes after the first noun or
pronoun.

There's a message for me.
    May mensahe para   mai men·*sa*·he *pa*·ra
    sa akin.   sa *a*·keen

Is there a message for me?
    May mensahe ba   mai men·*sa*·he ba
    para sa akin?   *pa*·ra sa *a*·keen

To answer yes/no to these types of questions, use the words *oo*
o·o (yes) and *hindî* heen·*dee* (not/no).

question words		
who	*sino*	*see·no*
Who's the manager?	*Sino ang mánedyer?*	*see·no ang ma·ned·yer*
what	*anó*	*a·no*
What's that?	*Anó iyan?*	*a·no ee·yan*
when	*kailán*	*ka·ee·lan*
When's he coming?	*Kailán siyá daratíng?*	*ka·ee·lan see·ya da·ra·teeng*
where	*saán/nasaán*	*sa·an/na·sa·an*
Where do you live?	*Saán ka nakatirá?*	*sa·an ka na·ka·tee·ra*
how	*paano*	*pa·a·no*
How did you do this?	*Paano mo ginawâ iyan?*	*pa·a·no mo gi·na·wa' ee·yan*
why	*bakit*	*ba·keet*
Why is it cancelled?	*Bakit nakanselá?*	*ba·keet na·kan·se·la*
how many	*ilán*	*ee·lan*
How many children do you have?	*Ilán ang anák mo?*	*ee·lan ang a·nak mo*
how much	*magkano*	*mag·ka·no*
How much is it?	*Magkano?*	*mag·ka·no*
whose	*kanino*	*ka·nee·no*
Whose back-pack is that?	*Kanino ang backpak na iyán*	*ka·nee·no ang bak·pak na ee·yan*

requests

giving orders/directions • making a request

Requests or commands in Filipino are straightforward. Start your request with the root form of the verb (given in the dictionary) and add *paki-* pa·kee· to the beginning. Using the polite particle *ngâ* nga when making a request makes it sound more gracious.

Please give me my passport.

Pakibigáy ngâ ang	pa·*kee*·bee·*gai* nga' ang
aking pasaporte.	a·*keeng* pa·sa·*por*·te
(lit: *paki*-give-**pv** *ngâ ang* my passport)	

tense & aspect

expressing time • doing things

Filipino verbs don't change for tense as English verbs do – instead they change according to aspect. Aspect in Filipino distinguishes between actual and hypothetical events and complete and incomplete events. To show these changes, affixes (added syllables) are joined to the beginning, middle or end of a verb root.

aspect		english	filipino	
actual	complete	travelled has travelled	*naglakbáy* (*nag*-verb)	nag·lak·*bai*
	incomplete	travels is travelling was travelling	*naglalakbáy* (*nag*-**dup**-verb)	nag·la·lak·*bai*
hypothetical		will travel	*maglalakbáy* (*mag*-**dup**-verb)	mag·la·lak·*bai*

The symbol **dup** means repeating the first consonant and vowel of the verb root - in our example the '*la*' of '*lakbáy*'. See also **verbs**.

there is/are

The word *mayroón* mai·*ro*·on corresponds to both 'there is' and 'there are':

There's a café next door.
Mayroong café sa   mai·*ro*·ong ka·*pay* sa
kapitbahay.   ka·peet·*ba*·hai
(lit: there-is-*ng* café at next-door)

The word *walang* wa·*lang* corresponds to both 'there isn't' and 'there aren't':

There isn't a fan in my room.
Walang bentilador sa   wa·*lang* ben·tee·la·*dor* sa
kuwarto ko.   koo·*war*·to ko
(lit: there-isn't fan in room my)

verbs

Filipino verbs don't change form according to who is doing the action:

I'm eating.
Kumakain ako.   koo·ma·*ka*·een a·*ko*
(lit: eating-**av** I)

You're eating.
Kumakain ikáw.   koo·ma·*ka*·een ee·*kaw*
(lit: eating-**av** you)

However, verbs do change depending on whether they are patient voice verbs (**pv**) or actor voice verbs (**av**). For more information on verbs, see also **focus** and **tense & aspect**.

word order

In regular Filipino sentences the verb usually comes first. This is followed by the nouns or things involved in the event. There's quite a bit of flexibility with how these nouns are arranged after the verb, but generally the agent or the doer of the action comes directly after the verb.

I'll wait here.
    Maghihintay ako dito.   mag·hee·heen·*tay* a·*ko dee*·to
    (lit: will-be-waiting-**av** I here)

The particle *ay* ai is often used in sentences where English speakers would use the verb 'be', but using *ay* changes the order of the words in the phrase.

I'm a tourist.
    Ako **ay** *turista.*   a·*ko* ay too·*rees*·ta
    (lit: I *ay* tourist)

glossary

actor/agent	the person or thing responsible for doing the action
adjective	a word used for describing something, eg '**cold** weather'
affix	extra syllable(s) added to a word, eg '**re**-' in 'reorganise'
exclusive	refers to pronouns that include the person who is being spoken to
focus marker	something that marks a noun as the most prominent/important thing in the sentence
inclusive	refers to pronouns that include the person who is being spoken to
noun	the thing that is talked about, can be either a person, thing or something abstract like a concept
patient	the person or thing affected by the action
possessive pronoun	words such as 'mine', 'yours', 'theirs' that express ownership
pronoun	a word that means 'I', 'you', etc
subject	the thing or person in the sentence that does the action – 'the **police** entered the building'
transliteration	pronunciation guide for words and phrases
verb	the word that tells you what action happened – 'I **broke** the code'
verb root	the part of a verb which does not change – 'search' in '**search**ing' and '**search**ed'

Do you speak (English)?
*Marunong ka ba
ng (Inglés)?*
ma·*roo*·nong ka ba
nang (eeng·*gles*)

Does anyone speak (English)?
*May marunong bang
magsalitá ng (Inglés)?*
mai ma·*roo*·nong bang
mag·sa·lee·*ta* nang (eeng·*gles*)

Do you understand?
Náiintindihán mo ba?
na·ee·een·teen·dee·*han* mo ba

Yes, I understand.
Oo, náiintindihán ko.
o·o, na·ee·een·teen·dee·*han* ko

No, I don't understand.
*Hindí ko
náiintindihán.*
heen·*dee* ko
na·ee·een·teen·dee·*han*

Pardon?
Anó kamo?
a·*no* ka·mo

I speak (English).
*Marunong ako
ng (Inglés).*
ma·*roo*·nong a·*ko*
nang (eeng·*gles*)

I don't speak (Filipino).
*Hindî ako marunong
ng (Pilipino).*
heen·*dee'* a·ko ma·*roo*·nong
nang (pee·lee·*pee*·no)

I speak a little.
Kauntí lang.
ka·oon·*tee* lang

I would like to practise (Filipino).
*Gustó kong magpraktis
ng (Pilipino).*
goos·*to* kong mag·*prak*·tees
nang (pee·lee·*pee*·no)

35

Let's speak (Filipino).
Magsalitá tayo   mag·sa·lee·*ta* ta·yo
ng (Pilipino).   nang (pee·lee·*pee*·no)

What does 'aklatan' mean?
Anó ang ibig sabihin   a·*no* ang ee·beeg sa·*bee*·heen
ng 'aklatan'?   nang ak·*la*·tan

How do you pronounce this?
Paano mo bibigkasín   pa·*a*·no mo bee·beeg·ka·*seen*
itó?   ee·*to*

How do you write 'unggóy'?
Paano mo isusulat   pa·*a*·no mo ee·soo·*soo*·lat
ang 'unggóy'?   ang oong·*goy*

Could you please …?	*Pakí- …?*	pa·*kee*·…?
repeat that	*ulit mo*	*oo*·leet mo
speak more slowly	*bagalan mo ang salitâ*	ba·*ga*·lan mo ang sa·lee·*ta'*
write it down	*sulat mo*	*soo*·lat mo

---

speed it up!

The pronunciation of words can vary depending on how fast you talk. For example, whenever you see words like *Diyos* dee·yos (God) or *diyan* dee·yan (there), you can pronounce dee + y simply as a j (as in jump) when you speed up your speech – an alternative pronunciation would be jos for *Diyos* and jan for *diyan*.

cardinal numbers

		mga númerong pambilang
0	*sero*	se·ro
1	*isá*	ee·sa
2	*dalawá*	da·la·wa
3	*tatló*	tat·lo
4	*apat*	a·pat
5	*limá*	lee·ma
6	*anim*	a·neem
7	*pitó*	pee·to
8	*waló*	wa·lo
9	*siyám*	see·yam
10	*sampû*	sam·poo'
11	*labing-isá*	la·beeng·ee·sa
12	*labindalawá*	la·been·da·la·wa
13	*labintatló*	la·been·tat·lo
14	*labing-apat*	la·beeng·a·pat
15	*labinlimá*	la·been·lee·ma
16	*labing-anim*	la·beenq·a·neem
17	*labimpitó*	la·beem·pee·to
18	*labingwaló*	la·beeng·wa·lo
19	*labinsiyám*	la·been·see·yam
20	*dalawampû*	da·la·wam·poo'
21	*dalawampú't isá*	da·la·wam·poot ee·sa
22	*dalawampú't*	da·la·wam·poot
	dalawá	da·la·wa
30	*tatlumpû*	tat·loom·poo'
40	*apatnapû*	a·pat·na·poo'
50	*limampû*	lee·mam·poo'
60	*animnapû*	a·neem·na·poo'
70	*pitumpû*	pee·toom·poo'

80	*walumpû*	wa·loom·*poo'*
90	*siyamnapû*	see·yam·na·*poo'*
100	*sandaán*	san·da·*an*
101	*isáng daán at isá*	ee·*sang*·da·*an* at ee·*sa*
105	*isáng daán at limá*	ee·*sang*·da·*an* at lee·*ma*
200	*dalawándaán*	da·la·*wan*·da·*an*
1,000	*isáng libo*	ee·*sang* lee·bo
1,000,000	*isáng milyón*	ee·*sang* meel·yon
1,000,000,000	*isáng bilyón*	ee·*sang* beel·yon

a number of choices

You can talk about numbers in three different ways in the Philippines. As well as counting in Filipino, you can count in English and Spanish and still be understood.

It's important to know your basic Spanish numbers, as they're normally used when telling the time. Below are the numbers borrowed from Spanish, but spelled in Filipino.

1	*uno*	*oo*·no
2	*dos*	dos
3	*tres*	tres
4	*kwatro*	*kwa*·tro
5	*singko*	*seeng*·ko
6	*seis*	seys
7	*siyete*	see·*ye*·te
8	*otso*	*ot*·so
9	*nuweve*	noo·*we*·ve
10	*diyés*	dee·*yes*
11	*onse*	*on*·se
12	*dose*	*do*·se

To learn more about how to tell the time, see **time & dates**, page 41.

To learn more about how to tell the time, see **time & dates**, page 41.

BASICS

ordinal numbers

Ordinals, with the exception of '1st', are formed by adding the prefix *ika-* ee·ka· to the cardinal number – *ikaapat* ee·ka·*a*·pat, (fourth), is formed by adding *ika-* to the number *apat* a·pat (four). If the cardinal number begins with a *d* or *t* delete the first consonant before adding the prefix, and add *ik-* ik· instead of *ika-*, eg *tatló* tat·*lo* (three), becomes *ikatló* ee·kat·*lo* (third) by deleting the first consonant and then adding *ik-*.

1st	*una*	*oo*·na
2nd	*ikalawá*	ee·ka·la·*wa*
3rd	*ikatló*	ee·kat·*lo*
4th	*ikaapat*	ee·ka·*a*·pat
5th	*ikalimá*	ee·ka·lee·*ma*
10th	*ikasampû*	ee·ka·sam·*poo*
11th	*ikalabing-isá*	ee·ka·la·bing·ee·*sa*
12th	*ikalabing-dalawá*	ee·ka·la·bing·da·la·*wa*
20th	*ikadalawampû*	ee·ka·da·la·wam·*poo*
30th	*ikatatlumpû*	ee·ka·tat·lum·*poo*

fractions

a quarter	*sangkapat*	sang·*ka*·pat
a third	*ikatlóng*	ee·kat·*long*
	bahagi	ba·*ha*·gee
a half	*kalahatì*	ka·la·*ha*·tee'
three-quarters	*tatlóng*	tat·*long*
	sangkapat	sang·*ka*·pat
all	*kabuuán*	ka·boo·oo·*an*
none	*walâ*	wa·*la*'

useful amounts

How much?	*Magkano?*	mag·*ka*·no
How many?	*Ilán?*	ee·*lan*
Please give me ...	*Pakibigyán mo ako ng ...*	pa·kee·beeg·*yan* mo a·*ko* nang ...
(100) grams	*(sandaáng) gramo*	(san·da·*ang*) *gra*·mo
half a dozen	*kalahating dosena*	ka·la·*ha*·teeng do·*se*·na
half a kilo	*kalahating kilo*	ka·la·*ha*·teeng *kee*·lo
a kilo	*isáng kilo*	ee·*sang kee*·lo
a bottle	*isáng bote*	ee·*sang* bo·*te*
a jar	*isáng garapón*	ee·*sang* ga·ra·*pon*
a packet	*isáng pakete*	ee·*sang* pa·*ke*·te
a slice	*isáng hiwà*	ee·*sang hee*·wa'
a tin	*isáng lata*	ee·*sang la*·ta
a few	*kauntî*	ka·oon·*tee'*
less	*kulang*	*koo*·lang
(just) a little	*kauntí (lang)*	ka·oon·*tee* (lang)
a lot/many	*marami*	ma·*ra*·mee
more	*higít pa*	hee·*geet* pa
some	*ilán*	ee·*lan*

If you want to find out how to put these amounts into use, see **self-catering**, page 171.

telling the time

Telling the time in Filipino is easy, once you get the hang of it. For the hour use *alás* a·*las* (lit: at-the) plus the number. For times past the hour say the number of minutes plus *minuto makalampás ang* mee·*noo*·to ma·ka·lam·*pas* ang (lit: minute(s) past *ang*) then the hour. For times before the hour say the number of minutes plus *minuto bago mag-* mee·*noo*·too *ba*·go mag· (lit: minute(s) before turning) then the hour.

Instead of *tatlampùng minuto* tat·loom·*poong* mee·*noo*·to (30 minutes), use *kalahating oras* ka·la·*ha*·teeng o·ras (lit: half-of hour).

What time is it?
  Anóng oras na?   a·*nong* o·ras na

At what time ...?
  Anóng oras ...?   a·*nong* o·ras ...

(Ten) o'clock.
  Alás-(diyés).   a·*las*·(dee·*yes*)

Five/Quarter past (ten).
  Limáng/Labinlimáng   lee·*mang*/la·been·lee·*mang*
  minuto makalampás   mee·*noo*·to ma·ka·lam·*pas*
  ang (alás-diyés).   ang (a·*las*·dee·*yes*)

same time but not the same place

In Filipino, the days of the week and months of the year have been 'borrowed' from Spanish, but spelled in Filipino.

The 12-hour clock is used in the Philippines – it's only for plane schedules at the airport that you'll see the 24-hour system used, and even then it's converted to the 12-hour clock when you say the times out loud.

Half past (ten).
   Kalahating oras maka-   ka·la·*ha*·teeng *o*·ras ma·ka·
   lampás ang (alás-diyés).   lam·*pas* ang (a·*las*·dee·*yes*)

Quarter to (ten).
   Labinlimáng minuto   la·been·lee·*mang* mee·*noo*·to
   bago mag-(alás-diyés).   *ba*·go mag-(a·*las*·dee·*yes*)

am	*ng umaga*	nang oo·*ma*·ga
pm (approx 12-2pm)	*ng tanghalì*	nang tang·*ha*·lee'
pm (approx 2-6pm)	*ng hapon*	nang *ha*·pon

the calendar

ang kalendaryo

days

Monday	*Lunes*	*loo*·nes
Tuesday	*Martés*	mar·*tes*
Wednesday	*Miyérkoles*	mee·*yer*·ko·les
Thursday	*Huwebes*	hoo·*we*·bes
Friday	*Biyernes*	bee·*yer*·nes
Saturday	*Sábado*	*sa*·ba·do
Sunday	*Linggó*	leeng·*go*

months

January	*Enero*	e·*ne*·ro
February	*Pebrero*	peb·*re*·ro
March	*Marso*	*mar*·so
April	*Abríl*	ab·*reel*
May	*Mayo*	*ma*·yo
June	*Hunyo*	*hoon*·yo
July	*Hulyo*	*hool*·yo
August	*Agosto*	a·*gos*·to
September	*Setyembre*	set·*yem*·bre
October	*Oktubre*	ok·*too*·bre
November	*Nobyembre*	nob·*yem*·bre
December	*Disyembre*	dees·*yem*·bre

dates

What date is it today?
   Anóng petsa ngayón?   a·*nong pet*·sa nga·*yon*

It's (18 May).
   Ngayon ay (ikalabing-   nga·*yon* ai (ee·ka·la·beeng·wa·*lo*
   waló ng Mayo).   nang *may*·yo)

seasons

spring	*tagsibol*	tag·*see*·bol
summer	*tag-aráw*	tag·a·*row*
autumn/fall	*taglagás*	tag·la·*gas*
winter	*taglamíg*	tag·la·*meeg*

present

                                                           ang kasalukuyan

now	*ngayón*	nga·*yon*
today	*sa araw na itó*	sa *a*·row na ee·*to*
tonight	*ngayóng gabí*	nga·*yong* ga·*bee*
this ...	*ngayóng ...*	nga·*yong* ...
morning	*umaga*	oo·*ma*·ga
afternoon	*hapon*	*ha*·pon
week	*linggóng itó*	leeng·*gong* ee·*to*
month	*buwán na itó*	boo·*wan* na ee·*to*
year	*taón na itó*	ta·*on* na ee·*to*

past

                                                           pangnagdaán

(three days) ago	*(kama)katló*	(ka·ma·)kat·*lo*
day before yesterday	*(kama)kalawá*	(ka·ma·)ka·la·*wa*
since (May)	*mulá noóng (Mayo)*	moo·*la* no·*ong* (*ma*·yo)

last ...	nang nakaraáng ...	nang na·ka·ra·ang ...
night	gabí	ga·bee
week	linggó	leeng·go
month	buwán	boo·wan
year	taón	ta·on
yesterday ...	kahapon ng ...	ka·ha·pon nang ...
morning	umaga	oo·ma·ga
afternoon	hapon	ha·pon
evening	gabí	ga·bee

future

day after	samakalawá	sa·ma·ka·la·wa
tomorrow	sa makalipas	sa ma·ka·lee·pas
in (six days)	ang (anim na araw)	ang (a·neem na a·row)
until (June)	hanggáng sa (Hunyo)	hang·gang sa (hun·yo)
next ...	sa súsunód na ...	sa soo·soo·nod na ...
week	linggó	leeng·go
month	buwán	boo·wan
year	taón	ta·on
tomorrow ...	bukas ng ...	boo·kas nang ...
afternoon	hapon	ha·pon
evening	gabí	ga·bee
morning	umaga	oo·ma·ga

during the day

morning	umaga	oo·ma·ga
midday	katánghalian	ka·tang·ha·lee·an
afternoon	hapon	ha·pon
day	araw	a·row
night/evening	gabí	ga·bee
midnight	hatinggabí	ha·teeng·ga·bee

How much is it?
Magkano? — mag·*ka*·no

Can you write down the price?
Pakisulat mo ang presyo? — pa·kee·*soo*·lat mo ang *pres*·yo

That's too expensive.
Masyadong mahál. — mas·*ya*·dong ma·*hal*

Do you accept ...?	*Tumatanggáp ka ba ng ...?*	too·ma·tang·*gap* ka ba nang ...
credit cards	*kredit kard*	*kre*·deet kard
debit cards	*debit kard*	*de*·beet kard
travellers cheques	*travellers check*	*tra*·be·lers tsek

Where can I ...?	*Saán akó ...?*	sa·*an* a·ko ...
I'd like to ...	*Gustó kong ...*	goos·*to* kong ...
cash a cheque	*magpalít ng tseke*	mag·pa·*leet* nang *tse*·ke
change a travellers cheque	*magpalít ng travellers check*	mag·pa·*leet* nang *tra*·be·lers tsek
change money	*magpalít ng pera*	mag·pa·*leet* nang *pe*·ra
get a cash advance	*kumuha ng abanse*	koo·*moo*·ha nang a·*ban*·se
withdraw money	*maglabás ng pera*	mag·la·*bas* nang *pe*·ra

Where's a/an ...?	*Násaán ang ...?*	*na*·sa·*an* ang ...
automated teller machine	*ATM*	*ay*·tee·em
foreign exchange office	*palitan ng pera*	pa·*lee*·tan nang *pe*·ra

What's the charge for that?
Anó ang bayad para diyán?   a·*no* ang *ba*·yad *pa*·ra dee·*yan*

What's the exchange rate?
Anó ang palít?   a·*no* ang pa·*leet*

Has my money arrived yet?
Dumatíng na ba ang   doo·ma·*teeng* na ba ang
pera ko?   *pe*·ra ko

Can I use my credit card to withdraw money?
Puwede ko bang   poo·*we*·de ko bang
gamitin ang aking   ga·*mee*·teen ang *a*·keeng
kredit kard para   *kre*·deet kard *pa*·ra
maglabás ng pera?   mag·la·*bas* nang *pe*·ra

Could I have a receipt please?
Puwedeng pakibigyán   poo·*we*·deng pa·kee·beeg·*yan*
mo akó ng resibo?   mo a·*ko* nang re·*see*·bo

I'd like …, please.	*Pakí lang,*	pa·*kee* lang
	gustó ko …	goos·*to* ko …
a refund	*na ibalík mo*	na ee·ba·*leek* mo
	ang pera ko	ang *pe*·ra ko
my change	*ng suklí ko*	nang sook·*lee* ko

---

talkin' about money money

The currency of the Philippines is the *piso* *pee*·so (peso). It's made up of 100 *séntimos* *sen*·tee·mos (centavos).

getting around

paglilibót

Which ... goes to (Bataan)?	*Alíng ... ang papuntá sa (Bataan)?*	a·*leeng* ... ang pa·poon·*ta* sa (ba·ta·*an*)
boat	*bapór*	ba·*por*
ferry	*ferry*	*pe*·ree
catamaran	*catamaran*	*ka*·ta·ma·ran
Is this the ... to (Baguío)?	*Itó ba ang ... na papuntá sa (Baguío)?*	ee·*to* ba ang ... na pa·poon·*ta* sa (ba·gee·o)
bus	*bus*	boos
jeepney	*dyipni*	*jeep*·nee
mega-taxi	*mega-taksi*	me·ga·*tak*·see
train	*tren*	tren
When's the ... (bus)?	*Kailán ang ... (bus)?*	ka·ee·*lan* ang ... (boos)
first	*unang*	*oo*·nang
last	*hulíng*	hoo·*leeng*
next	*súsunód na*	soo·soo·*nod* na

What time does the (bus) leave?
Anóng oras áalís ang (bus)?　a·nong o·ras a·a·lees ang (boos)

What time does the (boat) get to (Samal)?
Anóng oras daratíng ang (bapór) sa (Samal)?　a·nong o·ras da·ra·*teeng* ang (ba·por) sa (sa·mal)

How long will it be delayed?
Gaano katagál itó maaatraso?　ga·a·no ka·ta·gal ee·to ma·a·at·ra·so

Is this seat free?
May nakaupó ba dito?　mai na·ka·oo·po ba dee·to

bilihan ng tiket	bee·*lee*·han nang *tee*·ket	**ticket window**
kinanselá	kee·nan·se·*la*	**cancelled**
naatraso	na·at·*ra*·so	**delayed**
plataporma	pla·ta·*por*·ma	**platform**
punô	poo·*no'*	**full**
welga	*wel*·ga	**strike** n

That's my seat.
Upuan ko iyán.   oo·*poo*·an ko ee·*yan*

Please tell me when we get to (Tagaytay).

Pakisabi lang sa akin   pa·kee·*sa*·bee lang sa *a*·keen
pagdatíng natin sa   pag·da·*teeng na*·teen sa
(Tagaytay).   (ta·*gai*·tai)

Please stop here.
Sa tabi lang ho.   sa ta·*bee* lang ho

How long do we stop here?

Gaano katagál tayo   ga·*a*·no ka·ta·*gal ta*·yo
hihintó dito?   hee·heen·*to dee*·to

tickets

mga tiket

Where do I buy a ticket?

Saán ako bibilí ng   sa·*an a·ko* bee·bee·*lee* nang
tiket?   *tee*·ket

Do I need to book?

Dapat ba akóng mag-buk?   *da*·pat ba a·*kong* mag·*book*

I'd like to ... my ticket, please.	Pakí lang, gustó kong ... ang tiket ko.	pa·*kee* lang goos·*to* kong ... ang *tee*·ket ko
cancel	kanselahín	kan·se·la·*heen*
change	baguhin	ba·*goo*·heen
confirm	tiyakín	tee·ya·*keen*

A ... ticket (to Liliw).	Isáng tiket ... na (papuntá sa Liliw).	ee·*sang* tee·ket ... na (pa·poon·ta sa lee·lew)
1st/2nd-class	1st/2nd class	pers/*se*·kan klas
child's	pambatà	pam·*ba*·ta
one-way	one way	*wan*·way
return	balikan	ba·*lee*·kan
student	pang-estudyante	pang·es·tood·*yan*·te

I'd like a/an ... seat.	Gustó kong maupo sa ...	goos·to kong ma·*oo*·po sa ...
aisle	nasa daanan	*na*·sa da·*a*·nan
nonsmoking	waláng naníni-garilyó	wa·*lang* na·*nee*·nee·ga·reel·yo
smoking	puwedeng manigarílyo	poo·*we*·deng ma·nee·ga·*reel*·yo
window	may bintanà	mai been·*ta*·na'

Is there (a) ...?	Mayroón bang ...?	mai·ro·*on* bang ...
air conditioning	erkon	*er*·kon
sick bag	supot na sukahan	*soo*·pot na soo·*ka*·han
toilet	kubeta	koo·*be*·ta

How much is it?
Magkano? mag·*ka*·no

Is it a direct route?
Diretso ba ang biyahe? dee·*ret*·so ba ang bee·*ya*·he

How long does the trip take?
Gaano katagál ang biyahe? ga·*a*·no ka·ta·*gal* ang bee·*ya*·he

Can I get a stand-by ticket?
Puwede bang bumilí ng istambay na tiket? poo·*we*·de bang boo·mee·*lee* nang ees·*tam*·bai na *tee*·ket

Can I get a sleeping berth?
Puwede ba akóng kumuha ng tulugán? poo·*we*·de ba a·*kong* koo·*moo*·ha nang too·loo·*gan*

What time should I check in?
Anóng oras akó dapat mag-check in? a·*nong* o·ras a·*ko* da·*pat* mag·*tsek* een

luggage

Where can I find …?	Saán ko makikita ang …?	sa·an ko ma·kee·kee·ta ang …
the baggage claim	kuhanán ng bagahe	koo·ha·nan nang ba·ga·he
the left-luggage office	upisina ng naiwang bagahe	oo·pee·see·na nang na·ee·wang ba·ga·he
a luggage locker	isáng laker ng bagahe	ee·sang la·ker nang ba·ga·he
a trolley	isáng trole	ee·sang tro·lee

My luggage has been …	Ang bagahe ko ay …	ang ba·ga·he ko ai …
damaged	nasirà	na·see·ra'
lost	nawalâ	na·wa·la'
stolen	nanakaw	na·na·kow

That's (not) mine.
(Hindî) Akin iyán.   (heen·dee') a·keen ee·yan

Can I have some coins/tokens?
Puwede mo ba akóng bigyán ng koyn/token?   poo·we·de mo ba a·kong beeg·yan nang koyn/to·ken

listen for …

bording pas	bor·deeng pas	boarding pass
pasaporte	pa·sa·por·te	passport
pasulóng na bagahe	pa·soo·long na ba·ga·he	carry-on baggage
sobrang bagahe	sob·rang ba·ga·he	excess baggage
transit	tran·seet	transit
transper	trans·per	transfer

plane

Is there a bus to the airport?
May bus bang papuntá   mai boos bang pa·poon·*ta*
sa erport?   sa *er*·port

Is there a flight to (Cebu)?
May eruplano bang   mai e·roo·*pla*·no bang
palipád sa (Cebu)?   pa·lee·*pad* sa (se·*boo*)

When's the next flight to (San José)?
Kailán ang súsunód   ka·ee·*lan* ang soo·soo·*nod*
na flight sa (San José)?   na plait sa (*san* ho·*se*)

Where does flight (153) arrive/depart?
Saán ang datíng/alís ng   sa·*an* ang da·*teeng*/a·*lees* nang
flight (153)?   plait (wan paib tree)

Where's ...?	Násaán ang ...?	na·sa·an ang ...
the airport	siyatel na	see·*ya*·tel na
shuttle	pang-erport	pang·*er*·port
arrivals	datingan	da·tee·ngan
departures	alisan	a·*lee*·san
duty-free	duty-free	joo·tee·pree
gate (17)	gate (17)	gayt (se·ben·*teen*)

bus

How often do buses come?
Gaano kadalás ang   ga·*a*·no ka·da·*las* ang
datíng ng mga bus?   da·*teeng* nang ma·*nga* boos

How much to (Tuba)?
Magkano hanggáng   mag·*ka*·no hang·*gang*
sa (Tuba)?   sa (*too*·ba)

Does it stop at (Porac)?
Humihintó ba itó   hoo·mee·heen·*to* ba ee·*to*
sa (Porac)?   sa (*po*·rak)

What's the next stop?

    Saán ang súsunód na   sa·*an* ang *soo*·soo·*nod* na
    paghintô?   pag·heen·*to'*

I'd like to get off at (Rizal).

    Gustó kong bumabá   goos·*to* kong boo·ma·*ba*
    sa (Rizal).   sa (ree·*sal*)

My change, please.

    Ang suklí ko, pakibigay.   ang sook·*lee* ko pa·kee·bee·*gai*

city	*siyúdad*	see·yoo·*dad*
inter-city	*pang-siyudád*	pang·see·yoo·*dad*
local	*lokal*	*lo*·kal

Taking a *jeepney*? See **local transport**, page 60.

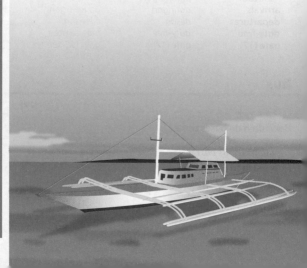

train

What station is this?
Alíng istasyón itó?
a·*leeng* ees·tas·*yon* ee·*to*

What's the next station?
Anó ang súsunód na istasyón?
a·*no* ang soo·soo·*nod* na ees·tas·*yon*

Does it stop at (Tarlac)?
Hihintó ba itó sa (Tarlac)?
hee·heen·*to* ba ee·*to* sa (tar·*lak*)

Do I need to change?
Kailangan ko bang lumipat?
ka·ee·*la*·ngan ko bang loo·*mee*·pat

Is it direct/express?
Itó ba ay diretso/eksprés?
ee·*to* ba ai dee·*ret*·so/eks·*pres*

Which carriage is (for) …?	*Alíng kompartment ang para sa …*	a·*leeng* kom·*part*·ment ang *pa*·ra sa …
1st class	*1st klas*	pers klas
dining	*kainan*	ka·*ee*·nan
San Fernando	*San Fernando*	san per·*nan*·do

boat

Can you recommend a reliable ferry operator?
May alám ka ba na mapagkakátiwalaang opereytor ng ferry?
mai a·*lam* ka ba na ma·pag·ka·*ka*·tee·wa·*la*·ang o·pe·*ray*·tor nang *pe*·ree

Could I hire a *banca* **for a day trip?**
Puwede ba akóng umarkilá ng bangkâ?
poo·*we*·de ba a·*kong* oo·mar·kee·*la* nang bang·*ka'*

Are there life jackets?
May mga layp dyaket ba?
mai ma·*nga* laip *ja*·ket ba

What's the sea like today?
> Anó ang lagáy ng dagat
> ngayón?

a·no ang la·*gay* nang *da*·gat
nga·*yon*

What island/beach is this?
> Anóng isla/baybayin itó?

a·nong ees·la/bai·*ba*·yeen ee·to

I feel seasick.
> Naliliyó akó.

na·lee·lee·*yo* a·ko

banca (native boat)	bangkâ	bang·*ka'*
cabin	kamarote	ka·ma·*ro*·te
captain	kapitán	ka·pee·*tan*
catamaran	katamaran	*ka*·ta·ma·ran
(car) deck	(car) deck	(kar) dek
(fast) ferry	(mabilís na) ferry	(ma·bee·*lees* na) *pe*·ree
hydrofoil	hydrofoil	*hai*·dro·poyl
lifeboat	lifeboat	*laip*·boht
life jacket	layp dyaket	laip *ja*·ket
yacht	yate	*ya*·te

taxi & tricycle

I'd like a taxi/tricycle ...	Gustó ko ng taksi/tráysikel ...	goos·*to* ko nang tak·see/trai·see·kel ...
at (9am)	sa (alás-nuwebe ng umaga)	sa (a·*las* noo·*we*·be nang oo·*ma*·ga)
now	ngayón	nga·*yon*
tomorrow	bukas	*boo*·kas

Where's the taxi/tricycle rank?
> Násaán ang paradahán
> ng taksi/tráysikel?

na·sa·*an* ang pa·ra·da·*han*
nang tak·see/trai·see·kel

Where can I get a tricycle to (Ángeles)?
> Saán akó kukuha ng
> tráysikel papuntá
> sa (Ángeles)?

sa·*an* a·ko koo·koo·ha nang
trai·see·kel pa·poon·*ta*
sa (*ang*·he·les)

Please take me to (this address).
Pakihatíd mo akó	pa·kee·ha·*teed* mo a·*ko*
sa (adrés na itó).	sa (a·*dres* na ee·*to*)

That's too expensive.
Masyadong mahál.	mas·*ya*·dong ma·*hal*

Is this taxi available?
Walá bang sakáy ang	wa·*la* bang sa·*kai* ang
taksing itó?	*tak*·seeng ee·*to*

How much is it (to …)?
Magkano (hanggáng …)?	mag·*ka*·no (hang·*gang* …)

Please put the meter on.
Pakilagáy ang metro.	pa·kee·la·*gai* ang *met*·ro

The meter isn't working properly.
Hindí pumapaták nang	heen·*dee'* poo·ma·pa·*tak* nang
tamà ang metro.	*ta*·ma ang *met*·ro

This isn't a direct route.
Hindî itó ang daáng	heen·*dee'* ee·*to* ang da·*ang*
tuwiran.	too·*wee*·ran

Stop the taxi/tricycle.
Ihintó mo ang	ee·heen·*to* mo ang
taksi/tráysikel.	*tak*·see/*trai*·see·kel

I want to get out.
Gustó kong bumabâ.	goos·*to* kong boo·ma·*ba'*

I'll give you …
Bibigyán kitá ng …	bee·beeg·*yan* kee·*ta* nang …

Please …	*Pakí …*	pa·*kee* …
slow down	*bagalan*	ba·*ga*·lan
stop here	*hintó dito*	heen·*to dee*·to
wait here	*hintáy dito*	heen·*tai dee*·to

---

road signs

Street signs in the Philippines are in English, and employ most internationally recognised symbols such as the red hexagon for 'stop'. Take special care when crossing at a 'pedestrian crossing' – vehicles don't actually stop for pedestrians, so you're crossing the street at your own risk!

car & motorbike

car & motorbike hire

I'd like to hire a/an …	Gustó kong umarkilá ng …	goos·to kong oo·mar·kee·la nang …
4WD	4WD	por weel draib
automatic	otomatik	o·to·ma·teek
car	kotse	kot·se
manual	manwal	man·wal
motorbike	motorsiklo	mo·tor·seek·lo

with a …	na may kasamang …	na mai ka·sa·mang …
air conditioning	erkon	er·kon
driver	tsupér	tsoo·per

How much for … hire?	Magkano ang arkiláng …?	mag·ka·no ang ar·kee·lang …
daily	arawán	a·ra·wan
weekly	lingguhan	leeng·goo·han

Does that include insurance/mileage?

Kasali ba ang seguro/kilometrahe?

ka·sa·lee ba ang se·goo·ro/kee·lo·met·ra·he

Do you have a guide to the road rules in English?

Mayroón ka bang giya sa Inglés tungkól sa mga pátakarán sa daán?

mai·ro·on ka bang gee·ya sa eeng·gles toong·kol sa ma·nga pa·ta·ka·ran sa da·an

Do you have a road map?

May mapa ka ba ng daán?

mai ma·pa ka ba nang da·an

Where can I get a helmet?

Saán ako kukuha ng helmet?

sa·an a·ko koo·koo·ha nang hel·met

on the road

What's the speed limit?
Anó ang takdáng bilís
ng takbó?
a·*no* ang tak·*dang* bee·*lees*
nang tak·*bo*

Is this the road to (Macabebe)?
Itó ba ang daán
patungo sa (Macabebe)?
ee·*to* ba ang da·*an*
pa·*too*·ngo sa (*ma*·ka·be·be)

Can I park here?
Puwede ba akóng
pumarada dito?
poo·*we*·de ba a·*kong*
poo·ma·*ra*·da dee·to

How long can I park here?
Gaano katagál akó
puwedeng pumarada
dito?
ga·*a*·no ka·ta·*gal* a·ko
poo·*we*·deng poo·ma·*ra*·da
dee·to

Do I have to pay?
Magbabayad ba akó?
mag·ba·*ba*·yad ba a·*ko*

Where's a petrol station?
Násaán ang istasyón
ng gasolina?
na·sa·*an* ang ees·tas·*yon*
nang ga·so·*lee*·na

Please fill it up.
Pakipunó ngâ.
pa·kee·poo·*no* nga'

I'd like ... litres.
... litro ngâ.
,,, *leet*·ro nga'

diesel	*disel*	*dee*·sel
(un)leaded	*(an)leded*	(an·)*le*·ded
LPG	*LPG*	*el*·pee·jee
regular	*regulár*	re·goo·*lar*
premium	*primyum*	*preem*·yoom

Can you check the ...?	*Pakitsék ngâ ang ...?*	pa·kee·*tsek* nga' ang ...
oil	*langís*	la·*ngees*
tyre pressure	*presyón ng gulóng*	pres·*yon* nang goo·*long*
water	*tubig*	*too*·beeg

problems

I need a mechanic.
Kailangan ko ng
mekániko.

ka·ee·*la*·ngan ko nang
me·*ka*·nee·ko

I've had an accident.
Náaksidente akó.

na·ak·see·*den*·te a·*ko*

I have a flat tyre.
Plat ang gulóng ko.

plat ang goo·*long* ko

The car/motorbike won't start.
Ayaw umandár ng
kotse/motorsiklo.

a·yaw oo·man·*dar* nang
kot·se/mo·tor·*seek*·lo

The (car) has broken down (at San Miguel).
Nasiraan ang (kotse)
sa (San Miguel).

na·see·*ra*·an ang (*kot*·se)
sa (san mee·*gel*)

I've lost my car keys.
Nawalâ ang susì ng
kotse ko.

na·wa·*la'* ang *soo*·see nang
kot·se ko

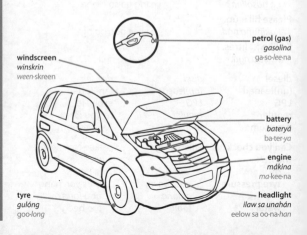

petrol (gas)
gasolina
ga·so·*lee*·na

windscreen
winskrin
ween·skreen

battery
bateryá
ba·ter·*ya*

engine
mákina
ma·kee·na

tyre
gulóng
goo·*long*

headlight
ilaw sa unahán
eelow sa oo·na·*han*

kilometro	kee·lo·*met*·ro	**kilometres**
libre	*lee*·bre	**free**
lisensiyá sa pagmamaneho	lee·sen·see·*ya* sa pag·ma·ma·*ne*·ho	**drivers licence**
metro sa pagparada	*met*·ro sa pag·pa·*ra*·da	**parking meter**

I've run out of petrol.
 Naubusan akó ng gasolina.
 na·oo·*boo*·san a·*ko* nang ga·so·*lee*·na

Can you fix it (today)?
 Kaya mo bang gawín itó (ngayón)?
 ka·ya mo bang ga·*ween* ee·*to* (nga·*yon*)

How long will it take?
 Gaano katagál?
 ga·*a*·no ka·ta·*gal*

bicycle

bisikleta

I'd like ...	*Gustó kong ...*	goos·*to* kong ...
my bicycle repaired	*ipagawâ ang aking bisikleta*	ee·pa·ga·*wa'* ang *a*·keeng bee·seek·*le*·ta
to buy a bicycle	*bumilí ng bisikleta*	boo·mee·*lee* nang bee·seek·*le*·ta
to hire a bicycle	*umarkilá ng bisikleta*	oo·mar·kee·*la* nang bee·seek·*le*·ta
I'd like a ... bike.	*Gustó ko ng bisikletang ...*	goos·*to* ko nang bee·seek·*le*·tang ...
mountain	*pambundók*	pam·boon·*dok*
racing	*pangkarera*	pang·ka·*re*·ra
second-hand	*segunda mano*	se·*goon*·da *ma*·no

How much is it per ...?	*Magkano sa isáng ...?*	mag·*ka*·no sa ee·*sang* ...
day	*araw*	*a*·row
hour	*oras*	*o*·ras

Do I need a helmet?
Kailangan ko ba ng helmet? ka·ee·*la*·ngan ko ba nang *hel*·met

Is there a bicycle-path map?
May mapa ba ng daanán ng bisikleta? mai *ma*·pa ba nang da·a·*nan* nang bee·seek·*le*·ta

I have a puncture.
Butás ang gulong ko. boo·*tas* ang goo·*long* ko

local transport

Are you waiting for more people?
Naghihintáy ka ba ng ibá pang sakáy? nag·hee·heen·*tai* ka ba nang ee·*ba* pang sa·*kai*

Can you take us around the city, please?
Pakilibot mo kamí sa siti. pa·kee·*lee*·bot mo ka·*mee* sa *see*·tee

How many people can ride on this?
Ilan ba itó? ee·*la*·nan ba ee·*to*

Is this leaving?
Áalís na ba? a·a·*lees* na ba

Will it take long?
Matagál pa ba? ma·ta·*gal* pa ba

Where can I catch a jeepney?
Saán akó sasakáy ng dyipni? sa·*an* a·ko sa·sa·*kai* nang *jeep*·nee

Where's this jeepney going?
Saán papuntá ang dyipning itó? sa·*an* pa·poon·*ta* ang *jeep*·neeng ee·*to*

border crossing

pagtawíd sa border

I'm ...	*Akó ay ...*	a·*ko* ai ...
in transit	*nakátransit*	na·ka·*tran*·seet
on business	*nasa trabaho*	*na*·sa tra·*ba*·ho
on holiday	*nakábakasyón*	na·ka·ba·kas·*yon*

I'm here for (two) ...	*Nárito akó nang (dalawàng) ...*	na·*ree*·to a·*ko* nang (da·la·*wang*) ...
days	*araw*	*a*·row
months	*buwán*	boo·*wan*
weeks	*linggó*	leeng·*go*

I'm going to (Cebu).
Pupuntá akó sa (Cebu). poo·poon·*ta* a·*ko* sa (se·*boo*)

I'm staying at (the Boracay Regency Resort).
Tútulóy akó sa (Boracay Regency Resort). too·too·*loy* a·*ko* sa (bo·ra·*kai* ree·jen·see re·*sort*)

The children are on this passport.
Ang mga batà ay nasa pasaporteng ito. ang ma·*nga ba*·ta' ai na·sa pa·sa·*por*·teng ee·to

listen for ...		
bisa	*bee*·sa	**visa**
grupo	*groo*·po	**group**
nag-íisá	nag·ee·ee·*sa*	**alone**
pamilya	pa·*meel*·ya	**family**
pasaporte	pa·sa·*por*·te	**passport**

at customs

I have nothing to declare.
Walâ akóng idédeklará.   wa·*la*' a·*kong* ee·*de*·dek·la·*ra*

I have something to declare.
Mayroón akóng   mai·ro·*on* a·*kong*
idédeklará.   ee·*de*·dek·la·*ra*

Do I have to declare this?
Dapat ko bang ideklará   *da*·pat ko bang ee·dek·la·*ra*
itó?   ee·*to*

I didn't know I had to declare it.
Hindí ko alám na dapat   heen·*dee* ko a·*lam* na *da*·pat
ko itóng ideklará.   ko ee·*tong* ee·dek·la·*ra*

That's (not) mine.
(Hindî) Akin iyán.   (heen·*dee*') a·keen ee·*yan*

signs		
Adwana	ad·*wa*·na	**Customs**
Duty-Free	*joo*·tee·pree	**Duty-Free**
Imigrasyón	ee·mee·gras·*yon*	**Immigration**
Kontrolan ng	kon·*trol*·an nang	**Passport**
Pasaporte	pa·sa·*por*·te	**Control**
Kuwárentenas	koo·*wa*·ren·*te*·nas	**Quarantine**

Can I have some help with directions, please?
Pakitulungan mo nga pa·kee·too·*loo*·ngan mo nga
akó sa direksiyón? a·*ko* sa dee·rek·see·*yon*

Where's a/the (market)?
Násaán ang (palengke)? na·sa·*an* ang (pa·*leng*·ke)

How do I get there?
Paano akó púpuntá doón? pa·*a*·no a·*ko* poo·poon·*ta* do·*on*

How far is it?
Gaano kalayo? ga·*a*·no ka·*la*·yo

What's the address?
Anó ang adrés? a·*no* ang a·*dres*

Can you show me (on the map)?
Maáari bang ipakita ma·*a*·a·ree bang ee·pa·*kee*·ta
mo sa akin (sa mapa)? mo sa *a*·keen (sa *ma*·pa)

It's …	*Iyón ay …*	ee·*yon* ai …
behind …	*nasa likurán ng …*	na·sa lee·koo·*ran* nang …
here	*nárito*	na·*ree*·to
in front of …	*sa harapán ng …*	sa·ha·ra·*pan* nang …
near (…)	*malapit (sa …)*	ma·*la*·peet (sa …)
next to …	*katabí ng …*	ka·ta·*bee* nang …
on the corner	*nasa kanto*	na·sa *kan*·to
opposite …	*katapát ng …*	ka·ta·*pat* nang …
straight ahead	*diretso*	dee·*ret*·so
there	*nároón*	na·ro·*on*

Turn …	*Lumikó sa …*	loo·mee·*ko* sa …
at the corner	*kanto*	*kan*·to
at the traffic lights	*ilaw-trápiko*	ee·low·*tra*·pee·ko
left	*kaliwâ*	ka·lee·*wa'*
right	*kanan*	*ka*·nan

typical addresses

avenue	*abenida*	a·be·*nee*·da
lane	*eskinita*	es·kee·*nee*·ta
street	*kalye*	*kal*·ye

north	*hilagà*	hee·*la*·ga'
south	*timog*	*tee*·mog
east	*silangan*	see·*la*·ngan
west	*kanluran*	kan·*loo*·ran

By ...	*Sa pamamagitan ng ...*	sa pa·ma·ma·*gee*·tan nang ...
bus	*bus*	boos
foot	*paglakad*	pag·*la*·kad
taxi	*taksi*	*tak*·see
train	*tren*	tren

What ... is this?	*Anóng ... itó?*	a·*nong* ... ee·*to*
street/road	*daán*	da·*an*
village	*baryo*	*bar*·yo

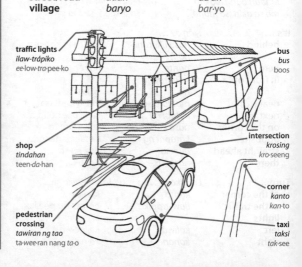

traffic lights
ilaw-trápiko
ee·low·*tra*·pee·ko

bus
bus
boos

shop
tindahan
teen·*da*·han

intersection
krosing
kro·seeng

corner
kanto
kan·to

pedestrian crossing
tawiran ng tao
ta·*wee*·ran nang *ta*·o

taxi
taksi
tak·see

finding accommodation

paghahanáp ng akomodasyón

Where's a ...?	*Násaán ang ...?*	na·sa·an ang ...
camping ground	*kampingan*	kam·*pee*·ngan
guesthouse	*bahay-bisita*	ba·hai·bee·*see*·ta
hotel	*otél*	o·*tel*
motel	*motél*	mo·*tel*
youth hostel	*hostel para*	*hos*·tel *pa*·ra
	sa kabataan	sa ka·ba·*ta*·an

Can you recommend	*May alám ka*	mai a·*lam* ka
somewhere ...?	*bang lugár na ...?*	bang loo·*gar* na ...
cheap	*mura*	*moo*·ra
clean	*malinis*	ma·*lee*·nees
good	*mainam*	ma·*ee*·nam
	marangyâ	ma·rang·ya'
nearby	*malapit*	ma·*la*·peet
romantic	*romántiko*	raw·*man*·tee·kaw

I'd like to arrange a homestay.
Gustó kong mag-ayos   goos·*to* kong mag·*a*·yos
ng panunuluyan sa   nang pa·noo·noo·*loo*·yan sa
isáng tahanan.   ee·*sang* ta·*ha*·nan

What's the address?
Anó ang adrés?   a·*no* ang a·*dres*

For responses, see **directions**, page 63.

local talk		
dive n	*di magandá*	dee ma·gan·*da*
haunted	*minumultó*	mee·noo·mool·*to*
rat-infested	*madagâ*	ma·da·*ga*'
top spot	*klas na klas*	klas na klas

booking ahead & checking in

I'd like to book a room, please.
Pakireserba mo akó
ng kuwarto.
pa·kee·re·*ser*·ba mo a·*ko*
nang koo·*war*·to

I have a reservation.
May reserbasyón akó.
mai re·ser·bas·yon a·*ko*

My name's ...
Akó si ...
a·*ko* see ...

For (three) nights/weeks.
(Tatlóng) gabí/linggó.
(tat·*long*) ga·*bee*/leeng·go

From (2 July) to (6 July).
Mulá (ika-2 ng
Hulyo) hanggáng
(ika-6 ng Hulyo).
moo·*la* (ee·ka·la·*wa* nang
hool·yo) hang·*gang*
(ee·ka·*a*·neem nang *hool*·yo)

Do I need to pay upfront?
Dapat ba akóng
magpaunang-bayad?
da·pat ba a·*kong*
mag·pa·*oo*·nang·*ba*·yad

Do you have a ... room?	Mayroón ba kayóng kuwartong ...?	mai·ro·*on* ba ka·*yong* koo·*war*·tong ...
double	pandalawahan	pan·da·la·*wa*·han
single	pang-isahan	pang·ee·*sa*·han
twin	may kambál na kama	mai kam·*bal* na *ka*·ma

How much is it per ...?	Magkano ba para sa isáng ...?	mag·*ka*·no ba *pa*·ra sa ee·*sang* ...
night	gabí	ga·*bee*
person	katao	ka·*ta*·o
week	linggó	leeng·*go*

Iláng gabí?	ee·lang ga·bee	**How many nights?**
pasaporte	pa·sa·por·te	**passport**
punô	poo·no'	**full**

Can I see it?
 Puwede ko bang tingnán? poo·we·de ko bang teeng·nan

I'll take it.
 Kukunin ko. koo·koo·neen ko

Can I pay by ...? *Puwede ba akóng* poo·we·de ba a·kong
 magbayad ng ...? mag·ba·yad nang ...
 credit card *kredit kard* kre·deet kard
 travellers cheque *travellers tsek* tra·be·lers tsek

For other methods of payment, see **shopping**, page 75.

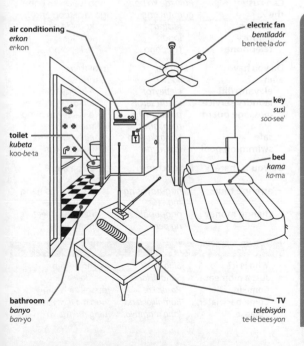

air conditioning
erkon
er·kon

electric fan
bentiladór
ben·tee·la·dor

key
susì
soo·see'

toilet
kubeta
koo·be·ta

bed
kama
ka·ma

bathroom
banyo
ban·yo

TV
telebisyón
te·le·bees·yon

accommodation

requests & queries

When is breakfast served?
Anóng oras ang agahan? a·*nong* o·ras ang a·*ga*·han

Where is breakfast served?
Saán ang agahan? sa·*an* ang a·*ga*·han

Please wake me at (seven).
Pakigising mo akó ng pa·kee·*gee*·seeng mo a·*ko* nang
(alás-siyete). (a·*las*·see·*ye*·te)

Can I use the ...?	*Puwede ko bang gamitin ang ...?*	poo·*we*·de ko bang ga·*mee*·teen ang ...
kitchen	*kusinà*	koo·*see*·na'
laundry	*londri*	*lon*·dree
telephone	*telépono*	te·*le*·po·no

Do you have a/an ...?	*Mayroón bang ...?*	mai·ro·*on* bang ...
elevator/lift	*elebeytor*	e·le·*bay*·tor
laundry service	*londri serbis*	*lon*·dree *ser*·bees
message board	*paskilan ng mensahe*	pas·*kee*·lan nang men·*sa*·he
safe	*kaha de yero*	*ka*·ha de *ye*·ro
swimming pool	*languyan*	la·*ngoo*·yan

Do you ... here?	*Kayó ba ang ... dito?*	ka·*yo* ba ang ... *dee*·to
arrange tours	*nag-aayos ng mga tur*	nag·a·*a*·yos nang ma·*nga* toor
change money	*nagpapalít ng pera*	nag·pa·pa·*leet* nang *pe*·ra

---

a knock at the door ...

Who is it?	*Sino iyán?*	*see*·no ee·*yan*
Just a moment.	*Sandalí lang.*	san·da·*lee* lang
Come in.	*Pasok ka.*	*pa*·sok ka
Come back later, please.	*Bumalík ka na lang mámayâ.*	boo·ma·*leek* ka na lang *ma*·ma·ya

resepsiyón	re·sep·see·*yon*	**reception**
susì	soo·see'	**key**

Could I have ..., please? — *Pakibigyán mo ako ng ...?* — pa·kee·beeg·*yan* mo a·*ko* nang ...

an extra blanket	*isá pang blangket*	ee·*sa* pang *blang*·ket
my key	*aking susì*	*a*·keeng soo·see'
a mosquito coil	*katól*	ka·*tol*
a mosquito net	*kulambô*	koo·lam·*bo*'
a receipt	*resibo*	re·*see*·bo
a towel	*tuwalya*	too·*wal*·ya
some soap	*sabón*	sa·*bon*

Is there a message for me?
May mensahe ba para sa akin? — mai men·*sa*·he ba *pa*·ra sa *a*·keen

Can I leave a message for someone?
Puwede ba akong mag-iwan ng mensahe? — poo·*we*·de ba a·*kong* mag·*ee*·wan nang men·*sa*·he

Could you put some drinking water in my room?
Puwede bang pakilagyán mo ng inumíng tubig ang aking kuwarto? — poo·*we*·de bang pa·kee·lag·*yan* mo ng ee·noo·*meeng* too·beeg ang *a*·keeng koo·*war*·to

I'm locked out of my room.
Nápagsarahán akó ng pintó ng aking kuwarto. — na·pag·sa·ra·*han* a·*ko* nang peen·*to* nang *a*·keeng koo·*war*·to

complaints

It's too ...
Masyadong ...
mas·*ya*·dong ...

  bright
maliwanag
ma·lee·*wa*·nag

  cold
malamíg
ma·la·*meeg*

  dark
madilím
ma·dee·*leem*

  dirty
marumí
ma·roo·*mee*

  expensive
mahál
ma·*hal*

  noisy
maingay
ma·*ee*·ngai

  small
maliít
ma·lee·*eet*

The ... doesn't work.
Hindî umaandár ang ...
heen·*dee'* oo·ma·an·*dar* ang ...

  air conditioning
erkon
er·kon

  electricity
koryente
kor·*yen*·te

  fan
bentiladór
ben·tee·la·*dor*

  toilet
kubeta
koo·*be*·ta

Can I get another (blanket)?
Makakukuha ba akó ng isá pang (blangket)?
ma·ka·koo·*koo*·ha ba a·*ko* nang ee·*sa* pang (*blang*·ket)

This (pillow) isn't clean.
Ang (unan) na ito ay hindî malinis.
ang (*oo*·nan) na ee·*to* ay heen·*dee* ma·*lee*·nees

There's no hot water.
Waláng mainit na tubig.
wa·*lang* ma·*ee*·neet na *too*·beeg

I can't open/close the window.
Hindí ko mabuksán/ máisara ang bintanà.
heen·*dee* ko ma·book·*san*/ ma·ee·sa·*ra* ang been·*ta*·na'

The fire escape isn't accessible.
Ang labasan sa oras ng sunog ay hindí maáabót.
ang la·*ba*·san sa *o*·ras nang *soo*·nog ai heen·*dee* ma·*a*·a·bot

checking out

What time is checkout?
Anóng oras ang tsek awt?   a·*nong* o·ras ang tsek owt

Can I have a late checkout?
Puwede ba akóng   poo·*we*·de ba a·*kong*
máhulí ng pagtsek awt?   ma·hoo·*lee* nang pag·*tsek* owt

Can you call a taxi for me (for 11 o'clock)?
Pakitawag mo akó ng   pa·kee·*ta*·wag mo a·*ko* nang
taksi (para sa alás-onse)?   tak·see (*pa*·ra sa a·*las* on·se)

I'm leaving now.
Áalís na akó.   a·a·*lees* na a·*ko*

Can I leave my bags here?
Puwede ko bang iwan ang   poo·*we*·de ko bang *ee*·wan ang
aking bagahe dito?   a·keeng ba·*ga*·he *dee*·to

There's a mistake in the bill.
May malí sa kuwenta.   mai ma·*lee* sa koo·*wen*·ta

I had a great stay, thank you.
Nasiyahán akó dito,   na·see·ya·*han* a·ko *dee*·to
salamat.   sa·*la*·mat

I'll recommend it to my friends.
Irerekomendá ko itó sa   ee·re·re·ko·men·*da* ko ee·*to* sa
mga kaibigan ko.   ma·*nga* ka·ee·*bee*·gan ko

Could I have my ..., please?	*Pakibigáy ngâ ang aking ...?*	pa·kee·bee·*gai* nga' ang *a*·keeng ...
deposit	*depósito*	de·*po*·see·to
valuables	*mga mahahalagáng bagay*	ma·*nga* ma·ha·ha·la·*gang* ba·gai

I'll be back ...	*Babalík ulî akó ...*	ba·ba·*leek* oo·*lee'* a·ko ...
in (three) days	*sa loób ng (tatlóng) araw*	sa lo·*ob* nang (tat·*long*) a·row
on (Tuesday)	*sa (Martés)*	sa (mar·*tes*)

71

camping

Do you have …?	Mayroón bang …?	mai·ro·*on* bang …
electricity	koryente	kor·*yen*·te
a laundry	londri	*lon*·dree
shower facilities	páliguán	pa·lee·goo·*an*
a site	lugár	loo·*gar*
tents for hire	mga tolda na máhihirám	ma·*nga* tol·da na ma·hee·hee·*ram*

How much is it per …?	Magkano ang isáng …?	mag·*ka*·no ang ee·*sang* …
caravan	káraban	*ka*·ra·ban
person	tao	*ta*·o
tent	tolda	*tol*·da
vehicle	sasakyán	sa·sak·*yan*

Can I …?	Puwede ba akóng …?	poo·*we*·de ba a·*kong* …
camp here	magkamping dito	mag·*kam*·peeng *dee*·to
park next to my tent	magparada sa tabí ng aking tolda	mag·pa·*ra*·da sa ta·*bee* nang a·*keeng* tol·da

Who do I ask to stay here?

Sino ang kákausapin para humintô akó dito?

see·no ang ka·ka·oo·*sa*·peen pa·ra hoo·meen·to' a·*ko* dee·to

Could I borrow …?

Puwede bang máhirám ang …

poo·*we*·de bang ma·hee·*ram* ang …

Is it coin-operated?

Umaandár ba itó pag-nilagyán ng bagól?

oo·ma·an·*dar* ba ee·*to* pag·nee·lag·*yan* nang ba·*gol*

Is the water drinkable?

Okey bang inumín ang tubig?

o·kay bang ee·noo·*meen* ang *too*·beeg

Babae	ba·*ba*·e	**Women**
Banyo	*ban*·yo	**Bathroom**
Kubeta	koo·*be*·ta	**Toilet**
Lalaki	la·*la*·kee	**Men**
May Bakante	mai ba·*kan*·te	**Vacancy**
Walá nang	wa·*la* nang	**No Vacancy**
Bakante	ba·*kan*·te	

renting

pagrenta

I'm here about the ... for rent.	*Nárito akó tungkól sa ... na 'for rent'.*	na·ree·to a·*ko* toong·*kol* sa ... na por rent
Do you have a/an ... for rent?	*Mayroón ka bang isáng ... na 'for rent'?*	mai·ro·*on* ka bang ee·*sang* ... na por rent
apartment	*apartment*	a·*part*·ment
cabin	*kubo*	*koo*·bo
dump	*lugar hindí maganda*	*loo*·gar heen·*dee* ma·gan·*da*
house	*bahay*	*ba*·hai
room	*kuwarto*	koo·*war*·to
villa	*bilya*	*beel*·ya
furnished	*may kasangkapan*	mai ka·sang·*ka*·pan
partly furnished	*may iláng kasangkapan*	mai ee·*lang* ka·sang·*ka*·pan
unfurnished	*waláng kasangkapan*	wa·*lang* ka·sang·*ka*·pan

accommodation

73

staying with locals

panunuluyan sa mga tagároón

Can I stay at your place?
Puwede ba akóng   poo·*we*·de ba a·*kong*
manuluyan sa iyóng   ma·noo·*loo*·yan sa ee·*yong*
lugár?   loo·*gar*

Is there anything I can do to help?
May maitutulong ba akó?   mai ma·ee·too·*too*·long ba a·*ko*

I have my own …	*Mayroón akóng*	mai·ro·on a·*kong*
	sariling …	sa·*ree*·leeng …
mattress	*kutsón*	koot·*son*
sleeping bag	*bag na tulugán*	bag na too·loo·*gan*

Can I …?	*Puwede ba*	poo·*we*·de ba
	akóng …?	a·*kong* …
bring anything for the meal	*magdalá ng anumán para sa kainan?*	mag·da·*la* nang a·noo·*man* pa·ra sa ka·*ee*·nan
do the dishes	*maghugas ng pinggán*	mag·*hoo*·gas nang peeng·*gan*
set/clear the table	*maghain/ maglinis ng mesa*	mag·*ha*·een/ mag·*lee*·nees nang *me*·sa
take out the rubbish	*magtapon ng basura*	mag·*ta*·pon nang ba·*soo*·ra

Thanks for your hospitality.
Salamat sa iyóng   sa·*la*·mat sa ee·*yong*
kagandahang-loób.   ka·gan·*da*·hang·lo·*ob*

For dining-related expressions, see **food**, page 159.

74

looking for ...

Where's a/the ...?	*Násaán ang ...?*	na·sa·an ang ...
department store	*department*	de·*part*·ment ees·*tor*
store	*istór*	
market	*palengke*	pa·*leng*·ke
supermarket	*supermarket*	soo·per·*mar*·ket

Where can I buy (a padlock)?
Saán akó makabíbilí ng (kandado)?
sa·*an* a·ko ma·ka·*bee*·bee·*lee* nang (kan·*da*·do)

For phrases on directions, see **directions**, page 63.

making a purchase

I'm just looking.
Tumitingín lang akó.
too·mee·tee·*ngeen* lang a·*ko*

I'd like to buy (an adaptor plug).
Gustó kong bumilí ng (adaptor plag).
goos·*to* kong boo·mee·*lee* nang (a·*dap*·tor plag)

How much is it?
Magkano?
mag·*ka*·no

Can you write down the price?
Pakisulat mo ang presyo?
pa·kee·*soo*·lat mo ang *pres*·yo

Do you have any others?
Mayroón ka bang ibá?
mai·ro·*on* ka bang ee·*ba*

Can I look at it?
Puwede ko bang tingnán?
poo·*we*·de ko bang teeng·*nan*

Makatutulong ba akó? ma·ka·too·*too*·long ba a·*ko*	**Can I help you?**
Iyán lang ba? ee·*yan* lang ba	**Anything else?**
Walá kamí. wa·*la* ka·*mee*	**No, we don't have any.**

Do you accept ...?	*Tumatanggáp ka* *ba ng ...?*	too·ma·tang·*gap* ka ba nang ...
credit cards	*kredit kard*	*kre*·deet kard
debit cards	*debit kard*	*de*·beet kard
travellers cheques	*travellers tsek*	*tra*·be·lers tsek

Could I have a ..., **please?**	*Puwedeng* *pakibigyán mo* *akó ng ...?*	poo·*we*·deng pa·kee·beeg·*yan* mo a·*ko* nang ...
bag	*bag*	bag
receipt	*resibo*	re·*see*·bo

I don't need a bag, thanks.
Hindí ko kailangan   heen·*dee* ko ka·ee·*la*·ngan
ng bag, salamat.   nang bag sa·*la*·mat

Could I have it wrapped?
Puwedeng pakibalot?   poo·*we*·deng pa·kee·*ba*·lot

Does it have a guarantee?
Mayroón ba itong   mai·ro·*on* ba ee·*tong*
garantiyá?   ga·ran·tee·*ya*

Can I have it sent overseas?
Puwede ko bang   poo·*we*·de ko bang
ipadalá sa ibáng bansâ?   ee·pa·da·*la* sa ee·*bang* ban·*sa'*

Can you order it for me?
Puwedeng paki-order   poo·*we*·deng pa·kee·*or*·der
mo para sa akin?   mo *pa*·ra sa *a*·keen

Can I pick it up later?
Puwede ko bang kunin   poo·*we*·de ko bang *koo*·neen
mámayâ?   *ma*·ma·ya'

It's faulty.	Sirâ itó.	see·ra' ee·to
I'd like ..., please.	Pakí lang,	pa·kee lang
	gustó ko ...	goos·to ko ...
my change	ng suklí ko	nang sook·lee ko
a refund	na ibalík mo	na ee·ba·leek mo
	ang pera ko	ang pe·ra ko
to return this	na isolì itó	na ee·so·lee' ee·to

bargaining

That's too expensive.
Masyadong mahál.   mas·ya·dong ma·hal

Can you lower the price?
Puwede mo bang ibabâ   poo·we·de mo bang ee·ba·ba'
ang presyo?   ang pres·yo

Do you have something cheaper?
Mayroón ka bang mas   mai·ro·on ka bang mas
mura?   moo·ra

I'll give you (five pesos).
Bibigyán kitá ng   bee·beeg·yan kee·ta nang
(limáng piso).   (lee·mang pee·so)

I don't want to pay the full price.
Ayokong magbayad ng   a·yo·kong mag·ba·yad nang
buóng presyo.   boo·ong pres·yo

clothes

mga damít

My size is …	Ang sukat ko ay …	ang *soo*·kat ko ai …
40	forty	*por*·tee
small	small	ees·*mol*
medium	medium	*meed*·yoom
large	large	lards

Can I try it on?
Puwede ko bang isukat?   poo·*we*·de ko bang ee·*soo*·kat

It doesn't fit.
Hindí hustó.   heen·*dee* hoos·to

Can you recommend a tailor?
May alám ka bang sastré?   mai a·*lam* ka bang sas·*tre*

For clothing items, see the **dictionary**.

repairs

pagkumpuní

Can I have my … repaired here?
Puwede ko bang   poo·*we*·de ko bang
ipakumpuní dito   ee·pa·koom·poo·*nee* dee·to
ang aking …?   ang *a*·keeng …

When will my … be ready?
Kailán mayayarì   ka·ee·*lan* ma·ya·*ya*·ree'
ang aking …?   ang *a*·keeng …

backpack	bakpak	*bak*·pak
camera	kámera	*ka*·me·ra
glasses	salamín sa mata	sa·la·*meen* sa ma·*ta*
shoes	sapatos	sa·*pa*·tos
sunglasses	sanglas	*san*·glas

PRACTICAL

hairdressing

pag-aayos ng buhók

I'd like (a) ...	Gustó ko ng ...	goos·to ko nang ...
blow wave	bloweyb	blo·wayb
colour	kulay	koo·lai
haircut	gupít	goo·peet
my beard trimmed	gupitán nang bahagyâ ang aking balbás	goo·pee·tan nang ba·hag·ya' ang a·keeng bal·bas
shave	ahit	a·heet
trim	bahagyáng gupít	ba·hag·yang goo·peet

Don't cut it too short.
Huwág mong gupitín nang maiklî.
hoo·wag mong goo·pee·teen nang ma·eek·lee'

Please use a new blade.
Puwede bang gumamit ka ng bagong talím?
poo·we·de bang goo·ma·meet ka nang ba·gong ta·leem

Shave it all off!
Ahitin mong lahát!
a·hee·teen mong la·hat

I should never have let you near me!
Ilindí kitá dapat pinalapit sa akin!
heen·dee kee·ta da·pat pee·na·la·peet sa a·keen

For colours, see the **dictionary**.

shopping

79

books & reading

Do you have …?	Mayroón ka bang …?	mai·ro·on ka bang …
a book by (Cesar Ruiz Aquino)	isáng libró ni (Cesar Ruiz Aquino)	ee·sang lee·bro nee (se·sar roo·ees a·kee·no)
an entertainment guide	isáng giya tungkól sa libangan	ee·sang gee·ya toong·kol sa lee·ba·ngan
Is there an English-language …?	Mayroón bang … na may Inglés?	mai·ro·on bang … na mai eeng·gles
bookshop	tindahan ng libró	teen·da·han nang lee·bro
section	isáng seksiyón	ee·sang seks·yon
I'd like a …	Gustó ko ng …	goos·to ko nang …
dictionary	diksiyunaryo	deek·see·yoo·nar·yo
newspaper (in English)	páhayagán (sa Inglés)	pa·ha·ya·gan (sa eeng·gles)
notepad	sulatáng-papél	soo·la·tang·pa·pel

Can you recommend a book for me?
May mairerekomendá
ka bang libró sa akin?
mai ma·ee·re·re·ko·men·da
ka bang lee·bro sa a·keen

Do you have Lonely Planet guidebooks?
Mayroón ka bang mga
giyang libró ng
Lonely Planet?
mai·ro·on ka bang ma·nga
gee·yang lee·bro nang
lon·lee pla·net

music

músika

I'd like a …	*Gustó ko ng …*	goos·*to* ko nang …
blank tape	*blangkong teyp*	*blang*·kong tayp
CD	*CD*	*see*·dee

I'm looking for something by (Lea Salonga).
Nagháhanáp akó ng gawá ng (Lea Salonga).
nag·ha·ha·*nap* a·ko nang ga·*wa* nang (*lee*·a sa·*long*·ga)

What's their best recording?
Anó ang pinakamagalíng niláng rekording?
a·*no* ang pee·na·*ka*·ma·ga·*leeng* nee·*lang* re·*kor*·deeng

Can I listen to this?
Puwede ko ba itóng pakinggán?
poo·*we*·de ko ba ee·*tong* pa·keeng·*gan*

electronic goods

mga bagay na elektronik

Will this work on any DVD player?
Puwede ba itó kahit alíng DVD player?
poo·*we*·de ba ee·*to* ka·heet a·*leeng* dee·*vee*·dee *play*·er

Is this a (PAL/NTSC) system?
Itó ba ay sistemang (PAL/NTSC)?
ee·*to* ba ai sees·*te*·mang (pal/en·tee·es·*see*)

Is this the latest model?
Itó ba ang pinakabagong modelo?
ee·*to* ba ang pee·na·ka·*ba*·gong mo·*de*·lo

Is this (240) volts?
Itó ba ay (240) boltahe?
ee·*to* ba ai (too·*por*·tee) bol·*ta*·he

Where can I buy duty-free electronic goods?
Saán akó makabíbilí ng dyutipring bagay na elektronik?
sa·*an* a·ko ma·ka·*bee*·bee·*lee* nang *joo*·tee·preeng *ba*·gay na e·lek·*tro*·neek

photography

I need ... film for this camera.	Kailangan ko ng ... pilm para sa kamerang itó.	ka·ee·la·ngan ko nang ... pilm pa·ra sa ka·me·rang ee·to
APS	APS	ay·pee·es
black & white	blak en wayt	blak en wait
colour	de-kolór	de·ko·lor
slide	isláyd	ees·laid
(200) speed	(200) ispid	(too han·dred) ees·peed

Can you ...?	Puwede ka bang ...?	poo·we·de ka bang ...
develop digital photos	magdebelop ng litratong dígitál	mag·de·be·lop nang leet·ra·tong dee·jee·tal
develop this film	magdibelop ng pilm na itó	mag·de·be·lop nang pilm na ee·to
load my film	magkargá ng aking pilm	mag·kar·ga nang a·keeng pilm
recharge the battery for my digital camera	mag-recharge ng bateryá para sa aking kamerang digitál	mag·ree·tsarj nang ba·ter·ya pa·ra sa a·keeng ka·me·rang dee·jee·tal
transfer photos from my camera to CD	magsalin ng litrato mulá sa aking kamera sa CD	mag·sa·leen nang leet·ra·to moo·la sa a·keeng ka·me·ra sa see·dee

When will it be ready?
Kailán ito matatapos?   ka·ee·lan ee·to ma·ta·ta·pos

I need a passport photo taken.
Kailangan ko ng litrato   ka·ee·la·ngan ko nang leet·ra·to
para sa pasaporte.   pa·ra sa pa·sa·por·te

I'm not happy with these photos.
Hindí ko gustó ang mga   heen·dee ko goos·to ang ma·nga
litratong itó.   leet·ra·tong ee·to

post office

tanggapan ng koreo

Generally, postal employees speak English, but if you want to practise some Filipino the phrases below should get you by.

I want to send a ...	Gustó kong magpadalá ng ...	goos·to kong mag·pa·da·la nang ...
fax	fax	paks
letter	sulat	soo·lat
parcel	pakete	pa·ke·te
postcard	poskard	pos·kard

I want to buy a/an ...	Gustó kong bumilí ng ...	goos·to kong boo·mee·lee nang ...
aerogram	érogram	e·ro·gram
envelope	sobre	so·bre
stamp	selyo	sel·yo

customs declaration	deklarasyón sa adwana	de·kla·ras·yon sa ad·wa·na
domestic	lokál	lo·kal
fragile	delikado	de·lee·ka·do
international	internasyonál	een·ter·nas·yo·nal
mail n	koreo	ko·re·o
mailbox	hulugán ng sulat	hoo·loo·gan nang soo·lat
postcode	postcode	pos·kohd

Please send it by air/surface mail to (Australia).

Pakipadalá itó nang air/surface mail sa (Australya).

pa·kee·pa·da·*la* ee·*to* nang er/*sar*·pays mayl sa (ows·*tral*·ya)

It contains (souvenirs).

May lamáng (mga subenír).

mai la·*mang* (ma·*nga* soo·be·*neer*)

Where's the poste restante section?

Saán ang kuhanán ng mga sulat ko?

sa·*an* ang koo·ha·*nan* nang ma·*nga* soo·*lat* ko

Is there any mail for me?

May sulat ba akó?

mai *soo*·lat ba a·*ko*

phone

What's your phone number?

Anó ang número ng telépono mo?

a·*no* ang *noo*·me·ro nang te·*le*·po·no mo

Where's the nearest public phone?

Násaán ang pinakamalapit na teléponong pampúbliko?

na·sa·*an* ang pee·na·*ka*·ma·la·*peet* na te·*le*·po·nong pam·*poob*·lee·ko

Where's the nearest regional telephone office?

Násaán ang pinakamalapit na pangrehiyóng upisina ng telépono?

na·sa·*an* ang pee·na·*ka*·ma·la·*peet* na pang·re·hee·*yong* oo·pee·*see*·na nang te·*le*·po·no

Do I need to call through an operator?

Kailangan ko bang dumaán sa opereytor?

ka·ee·*la*·ngan ko bang doo·ma·*an* sa o·pe·*ray*·tor

Can I look at a phone book?

Maáari ko bang tingnán ang phone book?

ma·*a*·a·ree ko bang teeng·*nan* ang pon book

I want to ...	Gustó kong ...	goos·to kong ...
buy a phonecard	bumilí ng phonecard	boo·mee·lee nang pon kard
call (Singapore)	tumawag sa (Singapore)	too·ma·wag sa (seeng·ga·por)
make a (local) call	tumawag sa lokal na número	too·ma·wag sa lo·kal na noo·me·ro
reverse the charges	irebérs ang bayad	ee·re·bers ang ba·yad
speak for (three) minutes	tumawag nang (tatlóng) minuto	too·ma·wag nang (tat·long) mee·noo·to

How much does ... cost?	Magkano ang ...?	mag·ka·no ang ...
a (three)-minute call	(tatlóng) minutong tawag	(tat·long) mee·noo·tong ta·wag
each extra minute	bawat ekstrang minuto	ba·wat eks·trang mee·noo·to

The number is ...
Ang número ay ...   ang noo·me·ro ai ...

What's the area/country code for (New Zealand)?
Anó ang area/country   a·no ang er·ya/kown·tree
code para sa (Nyu Siland)? kohd pa·ra sa (nyu see·lan)

It's engaged.
Bisi.   bee·see

I've been cut off.
Nawalâ ang koneksiyón.   na·wa·la' ang ko·nek·see·yon

The connection's bad.
Masamâ ang koneksiyón.   ma·sa·ma' ang ko·nek·see·yon

Hello.
Helów.   he·*loh*

It's (Josie).
Itó si (Josie).   ee·*to* see (jo·see)

Is (Marie) there?
Náriyán ba si (Marie)?   na·ree·*yan* ba see (ma·*ree*)

Can I speak to …?
Puwede maka-usap si …?   poo·*we*·de ma·ka·*oo*·sap si …

Can I leave a message?
Puwede ba akóng   poo·*we*·de ba a·*kong*
mag-iwan ng mensahe?   mag·*ee*·wan nang men·*sa*·he

Please tell him/her I called.
Pakisabi sa kanyá na   pa·kee·*sa*·bee sa kan·*ya* na
tumawag akó.   too·*ma*·wag a·*ko*

My number is …
Ang telépono ko ay …   ang te·*le*·po·no ko ai …

I don't have a contact number.
Walâ akóng kontak na   wa·*la*' a·*kong kon*·tak na
número.   *noo*·me·ro

I'll call back later.
Tatawag ulî akó.   ta·*ta*·wag oo·lee' a·*ko*

listen for …

Wrong number. rong *nam*·ber	**Wrong number.**
Sino itó? *see*·no ee·to	**Who's calling?**
Sino ang gustó mong kausapin? *see*·no ang goos·*to* mong ka·oo·*sa*·peen	**Who do you want to speak to?**
Sandalí lang. san·da·*lee* lang	**One moment.**
Walá siyá dito. wa·*la* see·*ya* dee·to	**He/She is not here.**
Walá si (Marie) dito. wa·*la* see (ma·*ree*) *dee*·to	**(Marie) is not here.**

mobile/cell phone

cell phone

I'd like a ...	Gustó ko ng ...	goos·to ko nang ...
charger for my phone	charger para sa aking telépono	tsar·jer pa·ra sa a·keeng te·le·po·no
mobile/cell phone for hire	mobile/cell phone na inaárkilá	mo·bail/sel·pon na ee·na·ar·kee·la
prepaid mobile/cell phone	prepaid na mobile/cell phone	pree·payd na mo·bail/sel pon
SIM card	SIM kard	seem kard

What are the rates?
Magkano ang presyo? — mag·ka·no ang pres·yo

(30c) per (30) seconds.
(Trenta séntimos) kada (trenta) segundo. — (tren·ta sen·tee·mos) ka·da (tren·ta) se·goon·do

the internet

ang ínternet

Where's the local Internet cafe?
Násaán ang lokal na ínternet café? — na·sa·an ang lo·kal na een·ter·net ka·pay

I'd like to check my email.
Gustó kong tsekin ang aking email. — goos·to kong tsek·een ang a·keeng ee·mayl

I'd like to use ...	Gustó kong gumamit ng ...	goos·to kong goo·ma·meet nang ...
the Internet	ínternet	een·ter·net
a printer	printer	preen·ter
a scanner	iskaner	ees·ka·ner

Do you have …?	Mayroón ka bang …?	mai·ro·on ka bang …
PCs	PC	pee·see
Macs	Mac	mak
a Zip drive	Zip drive	seep draib
How much per …?	Magkano kada …?	mag·ka·no ka·da …
hour	oras	o·ras
(five) minutes	(limáng) minuto	(lee·mang) mee·noo·to
page	pahina	pa·hee·na

How do I log on?

Paano akó maglo-log on? — pa·a·no a·ko mag·lo·log·on

Please change it to the English-language setting.

Pakipalitán mo itó ng seting na Inglés. — pa·kee·pa·lee·tan mo ee·to nang se·teeng na eeng·gles

It's crashed.

Nagkras itó. — nag·kras ee·to

I've finished.

Tapós na akó. — ta·pos na a·ko

---

an abrupt ending

Filipinos don't normally say goodbye on the phone. At the end of a phone conversation it's normal just to hear *okey* o·key or *sigé* see·ge (okay) and then the dial tone.

In the rural areas of the Philippines, such as the smaller towns in the provinces, banking facilities are somewhat limited and some stores may even reject payment with plastic.

It's best to make sure you have local currency and these useful phrases handy when venturing out of the city.

What time does the bank open?

Anóng oras ang bukás ng bangko?	a·*nong* o·ras ang boo·*kas* nang *bang*·ko

Where can I ...?	Saán akó ...?	sa·*an* a·ko ...
I'd like to ...	Gustó kong ...	goos·to kong ...
cash a cheque	magpalít ng tseke	mag·pa·*leet* nang *tse*·ke
change a travellers cheque	magpalít ng trábelers tsek	mag·pa·*leet* nang tra·be·lers tsek
change money	magpalít ng pera	mag·pa·*leet* nang *pe*·ra
get a cash advance	kumuha ng abanse	koo·*moo*·ha nang a·*ban*·se
withdraw money	maglabás ng pera	mag·la·*bas* nang *pe*·ra
Where's ...?	Násaán ang ...?	na·sa·*an* ang ...
an automated teller machine	ATM	*ay*·tee·em
a foreign exchange office	palitan ng pera	pa·*lee*·tan nang *pe*·ra

ID	*ai*·dee	**identification**
pasaporte	pa·sa·*por*·te	**passport**

May problema. — **There's a problem.**
  mai pro·*ble*·ma

Walá ka nang pera(ng nátitirá). — **You have no funds (left).**
  wa·*la* ka nang *pe*·ra(ng *na*·tee·tee·*ra*)

Hindí namin magagawâ iyán. — **We can't do that.**
  heen·*dee* na·meen ma·ga·ga·*wa*' ee·*yan*

Pumirma ka dito. — **Sign here.**
  poo·*meer*·ma ka *dee*·to

What's the ...?	*Anó ang ...?*	a·*no* ang ...
charge for that	*bayad para diyán*	*ba*·yad *pa*·ra dee·*yan*
exchange rate	*palít*	pa·*leet*

The automated teller machine took my card.
  Kinain ng ATM ang kard ko. — kee·*na*·een nang *ay*·tee·em ang kard ko

I've forgotten my PIN.
  Nakalimutan ko ang aking PIN. — na·ka·lee·*moo*·tan ko ang a·keeng peen

Can I use my credit card to withdraw money?
  Puwede ko bang gamitin ang aking kredit kard para maglabás ng pera? — poo·*we*·de ko bang ga·*mee*·teen ang a·keeng *kre*·deet kard pa·ra mag·la·*bas* nang *pe*·ra

Has my money arrived yet?
  Dumatíng na ba ang pera ko? — doo·ma·*teeng* na ba ang *pe*·ra ko

How long will it take to arrive?
  Gaano katagál bago itó dumatíng? — ga·*a*·no ka·ta·*gal* ba·go ee·to doo·ma·*teeng*

For other useful phrases, see **money**.

I'd like a/an ...	Gustó ko ng isang ...	goos·to ko nang ee·sang ...
audio set	audio set	o·dee·yo set
catalogue	katálogo	ka·ta·lo·go
guide	giya	gee·ya
guidebook	giyang-aklát	gee·yang·ak·lat
(in English)	(sa Inglés)	(sa eeng·gles)
(local) map	mapa	ma·pa
	(ng poók)	(nang po·ok)

Do you have information on ... sights?	May impormasyón ba kayó tungkól sa mga tanawing ...?	mai eem·por·mas·yon ba ka·yo toong·kol sa ma·nga ta·na·weeng ...
cultural	pangkultura	pang·kool·too·ra
historical	pang-istóriko	pang·ees·to·ree·ko
religious	pangrelihiyón	pang·re·lee·hee·yon

I'd like to see ...
Gustó kong makita ...   goos·to kong ma·kee·ta ...

What's that?
Anó iyán?   a·no ee·yan

Who made it?
Sino ang gumawâ?   see·no ang goo·ma·wa'

How old is it?
Ilang taón na iyan?   ee·lang ta·on na ee·yan

That's beautiful!
Iyon ay magandá!   ee·yon ay ma gan·da

Could you take a photo of me?
Puwede mo ba akóng   poo·*we*·de mo ba a·*kong*
kunan ng litrato?   *koo*·nan nang leet·*ra*·to

Can I take a photo (of you)?
Puwede bang kunan   poo·*we*·de bang *koo*·nan
(kitá) ng litrato?   (kee·*ta*) nang leet·*ra*·to

I'll send you the photo.
Padadalhán kita ng   pa·da·dal·*han* kee·*ta* nang
litrato.   leet·*ra*·to

Can you write down your name and address?
Puwede bang   poo·*we*·de bang
pakisulat mo ang   pa·kee·*soo*·lat mo ang
iyóng pangalan   ee·*yong* pa·*nga*·lan
at tirahan?   at tee·*ra*·han

getting in

What time does it open/close?

Anóng oras ang	a·*nong* o·ras ang	
bukás/sará?	boo·*kas*/sa·*ra*	

What's the admission charge?

Magkano ang pagpasok?	mag·*ka*·no ang pag·*pa*·sok

Is there a	*May diskuwento*	mai dees·koo·*wen*·to
discount for ...?	*ba para sa mga ...?*	ba *pa*·ra sa ma·*nga* ...
children	*bata*	*ba*·ta
families	*pamilya*	pa·*meel*·ya
groups	*grupo*	*groo*·po
older people	*matatandâ*	ma·ta·tan·*da'*
pensioners	*pensyonado*	pens·yo·*na*·do
students	*estudyante*	es·tood·*yan*·te

tours

Can you	*May*	mai
recommend a ...?	*mairerekomendá*	ma·ee·re·re·ko·men·*da*
	ka ba na ...?	ka ba na ...
When's the	*Kailán ang*	ka·ee·*lan* ang
next ...?	*súsunód na ...?*	*soo*·soo·*nod* na ...
boat trip	*biyahe ng*	bee·*ya*·he nang
	bapór	ba·*por*
day trip	*pang-araw na*	pang·*a*·row na
	biyahe	bee·*ya*·he
tour	*tur*	toor

Is ... included?	*Kasama ba ang ...?*	ka·*sa*·ma ba ang ...
accommodation	*akomodasyón*	a·ko·mo·das·*yon*
food	*pagkain*	pag·*ka*·een
transport	*sasakyán*	sa·sak·*yan*

sightseeing

93

The guide will pay.
Magbabayad ang giya.   mag·ba·*ba*·yad ang *gee*·ya

The guide has paid.
Nagbayad na ang giya.   nag·*ba*·yad na ang *gee*·ya

How long is the tour?
Iláng oras ang tour?   ee·*lang o*·ras ang toor

What time should we be back?
Anóng oras tayo dapat   a·*nong o*·ras *ta*·yo *da*·pat
bumalík?   boo·ma·*leek*

I'm with them.
Kasama nilá akó.   ka·*sa*·ma nee·*la* a·ko

I've lost my group.
Nawalâ ang aking grupo.   na·wa·*la'* ang *a*·keeng *groo*·po

---

signs

Many of the tourist signs and street signs you'll encounter
are in English. There are, however, a few interesting signs
written in Filipino.

Bawal tumae dito.   **No defecating here.**
  ba·wal too·*ma*·e *dee*·to

Huwag umihi dito.   **No urinating here.**
  hoo·*wag* oo·*mee*·hee *dee*·to

Bawal ang basura dito.   **Rubbish prohibited here.**
  ba·wal ang ba·*soo*·ra *dee*·to

When buying small souvenirs or a refreshment while sightseeing, you may see the following sign:

Barya lang pô.   **Small change only, please.**
  bar·*ya* lang po'

doing business

magnenegosyo

I'm attending a ...	Áatend akó ng ...	a·a·tend a·ko nang ...
conference	komperénsiya	kom·pe·ren·see·ya
course	kurso	koor·so
meeting	miting	mee·teeng
trade fair	pangnegosyong iksibisyón	pang·ne·gos·yong eek·see·bees·yon
I'm with ...	Kasama akó ng ...	ka·sa·ma a·ko nang ...
Shoe Mart	Shoe Mart	see·yoo mart
my colleague(s)	aking (mga) katrabaho	a·keeng (ma·nga) ka·tra·ba·ho
(two) others	(dalawá) pa	(da·la·wa) pa

I'm alone.
Nag-íisá akó.
nag·ee·ee·sa a·ko

I'm here for (two) days/weeks.
Nárito akó nang (dalawáng) araw/ linggó.
na·ree·to a·ko nang (da·la·wang) a·row/ leeng·go

I have an appointment with ...
May appointment akó kay ...
mai a·poynt·ment a·ko kai ...

Do you have a business card?
May business card ka ba?
mai bees·nees kard ka ba

Here's my …	Nárito ang aking …	na·ree·to ang a·keeng …
business card	business card	bees·nees kard
email address	email address	ee·mayl a·dres
mobile number	número ng mobayl	noo·me·ro nang mo·bail

What's your …?	Anó ang iyóng …?	a·no ang ee·yong …
address	tirahan	tee·ra·han
fax number	número ng paks	noo·me·ro nang paks
pager number	número ng pager	noo·me·ro nang pay·jer
work number	número sa trabaho	noo·me·ro sa tra·ba·ho

Where's the …?	Násaán ang …?	na·sa·an ang …
business centre	sentro ng bisnis	sen·tro nang bees·nees
conference	komperénsiya	kom·pe·ren·see·ya
meeting	miting	mee·teeng

I need …	Kailangan ko …	ka·ee·la·ngan ko …
a computer	ng kompyuter	nang komp·yoo·ter
an Internet connection	ng koneksiyón sa Internet	nang ko·nek·see·yon sa een·ter·net
an interpreter	ng tagasalin sa wikà	nang ta·ga·sa·leen sa wee·ka'
more business cards	ng marami pang business card	nang ma·ra·mee pang bees·nees kard
to send a fax	na magpadalá ng paks	na mag·pa·da·la nang paks

That went very well.
Magandá ang nangyari. ma·gan·da ang nang·ya·ree

Thank you for your time.
Salamat sa iyóng panahón. sa·la·mat sa ee·yong pa·na·hon

Shall we go for a drink/meal?
Halina at uminóm/ kumain tayo? ha·lee·na at oo·mee·nom/ koo·ma·een ta·yo

looking for a job

Where are jobs advertised?

Saán ináanunsiyó ang	sa·*an* ee·*na*·a·noon·see·*yo* ang
mga trabaho?	ma·*nga* tra·*ba*·ho

I'm enquiring about the position advertised.

Nagtatanóng akó tungkól	nag·ta·ta·*nong* a·ko toong·*kol*
sa trabahong	sa tra·*ba*·hong
ináanunsiyó.	ee·*na*·noon·see·*yo*

I'm looking for ... work.	*Naghahanáp akó ng ... na trabaho.*	nag·ha·ha·*nap* a·ko nang ... na tra·*ba*·ho
bar	*pang-bar*	pang·*bar*
casual	*casual*	*kas*·wal
English-teaching	*pagtuturó ng Inglés*	pag·too·too·*ro* nang eeng·*gles*
fruit-picking	*pamimitás ng prutas*	pa·mee·mee·*tas* nang *proo*·tas
full-time	*full-time*	*pool*·taim
office	*pang-upisina*	pang·oo·pee·*see*·na
part-time	*part-time*	*par*·taim
volunteer	*boluntaryo*	bo·loon·*tar*·yo
waitering	*pang-weyter*	pang·*way*·ter

Do I need ...?	*Kailangan ko ba ng ...?*	ka·ee·*la*·ngan ko ba nang ...
a contract	*kontrata*	kon·*tra*·ta
experience	*karanasán*	ka·ra·na·*san*
insurance	*seguro*	se·*goo*·ro
my own transport	*sariling sasakyán*	sa·*ree*·leeng sa·sak·*yan*
a work permit	*permiso na magtrabaho*	per·*mee*·so na mag·tra·*ba*·ho
work registration	*rehistrasyón sa pagtatrabaho*	re·hees·tras·*yon* sa pag·la·tra·*ba*·ho
a uniform	*uniporme*	oo·nee·*por*·me

I've had experience.
May karanasán akó.   mai ka·ra·na·*san* a·*ko*

What's the wage?
Magkano ang suweldo?   mag·*ka*·no ang soo·*wel*·do

Here is/are	*Nárito ang*	na·ree·to ang
my …	*aking …*	*a*·keeng …
bank account	*detalye ng*	de·*tal*·ye nang
details	*akáwnt sa*	a·*kownt* sa
	bangko	*bang*·ko
CV/résumé	*CV*	*see*·bee
work permit	*permiso na*	per·*mee*·so na
	magtrabaho	mag·tra·*ba*·ho
I can start …	*Makapagsisi-*	ma·ka·pag·see·see·
	mulâ akó …	moo·*la'* a·ko …
Can you	*Makapagsisi-*	ma·ka·pag·see·see·
start …?	*mulá ka ba …?*	moo·*la* ka ba …
at (8) o'clock	*ng (alás-otso)*	nang (a·*las* ot·so)
next week	*sa súsunód na*	sa soo·soo·*nod* na
	linggó	leeng·*go*
today	*ngayón*	nga·*yon*
tomorrow	*bukas*	*boo*·kas
What time	*Anóng oras*	a·*nong* o·ras
do I …?	*akó …?*	a·*ko* …
finish	*matatapos*	ma·ta·*ta*·pos
have a break	*magbebréyk*	mag·be·*brayk*
start	*magsisimulâ*	mag·see·see·moo·*la'*
advertisement	*anunsiyó*	a·noon·see·*yo*
contract	*kontrata*	kon·*tra*·ta
employee	*kawaní*	ka·wa·*nee*
employer	*ang pinág-*	ang pee·*nag*·
	lilingkurán	lee·leeng·koo·*ran*
job	*trabaho*	tra·*ba*·ho
work	*karanasán sa*	ka·ra·na·*san* sa
experience	*trabaho*	tra·*ba*·ho

senior & disabled travellers

I have a disability.
Mayroón akóng
disabilidád.
mai·ro·on a·kong
dees·a·bee·lee·dad

I need assistance.
Kailangan ko ng tulong.
ka·ee·la·ngan ko nang too·long

What services do you have for people with a disability?
Anóng mga
paglilingkód
ang mayroón ka para sa
mga taong may
disabilidád?
a·nong ma·nga
pag·lee·leeng·kod
ang mai·ro·on ka pa·ra sa
ma·nga ta·ong mai
dees·a·bee·lee·dad

Are there disabled toilets?
Mayroón bang kubeta
para sa may disabilidád?
mai·ro·on bang koo·be·ta
pa·ra sa mai dees·a·bee·lee·dad

Are there disabled parking spaces?
Mayroón bang páradahán
para sa may disabilidád?
mai·ro·on bang pa·ra·da·han
pa·ra sa mai dees·a·bee·lee·dad

Is there wheelchair access?
Mayroón bang daanan ng
silyang de-gulóng?
mai·ro·on bang da·a·nan nang
seel·yang de·goo·long

How wide is the entrance?
Gaano kaluwáng ang
pasukán?
ga·a·no ka·loo·wang ang
pa·soo·kan

How many steps are there?
Ilang baitáng mayroón?
ee·lang bai·tang mai·ro·on

Is there a lift/elevator?
Mayroón bang elebeytor?
mai·ro·on bang e·le·bay·tor

The official language of the deaf in the Philippines is Philippine Sign Language (*Wikang Pasenyas ng Pilipino* wee·kang pa·sen·*syas* nang pee·lee·*pee*·no) with American Sign Language a common second language.

Are there rails in the bathroom?
May hawakán ba sa banyo?   mai ha·wa·*kan* ba sa *ban*·yo

I'm deaf.
Bingí akó.   bee·*ngee* a·ko

I have a hearing aid.
Mayroón akóng hearing aid.   mai·ro·on a·*kong* hee·reeng ayd

Are guide dogs permitted?
Puwede ba ang mga asong taga-akay ng bulág?   poo·*we*·de ba ang ma·*nga* a·song ta·ga·*a*·kai nang boo·*lag*

Could you call me a disabled taxi?
Pakitawag mo akó ng taksi na para sa may disabilidád?   pa·kee·*ta*·wag mo a·ko nang *tak*·see na *pa*·ra sa mai *dees*·a·bee·lee·*dad*

Could you help me cross the street safely?
Pakitulungan mo akóng tumawíd sa kalye nang ligtás?   pa·kee·too·*loo*·ngan mo a·*kong* too·ma·*weed* sa *kal*·ye nang leeg·*tas*

Is there somewhere I can sit down?
Mayroón ba akóng maúupuán?   mai·ro·on ba a·*kong* ma·oo·oo·poo·an

guide dog	*asong taga-akay ng bulág*	*a*·song ta·ga·*a*·kai nang boo·*lag*
person with a disability	*taong may disabilidád*	*ta*·ong mai *dees*·a·bee·lee·*dad*
older person	*matandâ*	ma·tan·*da'*
ramp	*ramp*	ramp
walking frame	*gabáy panlakad*	ga·*bai* pan·*la*·kad
walking stick	*tungkód*	toong·*kod*
wheelchair	*silyang de-gulóng*	*seel*·yang de·goo·*long*

travelling with children

pagbibiyahe na may kasamang mga batà

Is there a …?	Mayroón bang …?	mai·ro·on bang …
baby change room	bihisán para sa beybi	bee·hee·san pa·ra sa bay·bee
child discount	pambatang diskuwento	pam·ba·tang dees·koo·wen·to
child-minding service	serbis na pagbabantáy ng batà	ser·bees na pag·ba·ban·tai nang ba·ta'
child's portion	pambatà	pam·ba·ta'
children's menu	pambatang menú	pam·ba·tang me·noo
crèche	álagaán ng batà	a·la·ga·an nang ba·ta
family ticket	pampamilyang tiket	pam·pa·meel·yang tee·ket

I need a/an …	Kailangan ko ng …	ka·ee·la·ngan ko nang …
baby seat	pambatang upuan	pam·ba·tang oo·poo·an
(English-speaking) babysitter	tagapag-alagá (na marunong ng Inglés)	ta·ga·pag·a·la·ga (na ma·roo·nong nang eeng·gles)
booster seat	pang-alsáng upuan	pang·al·sang oo·poo·an
cot	kuna	koo·na
highchair	highchair	hai·tser
plastic bag	plastik bag	plas·teek bag
plastic sheet	piraso ng plastik	pee·ra·so nang plas·teek
potty	arinola	a·ree·no·la
pram	pram	pram
sick bag	supot na sukahan	soo·pot na soo·ka·han

Where's the nearest ...?	Násaán ang pinakamalapit na ...?	na·sa·an ang pee·na·ka·ma·la·peet na ...
drinking fountain	inuman ng tubig	ee·noo·man nang too·beeg
park	parke	par·ke
playground	palaruan	pa·la·roo·an
swimming pool	languyan	la·ngoo·yan
tap	gripo	gree·po
toy shop	tindahan ng laruán	teen·da·han nang la·roo·an

Do you sell ...?	Nagtitindá ka ba ng ...?	nag·tee·teen·da ka ba nang ...
baby wipes	pamunas sa batà	pa·moo·nas sa ba·ta'
disposable nappies	dispósaból dayper	dees·po·sa·bol dai·per
infant painkillers	gamót na pangalís ng masakít sa batà	ga·mot na pang·a·lees nang ma·sa·keet sa ba·ta'
tissues	tisyu	tees·yoo

Do you hire out (prams)?
Nagpapaarkilá ka ba ng (pram)?
nag·pa·pa·ar·kee·la ka ba nang (pram)

Is there space for a pram?
May lugár ba para sa pram?
mai loo·gar ba pa·ra sa pram

Are there any good places to take children around here?
May maiinam bang lugár dito na puwedeng dalhín ang mga batà?
mai ma·ee·ee·nam bang loo·gar dee·to na poo·we·deng dal·heen ang ma·nga ba·ta

Are children allowed?
Puwede ba ang mga batà?
poo·we·de ba ang ma·nga ba·ta'

Where can I change a nappy?
Saán akó magpapalít ng lampín?
sa·an a·ko mag·pa·pa·leet nang lam·peen

Do you mind if I breast-feed here?
Puwede ba akóng magpasuso dito?
poo·we·de ba a·kong mag·pa·soo·so dee·to

Could I have some paper and pencils, please?
Pahingí nga ng papel   pa·hee·*ngee* nga nang pa·*pel*
at lapis?   at *la*·pees

Is this suitable for (2) year old children?
Tama ba itó sa mga   ta·ma ba ee·*to* sa ma·*nga*
batang (dalawáng)   *ba*·tang (da·la·*wang*)
taóng gulang?   ta·*ong* goo·lang

Do you know a dentist/doctor who is good with children?
May alám ka bang   mai a·*lam* ka bang
dentista/doktór na   den·*tees*·ta/dok·*tor* na
magalíng sa batà?   ma·ga·*leeng* sa *ba*·ta'

If your child is sick, see **health**, page 187.

talking with children

What's your name?
Anóng pangalan mo?   a·*nong* pa·*nga*·lan mo

When's your birthday?
Kailan ang bertdey mo?   ka·ee·*lan* ang *bert*·day mo

Do you go to school/kindergarten?
Pumapasok ka ba sa   poo·ma·*pa*·sok ka ba sa
eskuwelahán/kinder?   es·koo·we·la·*han*/*keen*·der

What grade are you in?
Anóng grado ka na?   a·*nong* *gra*·do ka na

Do you learn English?
Nag-aaral ka ba ng Inglés?   nag·a·*a*·ral ka ba nang eeng·*gles*

What do you do after school?
Anóng ginagawá mo   a·*nong* gee·na·ga·*wa* mo
ɲŋgkatapos ng eskuwela?   pag·ka·*ta*·pos nang es·koo·we·la

Do you like …!   *Gustó mo ba ang …?*   goos·*to* mo ba ang …
  school   *eskuwela*   es·koo·we·la
  sport   *larô*   la·*ro*'
  your teacher   *titser mo*   *teet*·ser mo

As a sign of respect, people *mano* ma·no (lit: hand) to their elders upon greeting them. This involves taking the back of an older person's hand and placing it on your forehead. To ask someone to offer their hand to you, say *Mano hô* ma·no ho (lit: hand please).

talking about children

pakikipag-usap tungkól sa mga batà

When's the baby due?
Kailán ang datíng ng beybi mo?
ka·ee·*lan* ang da·*teeng* nang *bay*·bee mo

What are you going to call the baby?
Anóng ipapangalan mo sa beybi?
a·*nong* ee·pa·pa·*nga*·lan mo sa *bay*·bee

How many children do you have?
Ilán ang anák mo?
ee·*lan* ang a·*nak* mo

What a beautiful child!
Kay gandáng batà!
kai gan·*dang* ba·ta'

Is it a boy or a girl?
Lalaki o babae?
la·*la*·kee o ba·*ba*·e

What's his/her name?
Anóng pangalan niyá?
a·*nong* pa·*nga*·lan nee·*ya*

How old is he/she?
Iláng taón na siyá?
ee·*lang* ta·*on* na see·*ya*

Does he/she go to school?
Pumapasok ba siyá sa eskuwelahán?
poo·ma·*pa*·sok ba see·*ya* sa es·koo·we·la·*han*

Is he/she well-behaved?
Mabaít ba siyá?
ma·ba·*eet* ba see·*ya*

He/She …	Siyá ay …	see·*ya* ai …
has your eyes	*kuha ang matá mo*	*koo*·ha ang ma·*ta* mo
looks like you	*kamukhá mo*	ka·mook·*ha* mo

PRACTICAL

SOCIAL > meeting people
pakikipagkilala

Polite forms (pol) are used for people who are older than yourself or have a higher social or professional status. In all other situations, you can use the informal form (inf). Both options have been provided where you're likely to use both. Unmarked phrases are in the informal form, as this is appropriate for most situations.

basics

Yes.	*Oo/Opò.* inf/pol	o·o/o·po'
No.	*Hindî.* inf	heen·dee'
	Hindí pô. pol	heen·dee' po'
Please.	*Plis.*	plees
Thank you (very much).	*(Maraming) Salamat.* inf	(ma·ra·meeng) sa·la·mat
	(Maraming) Salamat pô. pol	(ma·ra·meeng) sa·la·mat po'
You're welcome.	*Waláng anumán.* inf	wa·lang a·noo·man
	Walá pong anumán. pol	wa·la pong a·noo·man
Excuse me. (to get attention)	*Eksyus mi.*	eks·yoos mee
Excuse me. (to get past)	*Makikiraán nga.* inf	ma·kee·kee·ra·an nga
	Makikiraán nga pô. pol	ma·kee·kee·ra·an nga po'
Sorry.	*Sori.* inf	so·ree
	Sori pô. pol	so·ree po'
May I?	*Puwede ba?* inf	poo·we·de ba
	Puwede po ba? pol	poo·we·de po ba

polite & informal

You can add *pô* po or *hô* ho at the end of regular phrases if you want to make them more polite.

meeting people

105

greetings & goodbyes

There are no exact equivalents of 'hello' and 'goodbye' in Filipino. You would normally greet someone with *Kumusta?* koo·*moos*·ta (How are you?). To signal that you're about to leave, say *Sigé* see·*ge* (Alright then). The terms *helów* he·*loh* (hello) and *babay* ba·*bai* (bye-bye) are becoming more common in Filipino.

Hello.	*Helów.*	he·*loh*
Hi.	*Hi.*	hai
Good ...	*Magandáng ...*	ma·gan·*dang* ...
morning	*umaga* inf	oo·*ma*·ga
	umaga pô pol	oo·*ma*·ga po'
afternoon	*hapon* inf	*ha*·pon
	hapon pô pol	*ha*·pon po'
day	*araw* inf	*a*·row
	araw pô pol	*a*·row po'
evening	*gabí* inf	ga·*bee*
	gabí pô pol	ga·*bee* po'

Good morning to you too.
  Magandáng umaga   ma·gan·*dang* oo·*ma*·ga
  rin sa iyó/inyó. inf/pol   reen sa ee·*yo*/en·*yo*

How are you?
  Kumustá? inf   koo·moos·*ta*
  Kumustá po kayó? pol   koo·moos·*ta* po ka·*yo*

Fine.
  Mabuti. inf   ma·*boo*·tee
  Mabuti pô. pol   ma·*boo*·tee po'

And you?
  Ikáw? inf   ee·*kow*
  Kayó pô? pol   ka·*yo* po'

SOCIAL

What's your name?

Anó ang pangalan mo? inf	a·*no* ang pa·*nga*·lan mo
Anó pô ang pangalan ninyó? pol	a·*no* po' ang pa·*nga*·lan neen·*yo*

My name is …

Ang pangalan ko ay … inf	ang pa·*nga*·lan ko ai …
Ang pangalan ko pô ay … pol	ang pa·*nga*·lan ko po' ai …

I'd like to introduce you to …

Gustó kitáng ipakilala kay … inf	goos·*to* kee·*tang* ee·pa·kee·*la*·la kai …
Gustó ko po kayóng ipakilala kay … pol	goos·*to* ko po ka·*yong* ee·pa·kee·*la*·la kai …

This is my …

Itó ang aking … inf	ee·*to* ang *a*·keeng …
Itó pô ang aking … pol	ee·*to* po' ang *a*·keeng …

child	*anák*	a·*nak*
colleague	*katrabaho*	ka·tra·*ba*·ho
friend	*kaibigan*	ka·ee·bee·*gan*
husband	*asawa*	a·*sa*·wa
partner (intimate)	*kapartner*	ka·*part*·ner
wife	*asawa*	a·*sa*·wa

For family members, see **family**, page 114.

I'm pleased to meet you.

Nagagalák akóng makilala ka. inf	na·ga·ga·*lak* a·*kong* ma·kee·*la*·la ka
Nagagalák pô akóng makilala kayó. pol	na·ga·ga·*lak* po' a·*kong* ma·kee·*la*·la ka·*yo*

See you later.	*Sige.* inf	*see*·ge
	Sige pô. pol	*see*·ge po'
Goodbye.	*Babay.* inf	*ba*·bai
	Paalam na pô. pol	pa·*a*·lam na po'
Good night.	*Magandáng gabí.* inf	ma·gan·*dang* ga·*bee*
	Magandáng gabí pô. pol	ma·gan·*dang* ga·*bee* po'
Bon voyage!	*Maligayang paglalakbáy!*	ma·lee·*ga*·yang pag·la·lak·*bai*

addressing people

Honorifics and titles are important in Filipino because they mark status or seniority. Using first names isn't appropriate when you've just met someone, unless they indicate otherwise.

Mr/Sir	Ginoó/Mang	gee·no·o/mang
Mrs/Madam	Ginang/	gee·nang/
	Aling	a·leeng
Miss/Ms	Binibini/	bee·nee·bee·nee/
	Mis	mees

Attorney	Atorni	a·tor·nee
Doctor (MD/PhD)	Doktór	dok·tor
Father (priest)	Padre	pad·re
Governor	Gubernadór	goo·ber·na·dor
Head of the	Kapitán del	ka·pee·tan del
Barrio Council	Baryo	bar·yo
Judge	Judge	jads
Manager	Mánedyer	ma·ned·yer
Mayor	Meyor	me·yor
Pastor	Pastór	pas·tor
Professor	Propesór	pro·pe·sor
Sister (nun)	Sor/Sister	sor/sees·ter
Senator	Senadór	se·na·dor
Sister (nurse)	Nars	nars

different strokes for different folks

Filipinos sometimes ask direct questions upon introduction. These seemingly intrusive (and often personal) questions and comments serve the same function as a greeting, and are nothing more than a way of showing friendliness. If you're asked *Saan ka pupunta?* sa·an ka poo·poon·ta (Where are you going?), you're not expected to tell them your destination. Simply reply with *Diyan lang* dee·yan lang (Just there).

making conversation

Hey, how are you?
Oy, kumustá ka na?   oy, koo·moos·*ta* ka na

What a beautiful day!
Kay gandá ng araw!   kai gan·*da* nang *a*·row

Nice/Awful weather, isn't it?
Ang gandá/samá ng   ang gan·*da*/sa·*ma* nang
panahón, anó?   pa·na·*hon* a·*no*

You look dressed to kill!
Pustura ka yatà ngayón!   poos·*too*·ra ka *ya*·ta nga·*yon*

I haven't seen you for a long time.
Matagál na kitáng di   ma·ta·*gal* na kee·*tang* dee
nakita.   na·*kee*·ta

You seem to be in a hurry.
Nagmamadalî ka yata.   nag·ma·ma·da·*lee* ka *ya*·ta

Where are you going?
Saán ang puntá mo?   sa·*an* ang poon·*ta* mo

What are you doing?
Anó ang ginagawâ mo?   a·*no* ang gee·na·ga·*wa* mo

Where have you been?
Saán ka galing?   sa·*an* ka *ga*·leeng

Do you live here?
Dito ka ba nakatirá?   *dee*·to ka ba na·ka·tee·*ra*

Do you like it here?
Gustó mo ba dito?   goos·*to* mo ba *dee*·to

I love it here.
Gustúng-gustó ko dito.   goos·*toong*·goos·*to* ko *dee*·to

That's (beautiful), isn't it?
Ang (gandá), anó?   ang (gan·*da*) a·*no*

What's this called?
Anó ang tawag nito?   a·*no* ang *ta*·wag *nee*·to

Are you here on holiday?
    Bakasyón mo ba dito?   ba·kas·*yon* mo ba *dee*·to

I'm here ...	*Nárito akó para ...*	na·*ree*·to a·*ko* pa·ra ...
for a holiday	*magbakasyón*	mag·ba·kas·*yon*
on business	*sa trabaho*	sa tra·*ba*·ho
to study	*mag-aral*	mag·*a*·ral

How long are you here for?
    Gaano katagál ka dito?   ga·*a*·no ka·ta·*gal* ka *dee*·to

I'm here for (four) weeks/days.
    Nárito akó ng (apat)   na·*ree*·to a·*ko* nang (*a*·pat)
    na linggó/araw.   na leeng·*go*/a·row

What do you have there?
    Anó iyáng dalá-dalá mo?   a·no ee·*yang* da·*la*·da·*la* mo

Can I take a photo (of you)?
    Puwede ba (kitáng)   poo·*we*·de ba (kee·*tang*)
    kunan ng litrato?   *koo*·nan nang leet·*ra*·to

local talk		
Delicious!	*Masaráp!*	ma·sa·*rap*
Great!	*Magalíng!*	ma·ga·*leeng*
Hey!	*Oy!*	oy
I don't know.	*Éwan ko.*	*e*·wan ko
Jesus Mary Joseph!	*Súsmaryosep!*	soos·mar·yo·sep
Just a minute.	*Teka muna.*	*te*·ka *moo*·na
Just joking!	*Biro lang!*	*bee*·ro lang
Let's eat!	*Kain na!*	*ka*·een na
Maybe.	*Bakâ.*	ba·*ka'*
My God!	*Diyós ko!*	dee·*yos* ko
No problem.	*Waláng*	wa·*lang*
	problema.	pro·*ble*·ma
No way!	*Malayò!*	ma·*la*·yo'
Of course!	*Siyempre pa!*	see·*yem*·pre pa
Oh!	*Nakú!*	na·*koo*
Ouch!	*Arúy!*	a·*rooy*
Sure.	*Sigurado.*	see·goo·*ra*·do

nationalities

Where are you from?
  Tagá-saán ka?   ta·*ga*·sa·*an* ka

I'm from ...   *Akó ay tagá ...*   a·*ko* ai ta·*ga* ...
  Australia   *Australya*   ows·*tral*·ya
  Canada   *Kánada*   *ka*·na·da
  Singapore   *Síngapór*   *seeng*·ga·por

For other countries, see the **dictionary**.

age

edád

How old ...?	Iláng taon ...?	ee·lang ta·on ...
are you	ka na	ka na
is your	ang iyóng anák	ang ee·yong a·nak
son/daughter	na lalaki/babae	na la·la·kee/ba·ba·e

I'm ... years old.
Akó ay ... taóng gulang.   a·ko ai ... ta·ong goo·lang

He/She is ... years old.
Siyá ay ... taóng gulang.   see·ya ai ... ta·ong goo·lang

Too old!
Masyadong matandá na!   mas·ya·dong ma·tan·da na

I'm younger than I look.
Mas batà akó kesa sa   mas ba·ta' a·ko ke·sa sa
itsura ko.   eet·soo·ra ko

For your age, see **numbers & amounts**, page 37.

occupations & studies

mga hanapbuhay at pag-aaral

What's your occupation?
Anó ang hanapbuhay mo?   a·no ang ha·nap·boo·hai mo

I'm a ...	Akó ay ...	a·ko ai ...
chef	cook	kook
journalist	peryodista	per·yo·dees·ta
teacher	titser	teet·ser

I'm ...	Akó ay ...	a·ko ai ...
retired	retirado	re·tee·ra·do
self-employed	may sariling	mai sa·ree·leeng
	negosyo	ne·gos·yo
unemployed	waláng trabaho	wa·lang tra·ba·ho

I work in ...	Nagtatrabaho akó sa ...	nag·ta·tra·*ba*·ho a·*ko* sa ...
administration	*adminístrasyón*	ad·mee·*nees*·tras·yon
health	*kalusugan*	ka·loo·*soo*·gan
sales & marketing	*pagtitindá at márketíng*	pag·tee·teen·*da* at *mar*·ke·teeng
engineering	*engineering*	een·jee·*nee*·reeng
banking	*bangko*	*bang*·ko
IT	*IT*	*ai*·tee

What are you studying?

Anóng kurso ang kinukuha mo?	a·*nong koor*·so ang kee·noo·*koo*·ha mo

I'm studying ...	Nag-aaral akó ng ...	nag·a·*a*·ral a·*ko* nang ...
accountancy	*accounting*	a·*kown*·teeng
commerce	*komersyo*	ko·*mers*·yo
Filipino	*Pilipino*	pee·lee·*pee*·no
humanities	*humanities*	hee·yoo·*ma*·nee·tees
journalism	*pagka-mámahayág*	pag·ka·*ma*·ma·ha·*yag*
law	*abogasyá*	a·bo·gas·*ya*
nursing	*narsing*	*nar*·seeng
science	*aghám*	ag·*ham*

---

lost in translation

The English words 'hostess' (*hos*·tes) and 'tomboy' (*tam*·boy) have crept into the Filipino language, but have gained additional meaning. They're used as euphemisms – the word *hostess* means 'prostitute' and *tomboy* means 'lesbian'. Be sure not to tell your host that his wife has been a lovely hostess and that you think his daughter's a tomboy!

family

Do you have a/an ...?
Mayroón ka bang ...?   mai·ro·*on* ka bang ...

I have a/an ...
Mayroón akóng ...   may·ro·*on* a·*kong* ...

I don't have a/an ...
Walâ akóng ...   wa·*la'* a·*kong* ...

aunt	*ale*	*a*·le
brother	*kapatíd na lalaki*	ka·pa·*teed* na la·*la*·kee
cousin	*pinsan*	*peen*·san
daughter	*anák na babae*	a·*nak* na ba·*ba*·e
family	*pamilya*	pa·*meel*·ya
father	*amá*	a·*ma*
father-in-law	*biyanáng*	bee·ya·*nang*
	lalaki	la·*la*·kee
godchild	*ináanák*	ee·*na*·a·*nak*
godfather	*ninong*	*nee*·nong
godmother	*ninang*	*nee*·nang
granddaughter	*apó na babae*	a·*po* na ba·*ba*·e
grandfather	*lolo*	*lo*·lo
grandmother	*lola*	*lo*·la
grandson	*apó na lalaki*	a·*po* na la·*la*·kee
husband	*asawa*	a·*sa*·wa
mother	*iná*	ee·*na*
mother-in-law	*biyanáng*	bee·ya·*nang*
	babae	ba·*ba*·e
nephew	*pamangkíng*	pa·mang·*keeng*
	lalaki	la·*la*·kee
niece	*pamangkíng*	pa·mang·*keeng*
	babae	ba·*ba*·e
partner (intimate)	*kapartner*	ka·*part*·ner
sister	*kapatíd na babae*	ka·pa·*teed* na ba·*ba*·e
son	*anák na lalaki*	a·*nak* na la·*la*·kee
uncle	*amaín*	a·ma·*een*
wife	*asawa*	a·*sa*·wa

How many siblings do you have?
Ilán ang kapatíd mo?   ee·*lan* ang ka·pa·*teed* mo

How many children do you have?
Ilán ang anák mo?   ee·*lan* ang a·*nak* mo

I don't have any children.
Walâ akóng anák.   wa·*la'* a·*kong* a·*nak*

Are you married?
May asawa ka ba?   mai a·*sa*·wa ka ba

I live with someone.
May ka·lib-in akó.   mai ka·*leeb*·een a·*ko*

I'm ...	*Akó ay ...*	a·*ko* ai ...
married	*may asawa*	mai a·*sa*·wa
separated	*hiwaláy*	hee·wa·*lai*
single	*binatà/*	bee·*na*·ta'/
	dalaga m/f	da·*la*·ga

---

well-wishing

Bless you!
Pagpalain ka nawâ!   pag·pa·*la*·een ka na·*wa'*

Bon voyage!
Maligayang paglalakbáy!   ma·lee·*ga*·yang pag·la·lak·*bai*

Congratulations!
Maligayang batì!   ma·lee·*ga*·yang *ba*·tee'

Good luck!
Suwertihín ka nawâ!   soo·wer·tee·*heen* ka na·*wa'*

Happy birthday!
Maligayang kaarawán!   ma·lee·*ga*·yang ka·a·ra·*wan*

Happy New Year!
Manigong Bagong Taón!   ma·*nee*·gong *ba*·gong ta·*on*

Merry Christmas!
Maligayang Paskó!   ma·lee·*ga*·yang pas·*ko*

Happy Easter!
Maligayang Pasko ng Pagkabuhay!   ma·lee·*ga*·yang pas·*ko* nang pag·ka·boo·*hai*

farewells

Tomorrow is my last day here.
Bukas na ang hulíng
araw ko.

boo·kas na ang hoo·leeng
a·row ko

If you come to (Scotland) you can stay with me.
Kung púpuntá ka sa
(Eskosya) puwede kang
magtirá sa akin.

koong poo·poon·ta ka sa
(es·kos·ya) poo·we·de kang
mag·tee·ra sa a·keen

Keep in touch!
Huwág mo akóng
kalilimutan!

hoo·wag mo a·kong
ka·lee·lee·moo·tan

It's been great meeting you.
Mabuti na nakilala
kitá.

ma·boo·tee na na·kee·la·la
kee·ta

Here's my …	Eto ang aking …	e·to ang a·keeng …
What's your …?	Anó ang iyóng …?	a·no ang ee·yong …
address	adrés	a·dres
email address	email adrés	ee·mayl a·dres
phone number	número ng	noo·me·ro nang
	telépono	te·le·po·no

---

a cross to bear

Traditionally Easter is not a happy time for Filipinos, and wishing others 'Happy Easter' is a recent addition to the inventory of Filipino greetings. Filipinos feel it's appropriate to be mournful during the Easter period, so don't be too surprised if people of the older generation aren't as jovial as you are at this time …

Even though Filipino is the national language of the Philippines, for most Filipinos it's a second language that's learnt in high school and university, along with English. You'll find that most people you encounter can speak Filipino, but it may be handy to know a few phrases in the local language. The effort you make will definitely be appreciated, even if you do revert to Filipino or English as your main form of communication.

cebuano (visayan) & waray

Cebuano is the major language of the Visayan Islands and is often referred to as 'Visayan'. It's also spoken in Negros Oriental, Bohol, and parts of Mindanao. Almost a quarter of Filipinos speak Cebuano, so it may be handy to learn some of the basic phrases!

Waray is closely related to the Cebuano language and often the only difference between words in Waray and Cebuano is a difference in some sounds. Where it's not specified below as either Waray (w) or Cebuano (c), the phrases are in Cebuano.

Yes.	*Oo.* c&w	o·o
No.	*Dilì/Dirì.* c/w	dee·*lee*/dee·*ree*
Maybe.	*Tingali.*	tee·*nga*·lee
I'm sorry.	*Pasaylo-a ko.*	pa·sai·*lo*·a ko
Excuse me. (to get past)	*Paagi-a ko.*	pa·*a*·gee·a ko
Thank you.	*Salamat.*	sa·*la*·mat
You're welcome.	*Wa'y sapayan.*	way sa·*pai*·yan

meeting people

117

Hello! (announcing you're at someone's gate/door)
Maayo! ma·*a*·yo

Come in/Welcome!
Dayon! da·*yon*

How are you?
Kumusta ka? koo·moos·*ta* ka

Good morning. *Maayong buntag.* ma·*a*·yong *boon*·tag
Good afternoon. *Maayong hapon.* ma·*a*·yong *ha*·pon
Good evening. *Maayong gabii.* ma·*a*·yong ga·*bee*

Goodbye.
Babay. ba·bai

What's your name?
Unsay imong ngalan? oon·sai ee·mong *nga*·lan

I'm Alice.
Ako si Alice. a·*ko* si *a*·lees

Nice to meet you.
Nalipay ko nga nagkaila ta. na·*lee*·pai lo nga nag·ka·*ee*·la ta

Where are you from?
Taga-diin man ka? ta·ga·dee·*een* man ka

I'm from (Australia).
Taga-(Australia) ko. ta·ga·(ows·*tra*·lee·ya) ko

ilonggo (hiligaynon)

Ilonggo is spoken in Iloilo and Negros Occidental, as well as some parts of Panay and Mindanao.

Yes.	*Hu-ó.*	hoo·o
No.	*Indí.*	een·*dee*
Thank you.	*Salamat.*	sa·*la*·mat
You're welcome.	*Wala sang ano man.*	wa·*la* sang a·*no* man
Hello!	*Kamusta!*	ka·*moos*·ta
How are you?	*Kamusta ka?*	ka·*moos*·ta ka
Thank you.	*Palihug.*	pa·*lee*·hoog

Fine. And you?

Maayo man.	ma·*a*·yo·man
Kag ikaw?	kag ee·*kow*

Goodbye.

Sige, malakat na ako. inf	see·*ge* ma·la·*kat* na a·*ko*
Paalam na. pol	pa·*a*·lam na

What's the local speciality (in cuisine)?

Ano ang tumandok nga	a·*no* ang too·*man*·dok nga
espesyalidad nga	es·pes·*ya*·lee·*dad* nga
pagkaon?	pag·*ka*·on

You've been very kind.

Tama ka gid	*ta*·ma ka geed
ka-ma-abi-abihon.	ka·ma·a·*bee*·a·*bee*·hon

pampangan (kapampangan)

There are approximately 1 million speakers of this language, which is spoken in the province of Pampanga, north of Manila. It's the mother tongue of the first woman elected president of the Philippines, Corazon Aquino.

Yes.	*Wa/Opu.* inf/pol	wa/*o*·poo
No.	*Ali.* inf	a·*lee'*
	Ali pu. pol	a·*lee'* poo
I don't know.	*Tabalu.*	ta·*ba*·loo
Excuse me. (to get past)	*Pakilabas.*	pa·kee·*la*·bas
Thank you.	*Salamat.*	sa·*la*·mat
Hello. How are you?	*Komusta na ka?*	ko·moos·*ta* na ka
Goodbye.	*O sige!*	o see·*ge*
Good day.	*Masanting a aldo.*	ma·*san*·ting a *al*·do
Good evening.	*Masanting a bengi.*	ma·*san*·ting a *be*·ngi

What's your name?

Nanung pangalan mu?	na·noong pa·*nga*·lan moo

I'm Isaac.

Aku i Isaac.	a·koo ee *ai*·sak

Where are you from?
   Nokarin ka taga?   *no·*ka·reen ka ta·*ga*

I'm from (Australia).
   Taga ku (Australia).   ta·*ga* koo ows·*stra*·lee·ya

What are the local dishes here?
   Nanu ing pamangan   *na*·noo eeng *pa*·ma·ngan
   da keni?   da *ke*·nee

This is delicious!
   Manyaman ini.   man·*ya*·man ee·*nee*

Where am I?
   Nokarin ku?   *no·*ka·reen koo

Is this the road to (Ángeles)?
   Yapin ini ing dalan   *ya*·peen ee·*nee* eeng *da*·lan
   papunta (Angeles)?   pa·*poon*·ta (*ang*·he·les)

It's beautiful here!
   Masanting keni!   ma·san·ting ke·*nee*

pangasinan, ilokano & bikolano

The abbreviations p, i and b stand for Pangasinan, Ilokano and Bikolano respectively.

Hello.
   Kumusta. p&i&b   koo·*moos*·ta

Goodbye.
   Patanir. p   pa·ta·*neer*
   Innakon. i   *een*·na·kon
   Mahali na ako. b   ma·*ha*·lee na a·*ko*

Thank you.
   Salamat. p&i   sa·*la*·mat
   Mabalos. b   ma·*ba*·los

It's beautiful here!
   Marakep dia! p   ma·ra·*kep* dee·a
   Naimbag idtoy! i   na·eem·*bag* eed·toy
   Magayon digdi! b ma·ga·*yon* deeg·dee

common interests

mga karaniwang interés

What do you do in your spare time?
   Anó ang ginagawá mo   a·*no* ang gee·na·ga·*wa* mo
   sa libre mong oras?   sa *lee*·bre mong o·ras

Do you like …?
   Gustó mo ba ang …?   goos·*to* mo ba ang …

I like …   *Gustó ko ang …*   goos·*to* ko ang …
I don't like …   *Hindí ko gustó*   heen·*dee* ko goos·*to*
    ang …   ang …

cockfighting	*sabong*	*sa*·bong
cooking	*paglulutò*	pag·loo·loo·*to'*
dancing	*pagsasayáw*	pag·sa·sa·*yow*
drawing	*pagdodrowing*	pag·do·*dro*·weeng
films	*pelíkula*	pe·*lee*·koo·la
jai alai	*jai alaí*	hai a·*lai*
gambling	*pagsusugál*	pag·soo·soo·*gal*
gardening	*paggagarden*	pag·ga·*gar*·den
hiking	*puglalakád*	pag·la·la·*kad*
	nang mahabà	nang ma·ha·ba'
karaoke	*karayoke*	ka·ra·*yo*·ke
music	*músika*	*moo*·see·ka
painting	*pagpipintá*	pag·pee·peen·*ta*
photography	*potograpiya*	po·to·gra·*pee*·ya
reading	*pagbabasá*	pag·ba·ba·*sa*
shopping	*pamimilí*	pa·mee·mee·*lee*
sport	*sport*	sport
surfing the	*mag-surfing sa*	mag·*sar*·peeng sa
Internet	*ínternet*	een·ter·net
travelling	*paglalakbáy*	pag·la·lak·*bai*

For sporting activities, see **sport**, page 145 and the **dictionary**.

music

Do you …?	Ikáw ba ay …?	ee·kow ba ai …
dance	nagsásayáw	nag·sa·sa·yow
go to	nagpupuntá	nag·poo·poon·ta
concerts	sa konsiyerto	sa kon·see·yer·to
listen to music	nakikiníg sa	na·kee·kee·neeg sa
	músika	moo·see·ka
play an	tumutugtóg	too·moo·toog·tog
instrument	ng instrumento	nang eens·troo·men·to
sing	kumakantá	koo·ma·kan·ta
What …	Anóng mga …	a·nong ma·nga …
do you like?	ang gustó mo?	ang goos·to mo
bands	banda	ban·da
music	músika	moo·see·ka
singers	mang-aawit	mang·a·a·weet

blues	blues	bloos
classical music	músikang	moo·see·kang
	klásikal	kla·see·kal
electronic music	músikang	moo·see·kang
	elektronikó	e·lek·tro·nee·ko
jazz	jazz	jas
kundiman music	músikang	moo·see·kang
	kundiman	koon·dee·man
pop	pop	pap
rock	rock	rak
traditional music	músikang	moo·see·kang
	tradisyonál	tra·dees·yo·nal
world music	pangmundóng	pang·moon·dong
	músika	moo·see·ka

Planning to go to a concert? See **going out**, page 131.

SOCIAL

cinema & theatre

I feel like going to a/the …	*Parang gustó kong pumuntá sa …*	*pa*·rang goos·to kong poo·moon·*ta* sa …
Did you like the …?	*Nágustuhán mo ba ang …?*	*na*·goos·too·*han* mo ba ang …
ballet	*baléy*	ba·*lay*
concert	*konsyerto*	kon·*syer*·to
film	*pelíkula*	pe·*lee*·koo·la
play	*dulâ*	doo·*la'*

What's showing at the cinema/theatre tonight?

Anó ba ang palabás sa sinehán/teatro ngayóng gabí?

a·*no* ba ang pa·la·*bas* sa see·ne·*han*/te·*a*·tro nga·*yong* ga·*bee*

Is it in English?

Inglés ba?

eeng·*gles* ba

Does it have (English) subtitles?

Mayroón bang (Inglés na) subtitle?

mai·ro·*on* bang (eeng·*gles* na) sab·*tai*·tel

Have you seen …?

Nápanoód mo na ba ang …?

na·pa·no·*od* mo na ba ang …

Who's in it?

Sino ang lumabás doón?

see·no ang loo·ma·*bas* do·*on*

It stars …

Ang mga artista ay …

ang ma·*nga* ar·*tees*·ta ai …

Is this seat taken?

May nakaupó ba dito?

mai na·ka·oo·*po* ba *dee*·to

I thought it was …	*Akalà ko iyón ay …*	a·*ka*·la ko ee·*yon* ai …
excellent	*nápakagalíng*	*na*·pa·ka·ga·*leeng*
long	*mahabà*	ma·ha·*ba'*
(just) OK	*okey (lang)*	*o*·kay (lang)

interests

123

I like ...	Gustó ko ang ...	goos·to ko ang ...
I don't like ...	Hindí ko gustó ang ...	heen·dee ko goos·to ang ...
action movies	pelíkulang aksiyón	pe·lee·koo·lang ak·see·yon
animated films	pelíkulang cartoon	pe·lee·koo·lang kar·toon
comedies	komedya	ko·med·ya
documentaries	dokumentaryo	do·koo·men·tar·yo
drama	drama	dra·ma
(Filipino) cinema	sine(ng Pilipino)	see·ne(ng pee·lee·pee·no)
horror movies	pelíkulang katatákafter	pe·lee·koo·lang ka·ta·ta·koo·tan
sci-fi	sci fi	sai pai
short films	maiíklíng pelíkula	ma·ee·eek·leeng pe·lee·koo·la
thrillers	nakapag-pápákilíg	na·ka·pag·pa·pa·kee·leeg
war movies	giyerang pelíkula	gee·ye·rang pe·lee·koo·la

life imitates art

The USA isn't the only 'land of dreams' where an actor can become the country's most influential and powerful figure. Filipino Joseph Estrada, action film hero, was elected president in 1998. During his political career he headed the Anti-Crime Commission, a role that allowed him to transfer some of the tactics from his film roles into real life.

feelings

mga pakiramdám

Are you …?	*Ikáw ba ay …?*	ee·*kow* ba ai …
I'm not …	*(Hindî) Akó ay …*	(heen·*dee'*) a·*ko* ay …
cold	*ginigináw*	gee·nee·gee·*now*
embarrassed	*nahihiyâ*	na·hee·hee·*ya'*
happy	*masayá*	ma·sa·*ya*
hot	*naíinitan*	na·*ee*·ee·*nee*·tan
hungry	*gutóm*	goo·*tom*
sad	*malungkót*	ma·loong·*kot*
thirsty	*uháw*	oo·*how*
tired	*pagód*	pa·*god*
worried	*nag-áalalá*	nag·*a*·a·la·*la*

If you're not feeling well, see **health**, page 187.

mixed emotions

a little
medyo   *med·*yo

I'm a little sad.
Akó ay medyo malungkót.   a·*ko* ai *med*·yo ma·loong·*ko*

extremely
lubhâ   loob·*ha'*

I'm extremely sorry.
Akó ay lubháng   a·*ko* ai loob·*hang*
nagdaramdám.   nag·da·ram·*dam*

very
nápaka-   na·pa·ka·

I feel very lucky.
Nápakasuwerte   na·pa·ka·soo·*wer*·te
ng pakiramdám ko.   nang pa·kee·ram·*dam* ko

opinions

Did you like it?
Nagustuhán mo ba iyón?   na·goos·too·*han* mo ba ee·*yon*

What do you think of it?
Anó ang palagáy mo?   a·*no* ang pa·la·*gai* mo

I thought it was …	*Akalà ko iyón ay …*	a·ka·*la* ko ee·*yon* ai …
It's …	*Iyón ay …*	ee·*yon* ai …
awful	*nakapangíngi-labot*	na·ka·pa·*ngee*·ngee·*la*·bot
beautiful	*magandá*	ma·gan·*da*
boring	*nakabábagót*	na·ka·*ba*·ba·*got*
great	*magalíng*	ma·ga·*leeng*
interesting	*nakakawili*	na·ka·ka·*wee*·lee
OK	*okey*	o·kay
strange	*kakaibá*	ka·ka·ee·*ba*
too expensive	*napakamahál*	na·pa·ka·ma·*hal*

party on

Alliance of Hope
Alyansa ng Pagasa   al·*yan*·sa nang pa·*ga*·sa

Arise Philippines
Bangon Pilipinas   ba·*ngon* pee·lee·*pee*·nas

Coalition of Stability and Experience for the Future
Koalisyon ng Katatagan   ko·lee·*syon* nang ka·ta·*ta*·gan
at Karanasan para sa   at ka·ra·*na*·san *pa*·ra sa
Kinabukasan (K-4)   kee·na·boo·*ka*·san

Coalition of United Filipinos
Koalisyon ng   ko·a·lee·*syon* nang
Nagkakaisang   nag·ka·ka·*ee*·sang
Pilipino (KNP)   pee·lee·*pee*·no

Nationalist People's Coalition
Nationalist People's   na·syo·na·leest *pee*·pols
Coalition (NPC)   ko·a·*lee*·syon

Strength
Lakas   la·*kas*

politics & social issues

Who do you vote for?
Kanino ang boto mo?
ka·*nee*·no ang *bo*·to mo

I support	*Sinusuportahán*	see·noo·soo·por·ta·*han*
the … party.	*ko ang*	ko ang
	partidong …	par·*tee*·dong …
I'm a member of	*Miyembro akó*	mee·*yem*·bro a·*ko*
the … party.	*ng partidong …*	nang par·*tee*·dong …
communist	*komunista*	ko·moo·*nees*·ta
conservative	*konserbatibo*	kon·ser·ba·*tee*·bo
democratic	*demokrátiko*	de·mo·*kra*·tee·ko
green	*green*	green
liberal	*liberál*	lee·be·*ral*
social	*sosyalistang*	sos·ya·*lees*·tang
democratic	*demokrátiko*	de·mo·*kra*·tee·ko
socialist	*sosyalista*	sos·ya·*lees*·ta

Did you hear about …?
Náriníg mo ba ang
na·ree·*neeg* mo ba ang
tungkól sa …?
toong·*kol* sa …

Do you agree with it?
Sang-ayon ka ba doón?
sang·*a*·yon ka ba do·*on*

I don't agree with …
Hindî akó sang-ayon sa …
heen·*dee*' a·*ko* sang·*a*·yon sa …

I agree with …
Sang-ayon akó sa …
sang·*a*·yon a·*ko* sa …

How do people feel about …?
Anó ang palagáy ng mga
a·*no* ang pa·la·*gai* nang ma·*nga*
tao tungkól sa …?
ta·o toong·*kol* sa …

How can we protest against …?
Paano tayo magpoprotesta
pa·*a*·no *ta*·yo mag·po·pro·*tes*·ta
laban …?
la·*ban* …

How can we support …?
Paano natin
pa·*a*·no *na*·teen
masusuportahán ang …?
ma·soo·soo·por·ta·*han* ang …

abortion	*aborsyon*	a·*bors*·yon
animal rights	*karapatán ng*	ka·ra·pa·*tan* nang
	mga hayop	ma·*nga* ha·yop
birth control	*birth control*	bert kon·*trol*
crime	*krimen*	kree·*men*
discrimination	*diskriminasyón*	dees·kree·mee·nas·*yon*
drugs	*droga*	*dro*·ga
the economy	*ang ekonomiyá*	ang e·ko·no·mee·*ya*
education	*edukasyón*	e·doo·kas·*yon*
the environment	*ang kapaligirán*	ang ka·pa·lee·gee·*ran*
equal	*pantáy-pantáy na*	pan·*tai*·pan·tai na
opportunity	*oportunidád*	o·por·too·nee·*dad*
education	*edukasyón*	e·doo·kas·*yon*
euthanasia	*euthanasia*	yoo·ta·*nas*·ya
globalisation	*pangmundóng*	pang·moon·*dong*
	pakikipag-	pa·kee·kee·pag·
	ugnayan	oog·*na*·yan
human rights	*mga pantaong*	ma·*nga* pan·*ta*·ong
	karapatán	ka·ra·pa·*tan*
immigration	*imigrasyón*	ee·mee·gras·*yon*
inequality	*hindí pagkaka-*	heen·*dee* pag·ka·ka·
	pantáy-pantáy	pan·*tai*·pan·*tai*
party politics	*pulítika ng*	poo·*lee*·tee·ka nang
	partido	par·*tee*·do
poverty	*kahirapan*	ka·hee·*ra*·pan
privatisation	*gawíng pribado*	ga·*weeng* pree·*ba*·do
racism	*pagkapoót sa lahì*	pag·ka·po·*ot* sa *la*·hee'
sexism	*diskriminasyón*	dees·kree·mee·nas·*yon*
	ayon sa kasarián	*a*·yon sa ka·sa·ree·*an*
social welfare	*kapakanáng*	ka·pa·ka·*nang*
	panlipunan	pan·lee·*poo*·nan
terrorism	*terorismo*	te·ro·*rees*·mo
unemployment	*kawalán ng*	ka·wa·*lan* nang
	trabaho	tra·*ba*·ho
domestic	*karahasan sa*	ka·ra·ha·*san* sa
violence	*pamilya*	pa·*meel*·ya
the war in …	*ang giyera sa …*	ang gee·*ye*·ra sa …
the war on	*paglaban sa*	pag·*la*·ban sa
terrorism	*terorismo*	te·ro·*rees*·mo

the environment

Is this a	Itó ba ay	ee·to ba ai
protected …?	protektadong …?	pro·tek·ta·dong …
animal	hayop	ha·yop
area	pook	po·ok
forest	gubat	goo·bat
park	parke	par·ke
plant	halaman	ke·la·man
species	urì	oo·ree'

Is there a … problem here?

May problema ba dito   mai pro·ble·ma ba dee·to
sa … ?   sa …

What should be done about …?

Anó ang dapat gawín   a·no ang da·pat ga·ween
tungkól sa …?   toong·kol sa …

How can I find out about … issues?

Paano akó makakaalam   pa·a·no a·ko ma ka ka·a·lam
tungkól sa …?   toong·kol sa …

---

lost ancient script

Prior to the Spanish colonisation of the Philippines in the 16th century, the Filipino language had a unique writing system, which was probably of Indian origin. This script was a 'syllabary', which used symbols to represent syllables, not individual letters. The Filipino syllabary, called *alibatali* a·lee·ba·ta·lee, had 17 symbols – three of these represented vowels and the rest consonants. It was very aesthetically pleasing being made up of curving, scribbly lines.

feelings & opinions

129

conservation	konserbasyón	kon·ser·bas·yon
deforestation	pagkaubos ng gubat	pag·ka·oo·bos nang goo·bat
drought	tagtuyót	tag·too·yot
ecosystem	ekosistem	e·ko·sees·tem
endangered species	nanganganib na urì	na·nga·nga·neeb na oo·ree
genetically modified food	mga pagkaing binago ang kaanyuán	ma·nga pag·ka·eeng bee·na·go ang ka·an·yoo·an
hunting with guns/dogs	pamamaríl/ pangangasó	pa·ma·ma·reel/ pa·nga·nga·so
hydroelectricity	elektrisidád na likha ng tubig	e·lek·tree·see·dad na leek·ha nang too·beeg
immigration	imigrasyón	e·mee·gras·yon
indigenous issues	mga isyu tungkól sa mga taong katutubò	ma·nga ees·yoo toong·kol sa ma·nga ta·ong ka·too·too·bo'
irrigation	irigasyón	ee·ree·gas·yon
nuclear energy	enerhiyáng nukliyár	e·ner·hee·yang nook·lee·yar
nuclear testing	testing na nukliyár	tes·teeng na nook·lee·yar
ozone layer	susón ng ozone	soo·son nang o·son
pesticides	mga pamatáysalot	ma·nga pa·ma·tai·sa·lot
pollution	polusyón	po·loos·yon
recycling programme	programa ng pagre-recycle	pro·gra·ma nang pag·ree·ree·sai·kel
toxic waste	basurang nakalalason	ba·soo·rang na·ka·la·la·son
water supply	tustós na tubig	toos·tos na too·beeg

where to go

saán pupuntá

What's there to do in the evenings?
Anó ang magagawá   a·*no* ang ma·ga·ga·*wa*
sa gabí?   sa ga·*bee*

What's on ...?	*Anó ang*	a·*no* ang
	mayroón ...?	mai·ro·*on* ...
locally	*dito*	*dee*·to
this weekend	*ngayóng Sábado*	nga·*yong sa*·ba·do
	at Linggó	at leeng·*go*
today	*ngayón*	nga·*yon*
tonight	*ngayóng gabí*	nga·*yong* ga·*bee*

I feel like going	*Parang gustó kong*	pa·rang goos·*to* kong
to a ...	*magpuntá sa ...*	mag·*poon*·ta sa ...
bar	*bar*	bar
café	*kapiteryá*	ka·pee·ter·*ya*
concert	*konsiyerto*	kon·see·*yer*·to
film	*pelíkula*	pe·*lee*·koo·la
folk dance	*palahás na katu-*	pa·la·*bas* na ka·too-
performance	*tubong sayáw*	*too*·bong sa·*yow*
karaoke bar	*bar na may*	bar na mai
	karayoke	ka·ra·*yo*·ke
kundiman	*palabás na may*	pa·la·*bas* na mai
performance	*kundiman*	koon·*dee*·man
nightclub	*naytklab*	*nait*·klab
play	*dulâ*	doo·*la'*
restaurant	*restoran*	res·*to*·ran
tinikling	*palabás na*	pa·la·*bas* na
performance	*tiniklíng*	tee·neek·*leeng*

For more on eateries, bars and drinks, see **romance**, page 135, and **eating out**, page 159.

Where are the ...?	Saán akó makakakita ng ...?	sa·an a·ko ma·ka·ka·kee·ta nang ...
bars	bar	bar
(gay) clubs	club (para sa baklâ)	klab (pa·ra sa bak·la')
places to eat	kainan	ka·ee·nan

Is there a local ... guide?	Mayroón bang lokal na giyang ...?	mai·ro·on bang lo·kal na gee·yang ...
entertainment	pangliwalíw	pang·lee·wa·lew
film	pampelíkula	pam·pe·lee·koo·la
gay	pambaklâ	pam·bak·la'
music	pangmúsika	pang·moo·see·ka

invitations

mga imbitasyón

What are you doing ...?	Anó ang gagawín mo ...?	a·no ang ga·ga·ween mo ...
now	ngayón	nga·yon
tonight	ngayóng gabí	nga·yong ga·bee
this weekend	ngayóng Sabado at Linggó	nga·yong sa·ba·do at leeng·go

Would you like to go (for a) ...?	Gustó mo bang magpunta sa ...?	goos·to mo bang mag·poon·ta (sa) ...
I feel like going (for a) ...	Parang gustó kong ...	pa·rang goos·to kong ...
coffee	magkape	mag·ka·pe
dancing	magsayáw	mag·sa·yow
drink	mag-ínuman	mag·ee·noo·man
meal	kumain sa labás	koo·ma·een sa la·bas
out	lumabás	loo·ma·bas
somewhere	kahit saán	ka·heet sa·an
walk	maglakád	mag·la·kad

We're having a party.
May parti kamí.   mai par·tee ka·mee

You should come.
Dapat pumuntá ka.   da·pat poo·moon·ta ka

Do you know a good restaurant?
May alám ka bang — mai a·*lam* ka bang
masaráp na restoran? — ma·sa·*rap* na res·*to*·ran

Do you want to come to the concert with me?
Gustó mo bang sumama — goos·*to* mo bang soo·*ma*·ma
sa akin sa konsiyerto? — sa *a*·keen sa kon·see·*yer*·to

responding to invitations

pagsagót sa mga imbitasyón

Sure!
Sigé! — see·*ge*

Yes, I'd love to.
Oo, gustó ko. — o·o goos·*to* ko

Where shall we go?
Saán tayo pupuntá? — sa·*an* ta·yo poo·poon·*ta*

No, I'm afraid I can't.
Hindî akó puwede. — heen·*dee*' a·ko poo·*we*·de

What about tomorrow?
Bukas? — *boo*·kas

Sorry, I can't sing/dance.
Sori, hindî akó marunong — so·ree heen·*dee*' a·ko ma·*roo*·nong
kumantá/magsayáw. — koo·man·*ta*/mag·sa·*yow*

arranging to meet

pag-aayos na magkita

What time will we meet?
Anóng oras tayo — a·*nong o*·ras ta·yo
magkikita? — mag·kee·*kee*·ta

Where will we meet?
Saán tayo magkikita? — sa·*an* ta·yo mag·kee·*kee*·ta

Let's meet at …	*Magkita tayo …*	mag·*kee*·ta ta·yo …
(eight) o'clock	*nang alás-(otso)*	nang a·*las*·(ot·so)
the (entrance)	*sa (pintuan)*	sa (peen·*too*·an)

I'll pick you up.
Pípik·apín kitá. · pee·peek·a·peen kee·ta

Are you ready?
Handá ka na ba? · han·da ka na ba

I'm ready.
Handá na akó. · han·da na a·ko

I'll be coming later.
Daratíng akó mámayâ. · da·ra·teeng a·ko ma·ma·ya'

Where will you be?
Saán ka naroroón? · sa·an ka na·ro·ro·on

If I'm not there by (nine), don't wait for me.
Pag walâ akó nang · pag wa·la a·ko nang
alás-(nuwebe), huwág · a·las·(noo·we·be), hoo·wag
kang maghintáy sa akin. · kang mag·heen·tai sa a·keen

See you later/tomorrow.
Hanggáng mámayâ/bukas. · hang·gang ma·ma·ya'/boo·kas

I'm looking forward to it.
Maghihintáy akó. · mag·hee·heen·tai a·ko

Sorry I'm late. *Sori, hulí akó.* · so·ree hoo·lee a·ko
Never mind. *Walá iyón.* · wa·la ee·yon

drugs

droga

Do you have a light?
May layter ka? · mai lai·ter ka ba

I don't take drugs.
Hindî akó nagdodroga. · heen·dee' a·ko nag·do·dro·ga

asking someone out

pakikipag-deyt

Would you like to do something (tomorrow)?
Gustó mo bang may　　goos·*to* mo bang mai
gawin tayo (bukas)?　　ga·*ween* ta·yo (*boo*·kas)

Yes, I'd love to.
Oo, gustó ko.　　o·o goos·*to* ko

Sorry, I can't.
Sori, hindî akó puwede.　　so·ree heen·*dee*' a·ko poo·*we*·de

Where would you like to go (tonight)?
Saán mo gustóng　　sa·*an* mo goos·*tong*
pumuntá　　poo·moon·*ta*
(mámayáng gabi)?　　(*ma*·ma·*yang* ga·*bee*)

local talk

He/She is a babe.
Ang guwapo/gandá niyá.　　any goo·*wa*·po/gan·*da* nee·*ya*

He/She has no shame!
Walánghiyá siyá!　　wa·*lang*·hee·ya see·*ya*

He/She is up himself/herself.
Mayabang siyá.　　ma·*ya*·bang see·*ya*

As if he/she is somebody.
Akala mo kung sino siyá.　　a·*ka*·la mo koong *see*·no see·*ya*

He/She is annoying.
Siyá ay nakúkainís.　　see·*ya* ai na·*ka*·ka·ee·*nees*

Who? Him/Her?
Sino? Siyá?　　*see*·no see·*ya*

pick-up lines

Would you like a drink?
Gustó mo ba ng inumin?   goos·*to* mo ba nang ee·*noo*·meen

You look like someone I know.
Kamukhá ka nang   ka·*mook*·ha ka nang
kakilala ko.   ka·kee·*la*·la ko

You're a fantastic dancer.
Magalíng kang sumayáw.   ma·ga·*leeng* kang soo·ma·*yow*

I think we've met before.
Parang nagkita na tayo.   *pa*·rang nag·*kee*·ta na *ta*·yo

Aren't you (Joan)?
Di ba ikáw si (Joan)?   dee ba ee·*kaw* see (jo·*an*)

Are you doing anything (tomorrow)?
May gagawín ka ba   mai ga·ga·*ween* ka ba
(bukas)?   (*boo*·kas)

Can I ...?	*Puwede ba akóng ...?*	poo·*we*·de ba a·*kong* ...
dance	*makipagsayáw*	ma·kee·pag·sa·*yow*
with you	*sa iyó*	sa ee·*yo*
sit here	*maupó dito*	ma·oo·*po* dee·to
take you home	*maghatíd sa iyó*	mag·ha·*teed* sa ee·*yo*

---

local talk

I don't want to talk to you.
Ayokong   a·*yo*·kong
makipag-usap sa iyo.   ma·kee·pag·*oo*·sap sa ee·*yo*

My girlfriend/boyfriend is looking this way.
Nakatingín nga dito   na·ka·tee·*ngeen* nga *dee*·to
ang nobya/nobyo ko.   ang *nob*·ya/*nob*·yo ko

Leave me alone!
Iwan mo akóng mag-isá!   ee·wan mo a·*kong* mag·ee·*sa*

Piss off!
Lumayó ka!   loo·ma·*yo* ka

rejections

No, thank you.
    Hindí, salamat.   heen·*dee* sa·*la*·mat

I'd rather not.
    Ayoko.   a·*yo*·ko

Excuse me, I have to go now.
    Eksyus mi, áalís na akó.   eks·*yoos* mee, *a·a*·lees na a·*ko*

I'm here with my girlfriend/boyfriend.
    Kasama ko ang aking   ka·*sa*·ma ko ang *a*·keeng
    nobya/nobyo.   *nob*·ya/*nob*·yo

I'm married already.
    May asawa na akó.   mai a·*sa*·wa na a·*ko*

Talk to someone else.
    Sa iba ka na lang   sa ee·*ba* ka na lang
    makipag-usap.   ma·kee·pag·*oo*·sap

getting closer

I like you very much.
    Gustúng-gustó kitá.   goos·*toong*·goos·*to* kee·*ta*

Can I kiss you?
    Puwede ba kitáng   poo·*we*·de ba kee·*tang*
    halikán?   ha·lee·*kan*

Do you want to come inside for a while?
    Gustó mo bang pumasok goos·*to* mo bang poo·*ma*·sok
    muna sandalî?   *moo*·na san·da·*lee'*

Do you want a massage?
    Gustó mo ba ng masahe? goos·*to* mo ba nang ma·*sa*·he

Can I stay over?
    Puwede ba akóng   poo·*we*·de ba a·*kong*
    maghintó dito?   mag·heen·*to dee*·to

romance

sex

seks

Kiss me.
Halikan mo akó.   ha·lee·*kan* mo a·*ko*

I want you.
Nais kitá.   *na*·ees kee·*ta*

Let's go to bed.
Halina sa kama.   ha·*lee*·na sa *ka*·ma

Do you like this?
Gustó mo ba itó?   goos·*to* mo ba ee·*to*

I like that.
Gustó ko iyan.   goos·*to* ko ee·*yan*

I don't like that.
Hindí ko gustó iyan.   heen·*dee* ko goos·*to* ee·*yan*

I think we should stop now.
Dapat ay humintó na tayo ngayón.   *da*·pat ai hoo·meen·*to* na *ta*·yo nga·*yon*

Do you have a (condom)?
May (kondom) ka ba?   mai (*kon*·dom) ka ba

I won't do it without protection.
Hindî akó papayag kung waláng proteksiyón.   heen·*dee* a·ko pa·*pa*·yag koong wa·*lang* pro·teks·*yon*

That was ...   *Iyón ay ...*
ee·*yon* ai ...

amazing	*kahanga-hanga*	ka·*ha*·nga·*ha*·nga'
romantic	*romantiko*	ro·*man*·tee·ko
wild	*nakahíhibáng*	na·ka·*hee*·hee·*bang*

SOCIAL

138

love

I think we're good together.
 Sa palagáy ko ay   sa pa·la·*gai* ko ai
 bagay tayo.   *ba*·gai *ta*·yo.

I love you.
 Mahál kitá.   ma·*hal* kee·*ta*

Will you …?	*Puwede ka bang …*	poo·*we*·de ka bang …
go out	*makipag-deyt*	ma·kee·pag·*dayt*
with me	*sa akin*	sa *a*·keen
marry me	*magpakasál*	mag·pa·ka·*sal*
	sa akin	sa *a*·keen
meet my	*makipagkilala sa*	ma·kee·pag·kee·*la*·la sa
parents	*aking mga*	*a*·keeng ma·*nga*
	magulang	ma·*goo*·lang

sweet nothings		
babe	*babe*	bayb
cutie-pie	*cutie-pie*	*kyoo*·tee·pai
dearest	*giliw*	gee·*lew*
love	*mahál*	ma·*hal*

problems

Are you seeing someone else?
*May ka-déyt ka na
bang ibá?*
mai ka·*dayt* ka na
bang ee·*ba*

He/She is just a friend.
Kaibigan ko lang siyá.
ka·ee·*bee*·gan ko lang see·*ya*

I never want to see you again.
*Ayoko na kitáng makita
pa ulî.*
a·*yo*·ko na kee·*tang* ma·*kee*·ta
pa oo·*lee'*

I don't think it's working out.
*Tila hindí nangyayari
nang tamà sa atin.*
tee·la heen·*dee* nang·ya·*ya*·ree
nang *ta*·ma sa *a*·teen

We'll work it out.
Titingnán natin.
tee·teeng·*nan* na·teen

leaving

I have to leave (tomorrow).
*Kailangan ko nang
umalís (bukas).*
ka·ee·*la*·ngan ko nang
oo·ma·lees (*boo*·kas)

I'll …   *Akó ay … sa iyó.*   a·*ko* ai … sa ee·*yo*
  keep in touch   *makikipag-alám*   ma·kee·kee·pag·a·*lam*
  miss you   *mangungulila*   ma·ngoo·ngoo·*lee*·la
  visit you   *dadalaw*   da·*da*·low

religion

relihiyón

What's your religion?
Anó ang relihiyón mo?   a·no ang re·lee·hee·*yon* mo

I'm not religious.
Hindî akó relihiyoso.   heen·*dee'* a·ko re·lee·hee·*yo*·so

I'm (a/an) ...	Akó ay ...	a·ko ai ...
agnostic	agnóstiko	ag·*nos*·tee·ko
atheist	hindí	heen·*dee*
	naniniwala	na·nee·nee·*wa*·la
	sa Diyós	sa dee·*yos*
Buddhist	Budista	boo·*dees*·ta
Catholic	Katóliko	ka·*to*·lee·ko
Christian	Kristiyano	krees·tee·*ya*·no
Church of Christ	Iglesya ni Kristo	eeg·*les*·ya nee *krees*·to
Hindu	Hindu	*heen*·doo
Jewish	Hudyó	hood·*yo*
Muslim	Muslím	moos·*leem*
Seventh Day Adventist	Sabadista	sa·ba·*dees*·ta

Can I ... here?	Maáarì ba akóng ... dito?	ma·a·a·ree ba a·*kong* ... *dee*·to
Where can I ...?	Saán akó puwedeng ...	sa·*an* a·ko poo·we·deng ...
attend mass	makapagsísimbá	ma·ka·pag·*see*·seem·ba
attend a service	makadádalo sa kulto	ma·ka·*da*·da·lo sa *kool*·to
meditate	magmunimuni	mag·*moo*·nee·moo·*nee'*
pray	makapagdádasál	ma·ka·pag·*da*·da·sal
worship	makasásambá	ma·ka·*sa*·sam·ba

I (don't)	Akó ay (hindí)	a·ko ay (heen·dee)
believe in ...	naniniwala sa ...	na·nee·nee·wa·la sa ...
astrology	astrolohiyá	as·tro·lo·hee·ya
fate	kapalaran	ka·pa·la·ran
God	Diyós	dee·yos

cultural differences

pagkákaibá ng kultura

Is this a local or national custom?
Itó ba ay kaugalián dito
o sa buong bansâ?
ee·to ba ai ka·oo·ga·lee·an dee·to
o sa boo·ong ban·sa

I don't want to offend you.
Hindí ko gustóng saktán
ang iyóng damdamin.
heen·dee ko goos·tong sak·tan
ang ee·yong dam·da·meen

I'd rather not join in.
Mas mainam na hindî
akó sumali.
mas ma·ee·nam na heen·dee'
a·ko soo·ma·lee

I'll try it.
Súsubukan ko.
soo·soo·boo·kan ko

I didn't mean to do/say anything wrong.
Hindí ko sinadyáng
gawín/sabihin ang
anumáng hindí tamà.
heen·dee ko see·nad·yang
ga·ween/sa·bee·heen ang
a·noo·mang heen·dee ta·ma'

I'm sorry, it's	Sori, laban itó sa	so·ree, la·ban ee·to sa
against my ...	aking ...	a·keeng ...
beliefs	paniniwalà	pa·nee·nee·wa·la'
religion	relihiyón	re·lee·hee·yon

This is ...	Itó ay ...	ee·to ai ...
different	ibá	ee·ba
fun	katuwaan	ka·too·wa·an
interesting	nakakawili	na·ka·ka·wee·lee

When's the gallery/museum open?

Kailán bukás ang galeryá/museo?	ka·ee·*lan* boo·*kas* ang ga·ler·*ya*/moo·*se*·o

What kind of art are you interested in?

Anóng klase ng arte ang gustó mo?	a·*nong kla*·se nang *ar*·te ang goos·*to* mo

What's in the collection?

Anó ang nasa koleksiyón?	a·*no* ang *na*·sa ko·lek·see·*yon*

What do you think of …?

Anó ang palagáy mo sa …?	a·*no* ang pa·la·*gai* mo sa …

abstract expressionism	*ekspresyonismo na abstrak*	eks·pres·yo·*nees*·mo na *abs*·trak
Christian art	*arte ng Kristiyano*	*ar*·te nang krees·tee·*ya*·no
contemporary Philippine painting	*Pilipinong pintá na kapanahón*	pee·lee·*pee*·nong peen·*ta* na ka·pa·na·*hon*
graphic	*grápiko*	*gra*·pee·ko
impressionism	*impresyonismo*	eem·pres·yo·*nees*·mo
modernism	*modernismo*	mo·der·*nees*·mo
Neorealism	*Niyoriyalismo*	nee·yo·ree·ya·*lees*·mo
the performing arts	*sining palabás*	*see*·neeng pa·la·*bas*
secular art	*arte na waláng kaugnayan sa relihiyón*	*ar*·te na wa·*lang* ka·oog·*na*·yan sa re·lee·hee·*yon*

lip service

In the Philippines you point things out with your mouth – purse your lips together and extend them out, Mick Jagger style, then jerk your chin slightly in the direction of the person or thing in question.

I'm interested in …
 Interesado akó sa … — een·te·re·*sa*·do a·*ko* sa …

It's an exhibition of …
 Iksibisyón itó ng … — eek·see·bees·*yon* ee·*to* nang …

I like the works of …
 Gustó ko ng mga — goos·*to* ko ng ma·*nga*
 likhá ni … — leek·*ha* nee …

Do they sell …?
 Nagtitindá ba — nag·tee·teen·*da* ba
 silá ng …? — (see·*la*) nang …

I want to see a demonstration of …
 Gusto kong makakita ng — goos·*to* kong ma·ka·*kee*·ta nang
 demonstrasyón ng … — de·mons·tras·*yon* nang …

architecture	*arkitektura*	ar·kee·tek·*too*·ra
art(work)	*(likháng) arte*	(leek·*hang*) *ar*·te
etching	*pag-uukit*	pag·oo·*oo*·keet
exhibition hall	*bulwagang*	bool·*wa*·gang
	pang-iksibisyón	pang·eek·see·bees·*yon*
metalwork	*gawáng*	ga·*wang*
	ginamitan ng	gee·na·*mee*·tan nang
	metál	me·*tal*
painter	*pintór*	peen·*tor*
painting (artwork)	*piníntura*	pee·neen·*too*·ra
painting (technique)	*pagpipintá*	pag·pee·peen·*ta*
period	*panahón*	pa·na·*hon*
permanent collection	*permanenteng*	per·ma·*nen*·teng
	koleksyón	ko·leks·*yon*
pottery	*palayók*	pa·la·*yok*
print n	*imprenta*	eem·*pren*·ta
sculptor	*iskultór*	ees·kool·*tor*
sculpture	*iskultura*	ees·kool·*too*·ra
statue	*istátuwa*	ees·*ta*·too·wa
woodcarvings	*inukit na kahoy*	ee·*noo*·keet na *ka*·hoy
embroidery	*burdá*	boor·*da*
woven cloth	*telang hinabì*	*te*·lang hee·*na*·bee'
sketching	*pagguhit*	pag·*goo*·heet

sporting interests

pang-ispórt na interés

What sport do you play/follow?
Anóng ispórt ang nilalaró/ sinúsundán mo? a·nong ees·port ang nee·la·la·ro/ see·noo·soon·dan mo

I play (football).
Naglalarô akó ng (football). nag·la·la·ro' a·ko nang (put·bol)

I follow (tennis).
Sinúsundán ko ang (tenis). see·noo·soon·dan ko ang (te·nees)

I ...	*Akó ay ...*	a·ko ai ...
cycle	*nagbibisikleta*	nag·bee·bee·seek·le·ta
run	*tumatakbó*	too·ma·tak·bo
walk	*naglalakád*	nag·la·la·kad

Do you like (badminton)?
Gustó mo ba ng laróng (badminton)? goos·to mo ba nang la·rong (bad·meen·ton)

Who's your favourite sportsperson?
Sino ang paborito mong tagapaglarô? see·no ang pa·bo·ree·to mong ta·ga·pag·la·ro'

sport

The names for sporting activities are very easy to remember in Filipino – they're the same as in English. The top 8 favourite sports in the Philippines are:

basketball	bas·ket·bol	softball	sop·bol
baseball	bays·bol	boxing	bok·seeng
badminton	bad·meen·ton	tennis	te·nees
tenpin bowling	ten·peen bo·leeng	volleyball	ba·lee·bol

going to a game

Would you like to go to a game?
Gustó mo bang magpuntá
sa isáng game?

goos·*to* mo bang mag·poon·*ta*
sa ee·*sang* gaym

Who are you supporting?
Sino ang sinú-
suportahán mo?

see·no ang see·*noo*·
soo·por·ta·*han* mo

Who's ...?	Sino ang ...?	*see*·no ang ...
playing	naglalarô	nag·la·la·*ro'*
winning	nananalo	na·na·*na*·lo

That was a ...	lyón ay ...	ee·*yon* ai ...
game!	na game!	na gaym
bad	waláng kuwenta	wa·*lang* koo·*wen*·ta
boring	nakababagót	na·ka·ba·ba·*got*
great	magalíng	ma·ga·*leeng*

sports talk

What a ...!	Ang galíng na ...!	ang ga·*leeng* na ...
goal	goal	gohl
hit	tira	*tee*·ra
kick	sipà	*see*·pa'
pass	pasa	*pa*·sa
performance	pakita	pa·*kee*·ta

playing sport

Do you want to play (soccer)?
Gustó mo bang maglarô
(ng soccer)?

goos·*to* mo bang mag·la·*ro'*
(nang *sa*·ker)

Can I join in?
Puwede ba akóng sumali?

poo·*we*·de ba a·*kong* soo·*ma*·lee

I can't.
Hindî akó puwede.   heen·*dee*'·a·ko poo·*we*·de

I have an injury.
May masakít sa akin.   mai ma·sa·*keet* sa *a*·keen

Your/My point.
Puntos mo/ko.   *poon*·tos mo/ko

You're a good player.
Magalíng kang player.   ma·ga·*leeng* kang *ple*·yer

Where's the nearest (swimming pool)?
Násaán ang   na·sa·*an* ang
pinakamalapit   pee·na·ka·ma·*la*·peet
na (palanguyan)?   na (pa·la·*ngoo*·yan)

Do I have to be a member to attend?
Kailangan bang akó uy   ka·ee·*la*·ngan bang a·ko ai
miyembro para dumaló?   mee·*yem*·bro *pa*·ra doo·ma·*lo*

Where are the changing rooms?
Násaán ang bihisán?   na·sa·*an* ang bee·hee·*san*

What's the charge per ...?	*Magkano ang upa kada ...?*	mag·*ka*·no ang *oo*·pa *ka*·da ...
day	*araw*	*a*·row
game	*game*	gaym
hour	*oras*	*o*·ras
visit	*bisita*	bee·*see*·ta

Can I hire (a) ...?	*Puwede ba akóng humirám ng ...?*	poo·*we*·de ba a·*kong* hoo·mee·*ram* nang ...
ball	*bola*	*bo*·la
bicycle	*bisikleta*	bee·seek·*le*·ta
racquet	*raketa*	ra·*ke*·ta
shoes	*sapatos*	sa·*pa*·tos

scoring

What's the score?	*Anó ang score?*	a·*no* ang ees·*kor*
draw	*patas*	*pa*·tas
even	*pantáy*	pan·*tai*
love/nil (zero)	*walâ*	wa·*la*'

basketball

What's your favourite team?
  Sino ang paborito mong team? — see·no ang pa·bo·ree·to mong teem

What position do you play?
  Ano ang posisyóng nilalaró mo? — a·no ang po·sees·yong nee·la·la·ro mo

centre	sentro	sen·tro
defence	depensa	de·pen·sa
guard	bantáy	ban·tai

cockfighting

sabong

Visitors may find *sabong* sa·bong (cockfighting) gruesome, but whatever your opinion, it's a noteworthy cultural experience.

arbiter	sentensiyadór	sen·ten·see·ya·dor
bet n	pustahan	poos·ta·han
bet v	pumustá	poo·moos·ta
chicken (any poultry)	manok	ma·nok
cockpit	sabungan	sa·boo·ngan
cock spur n	tarî	ta·ree
rooster	tandáng	tan·dang
sabong punter	sabungero	sa·boo·nge·ro

diving

daybing

Where's a good diving site?
Saán may magandáng	sa·*an* mai ma·gan·*dang*
lugár para mag-diving?	loo·*gar* pa·ra mag-*dai*·beeng

I'd like to …	*Gustó kong …*	goos·to kong …
do a reef dive	*dumayb sa*	doo·*maib* sa
	batuhán	ba·too·*han*
explore	*maggalugad*	mag·ga·*loo*·gad
caves/wrecks	*ng mga*	nang ma·*nga*
	kuweba/labí	koo·*we*·ba/la·*bee*
go night diving	*dumáyb sa*	doo·*maib* sa
	gabí	ga·*bee*
go scuba diving	*mag-scuba*	mag·ees·*koo*·ba
	daybing	*dai*·beeng
go snorkelling	*mag-snorkel*	mag·ees·*nor*·kel
join a diving tour	*sumama sa*	soo·*ma*·ma sa ee
	daybing tour	*dai*·beeng toor
learn to dive	*matutong*	ma·*too*·tong
	dumáyb	doo·*maib*

Is the visibility good?
  Malinaw ba? ma·*lee*·now ba

How deep is the dive?
  Gaano kalalim ang dayb? ga·*a*·no ka·*la*·leem ang daib

Is it safe?
  Ligtas ba? *leeg*·tas ba

I need an air fill.
  Kailangan kong ka·ee·*la*·ngan kong
  magpapunó ng hangin. mag·pa·poo·*no* nang *ha*·ngeen

I want to hire (a) …	Gustó kong umarkilá ng …	goos·*to* kong oo·mar·kee·*la* nang …
buoyancy vest	*pampalutang na kasuotan*	pam·pa·*loo*·tang na ka·soo·*o*·tan
diving equipment	*kagamitáng pang-dayb*	ka·ga·mee·*tang* pang·*daib*
tank	*tangké*	tang·*ke*
weight belt	*pampabigát na belt*	pam·pa·bee·*gat* na belt

Are there …?	Mayroón bang mga …?	mai·ro·*on* bang ma·*nga* …
currents	*agos*	*a*·gos
sharks	*patíng*	pa·*teeng*
whales	*balyena*	bal·*ye*·na

buddy	*kapareha*	ka·pa·*re*·ha
cave	*kuweba*	koo·*we*·ba
dive n	*dayb*	daib
dive v	*dumayb*	doo·*maib*
diving boat	*bangkáng pang-dayb*	bang·*kang* pang·*daib*
diving course	*kurso ng pag-dayb*	*koor*·so nang pag·*daib*
gas tank	*tangke ng gás*	*tang*·ke nang gas
googles	*mga gogel*	ma·*nga go*·gel
night dive	*pag-dayb sa gabí*	pag·*daib* sa ga·*bee*
sea	*dagatan*	da·*ga*·tan
wreck	*labí*	la·*bee*

horse racing

karera ng kabayo

Where is the racetrack?
Násaán ang kárerahán?   na·sa·an ang ka·re·ra·han

I'd like to bet on (Royal Catch) for a place/win.
Gustó kong pumustá   goos·to kong poo·moos·ta
kay (Royal Catch) para sa   kay (ro·yal cats) pa·ra sa
puwesto/panalo.   poo·wes·to/pa·na·lo

Which horse is favourite?
Alíng kabayo ang   a·leeng ka·ba·yo ang
paborito?   pa·bo·ree·to

Which horse should I back?
Alíng kabayo dapat kong   a·leeng ka·ba·yo da·pat kong
pustahán?   poos·ta·han

What are the odds?
Anó ang laban?   a·no ang la·ban

This horse is (five to one).
Ang kabayong itó ay   ang ka·ba·yong ee·to ai
(5 sa 1).   (lee·ma sa ee·sa)

What weight is the horse carrying?
Anó ang daláng   a·no ang da·lang
timbáng ng kabayo?   teem·bang nang ka·ba·yo

bet n	*pustá*	poos·ta
bookmaker	*tagakuha ng*	ta·ga·koo·ha nang
	pustá	poos·ta
horse	*kabayo*	ka·ba·yo
jockey	*hinete*	hee·ne·te
luck	*suwerte*	soo·wer·te
race n	*karera*	ka·re·ra

horse riding

How long is the ride?
   Gaano katagál ang   ga·a·no ka·ta·gal ang
   pagsakáy?   pag·sa·kai

I'm (not) an experienced rider.
   (Hindî) Akó ay sanáy na   (heen·dee') a·ko ay sa·nai na
   sakáy.   sa·kai

Can I rent a hat and boots?
   Puwede ba akóng   poo·we·de ba a·kong
   umarkilá ng   oo·mar·kee·la nang
   sombrero at bota?   som·bre·ro at bo·ta

bit	*pangatngát*	pa·ngat·ngat
bridle	*kabisada*	ka·bee·sa·da
canter n	*yagyág*	yag·yag
crop	*paltík*	pal·teek
gallop n	*yagyág*	yag·yag
groom	*tagapag-alaga*	ta·ga·pag·a·la·ga
	ng kabayo	nang ka·ba·yo
horse	*kabayo*	ka·ba·yo
reins	*renda*	ren·da
saddle	*siya*	see·ya
stable	*kwadra*	kwa·dra
stirrup	*estribo*	es·tree·bo
trot n	*paso*	pa·so
walk n	*lakad*	la·kad

hiking

paglalakád nang mahabà

Where can I …?	*Saán akó …?*	sa·*an* a·ko …
buy supplies	*makabíbilí*	ma·ka·*bee*·bee·*lee*
	ng kailangang	nang ka·ee·*la*·ngang
	bagay	*ba*·gay
find someone	*hahanap ng*	ha·*ha*·nap nang
who knows	*taong alám ang*	*ta*·ong a·*lam* ang
this area	*lugár na itó*	loo·*gar* na ee·*to*
get a map	*kukuha ng*	koo·*koo*·ha nang
	mapa	*ma*·pa
hire hiking	*aarkilá ng*	a·ar·kee·*la* nang
gear	*kagamitán para*	ka·ga·mee·*tan pa*·ra
	sa paglalakád	sa pag·la·la·*kad*
	nang mahabà	nang ma·*ha*·ba'
How …?	*Gaano …?*	ga·*a*·no …
high is the	*kataás ang*	ka·ta·*as* ang
climb	*áakyatín*	a·ak·ya·*teen*
long is the	*kahabà ang*	ka·*ha*·ba' ang
trail	*landás*	lan·*das*

Is it safe?
Ligtás ba itó?   leeg·*tas* ba ee·*to*

Do we need a guide?
Kailangan ba natin   ka·ee·*la*·ngan ba *na*·teen
ng giya?   nang *gee*·ya

Are there guided treks?
Mayroón bang paglalakád   mai·ro·*on* bang pag·la·la·*kad*
na may giya?   na mai *gee*·ya

When does it get dark?
Kailán dídilim?   ka·ee·*lan* dee·dee·leem

Is there a hut?
Mayroón bang kubo?   mai·ro·*on* bang *koo*·bo

Is the volcano active?
Buháy ba ang bulkán?   boo·*hai* ba ang bool·*kan*

Do we need to take …?	*Kailangan ba nating magdalá ng …?*	ka·ee·*la*·ngan ba na·teeng mag·da·*la* nang …
bedding	*higaan*	hee·*ga*·an
food	*pagkain*	pag·*ka*·een
water	*tubig*	*too*·beeg

Is the track …?	*Ang landás ba ay …?*	ang lan·*das* ba ai …
well-marked	*markadong mabuti*	mar·*ka*·dong ma·*boo*·tee
open	*bukás*	boo·*kas*
scenic	*matanawin*	ma·ta·*na*·ween

Where have you come from?
Saán ka galing?   sa·*an* ka *ga*·leeng

How long did it take (you to walk)?
Gaano katagál (mo nilakad)?   ga·*a*·no ka·ta·*gal* (mo nee·*la*·kad)

Does this path go to …?
Ang landás bang itó ay papuntá sa …?   ang lan·*das* bang ee·*to* ai pa·poon·*ta* sa …

Can I go through here?
Puwede ba akóng magdaán dito?   poo·*we*·de ba a·*kong* mag·da·*an* dee·to

Is the water OK to drink?
Okey bang inumín ang tubig?   o·kay bang ee·noo·*meen* ang *too*·beeg

I'm lost.
Nawawalá akó.   na·wa·wa·*la* a·ko

SOCIAL

Which is the ... route?	Alín ang daán na ...?	a·*leen* ang da·*an* na ...
easiest	pinakamadalî	pee·na·ka·ma·da·*lee'*
most interesting	pinaka-nakaáalíw	pee·na·ka·na·ka·*a·a*·lew
shortest	pinakamaiklî	pee·na·ka·ma·eek·*lee'*

Where can I find the ...?	Saán akó makakikita ng ...?	sa·*an* a·*ko* ma·ka·kee·*kee*·ta nang ...
camping ground	kampingan	kam·*pee*·ngan
nearest village	pinakamalapit na baryo	pee·na·ka·ma·*la*·peet na *bar*·yo
showers	páliguan	*pa*·lee·goo·an
toilets	kubeta	koo·*be*·ta

beach

Where's the ... beach?	Násaán ang ... na dalámpasigan?	na·sa·*an* ang ... na da·*lam*·pa·*see*·gan
best	pinakamagalíng	pee·na·ka·ma·ga·*leeng*
nearest	pinakamalapit	pee·na·ka·ma·*la*·peet
nudist	panghubót hubád	pang·hoo·*bot* hoo·*bad*
public	pampúbliko	pam·*poob*·lee·ko

Is it safe to dive/swim here?
Ligtás bang
dumáyb/lumangóy?
leeg·*tas* bang
doo·*maib*/loo·ma·*ngoy*

What time is high/low tide?
Anóng oras ang paglakí/
pagkati ng tubig?
a·*nong* o·ras ang pag·la·*kee*/
pag·*ka*·tee nang *too*·beeg

signs

Warning signs around beaches, such as 'No Diving', are usually in English. A sign more often seen in Filipino is *Bawal Lumangoy* ba·wal loo·ma·*ngoy* (No Swimming).

Do we have to pay?
*Kailangan ba nating   *ka·ee·*la*·ngan ba *na*·teeng
magbayad?   mag·*ba*·yad

How much for a/an ...?	*Magkano ang isáng ...?*	mag·*ka*·no ang ee·*sang* ...
chair	*upuan*	oo·*poo*·an
hut	*kubo*	*koo*·bo
umbrella	*payong*	*pa*·yong

weather

panahón

What's the weather like?
*Anóng klase ng   *a·*nong kla*·se nang
panahón?   pa·na·*hon*

What will the weather be like tomorrow?
*Magiging anóng klase   *ma·*gee*·geeng a·*nong kla*·se
ang panahón bukas? ang pa·na·*hon boo*·kas

dry season	*tag-aráw*	tag·a·*row*
monsoon/wet season	*tag-ulán*	tag·oo·*lan*

For words and phrases relating to seasons, see **times & dates**, page 41.

SOCIAL

It's ...	Itó ay ...	ee·to ai ...
cloudy	maulap	ma·oo·lap
cold	malamíg	ma·la·meeg
fine	mabuti	ma·boo·tee
freezing	magináw na	ma·gee·now na
	magináw	ma·gee·now
hot	mainit	ma·ee·neet
raining	umúulán	oo·moo·oo·lan
sunny	maaraw	ma·a·row
warm	mainit	ma·ee·neet
windy	mahangin	ma·ha·ngeen
Where can I buy a/an ...?	Saán ako bíbilí ng ...?	sa·an a·ko bee·bee·lee nang ...
raln jacket	kapote	ka·po·te
umbrella	payong	pa·yong

flora & fauna

mga halaman at hayop

What ... is that?	Anóng ... iyán?	a·nong ... ee·yan
animal	hayop	ha·yop
flower	bulaklák	boo·lak·lak
plant	halaman	ha·la·man
tree	punò	poo·no'
Is it ...?	Itó ba ay ...?	ee·to ba ai ...
common	pangkaraniwan	pang·ka·ra·nee·wan
dangerous	peligroso	pe·leeg·ro·so
endangered	nanganganib	na·nga·nga·neeb
poisonous	nakalalason	na·ka·la·la·son
protected	protektado	pro·tek·ta·do

What's it used for?
Anó ang gamit nitó?   a·no ang ga·meet nee·to

Can you eat the fruit?
Makakain ba ang prutas?   ma·ka·ka·een ba ang proo·tas

local plants & animals

bat	kabág-kabág	ka·bag·ka·bag
cow	baka	ba·ka
chameleon	tukô	too·ko'
deer	usá	oo·sa
dolphin	dolpin	dol·peen
flying lizard	lumilipád na butikî	loo·mee·lee·pad na boo·tee·kee'
gecko	butikî	boo·tee·kee'
goat	kambíng	kam·beeng
haribon (Philippine eagle)	ágila	a·gee·la
iguana	bayawak	ba·ya·wak
jasmine (national flower)	sampagita	sam·pa·gee·ta
milkfish (national fish)	bangús	ba·ngoos
narra (national tree)	nara	na·ra
owl	kuwago	koo·wa·go
Palawan peacock pheasant	paboreál ng Palawan	pa·bo·re·al nang pa·la·wan
python	sawá	sa·wa
quail	pugò	poo·go'
sea snake	ahas dagat	a·has da·gat
shark	patíng	pa·teeng
snake	ahas	a·has
Sulu hornbill	kaláw	ka·low
tamaraw (type of water buffalo)	támaraw	ta·ma·row
water buffalo (national animal)	kalabáw	ka·la·bow
whale	balyena	bal·ye·na
whale shark	butanding	boo·tan·deeng

FOOD > eating out

pagkain sa labás

basics

mga pangunahing bagay

breakfast	*almusál*	al·moo·*sal*
lunch	*tanghalian*	tang·ha·*lee*·an
dinner	*hapunan*	ha·*poo*·nan
snack n	*meryenda*	mer·*yen*·da
eat v	*kumain*	koo·*ma*·een
drink v	*uminóm*	oo·mee·*nom*

I'd like …
Gustó ko ng …   goos·*to* ko nang …

Please. (when making a request)
Pakí lang.   pa·*kee* lang

Thank you.
Salamat.   sa·*la*·mat

I'm starving!
Gutóm na gutóm na akó.   goo·*tom* na goo·*tom* na a·*ko*

finding a place to eat

paghahanáp ng makakainan

Can you recommend a …	*May alám ka bang …*	mai a·lam ka bang …
bar	*bar*	bar
café	*kapiteryá*	ka·pee·ter·*ya*
Chinese restaurant	*restorang Intsík*	res·*to*·rang een·*tseek*
restaurant	*restoran*	res·*to*·ran
turo turo restaurant	*turo turò*	*too*·ro too·ro'

eating out

159

Where would you go for ...?	Saán ka púpuntá para sa ...?	sa·an ka poo·poon·ta pa·ra sa ...
a celebration	selebrasyón	se·leb·ras·yon
a cheap meal	murang pagkain	moo·rang pag·ka·een
local specialities	espesyál na luto dito	es·pes·yal na loo·to dee·to
Western food	pagkaing Kanô	pag·ka·eeng ka·no'

I'd like to reserve a table for ...	Gustó kong mag-reserba ng mesa para sa ...	goos·to kong mag·re·ser·ba nang me·sa pa·ra sa ...
(two) people	(dalawáng) tao	(da·la·wang) ta·o
(eight) o'clock	(alás-otso)	(a·las·ot·so)

I'd like (a) ..., please.	Paki lang, gusto ko ng ...	pa·kee lang goos·to ko nang ...
half portion	kalahati lang	ka·la·ha·tee lang
table for (five)	mesa para sa (limáng) tao	me·sa pa·ra sa (lee·mang) ta·o
nonsmoking	mesang waláng naninigarilyó	me·sang wa·lang na·nee·nee·ga·reel·yo
smoking	mesang puwedeng manigarilyó	me·sang poo·we·deng ma·nee·ga·reel·yo

I'd like a/the ..., please.	Pakitingín nga ng ...	pa·kee·tee·ngeen nga nang ...
children's menu	pambatang menú	pam·ba·tang me·noo
drink list	listahan ng inumin	lees·ta·han nang ee·noo·meen
menu (in English)	menú(ng Inglés)	me·noo(ng eeng·gles)

Are you still serving food?
Nagsisilbí pa ba kayó ng pagkain?
nag·see·seel·bee pa ba ka·yo nang pag·ka·een

How long is the wait?
Gaano katagál ang paghihintáy?
ga·a·no ka·ta·gal ang pag·hee·heen·tai

at the restaurant

sa restoran

What would you recommend?
Anó ang mairerekomendá mo? — a·*no* ang ma·ee·re·re·ko·men·*da* mo

What's in that dish?
Anó iyán? — a·*no* ee·*yan*

What's that called?
Anó ang tawag diyán? — a·*no* ang *ta*·wag dee·*yan*

I'll have that.
Gustó ko iyán. — goos·*to* ko ee·*yan*

Does it take long to prepare?
Matagál bang ihandâ? — ma·ta·*gal* bang ee·han·*da'*

Is it self-serve?
Akó ba ang kukuha? — a·*ko* ba ang koo·*koo*·ha

Is there a cover charge?
May bayad ba ang mesa? — mai *ba*·yad ba ang *me*·sa

Is service included in the bill?
Kasama na ba ang serbisyo sa tsit? — ka·*sa*·ma na ba ang ser·*bees*·yo sa tseet

Are these complimentary?
Libre ba itó? — *lee*·bre ba ee·*to*

eating out

161

I'd like ...	Gustó ko ng ...	goos·to ko nang ...
a local speciality	espesyál na luto dito	es·pes·yal na loo·to dee·to
a meal fit for a king	pagkaing pang-mayaman	pag·ka·eeng pang·ma·ya·man
a sandwich	sanwits	san·weets
that dish	lutong iyán	loo·tong ee·yan
the chicken	manók	ma·nok
the menu	menú	me·noo

I'd like it with/without ...	Gustó ko ng may/waláng ...	goos·to ko nang mai/wa·lang ...
butter	mantikilya	man·tee·keel·ya
cheese	keso	ke·so
chilli (sauce)	sili (sows)	see·lee (sohs)
garlic	bawang	ba·wang
ketchup	ketsap	ket·sap
nuts	manê	ma·ne'
oil	mantikà	man·tee·ka'
pepper	pamintá	pa·meen·ta
salt	asín	a·seen
tomato sauce	tomeyto sows	to·may·to sohs
vinegar	sukà	soo·ka'

For more menu items, see the **menu decoder**, page 175. For other specific meal requests, see **vegetarian & special meals**, page 173.

---

listen for ...

Gustó mo ba ng ...? goos·to mo ba nang ...	Do you like ...?
Mairerekomendá ko ang ... ma·ee·re·re·ko·men·da ko ang ...	I suggest the ...
Paano mo gustó ang luto nitó? pa·a·no mo goos·to ang loo·to nee·to	How would you like it cooked?

look for ...

Pampagana	pam·pa·*ga*·na	**Appetisers**
Sopas	*so*·pas	**Soups**
Salad	*sa*·lad	**Salads**
Mga Handáng Putahe	ma·*nga* han·*dang* poo·*ta*·he	**Main Courses**
Matamís	ma·ta·*mees*	**Desserts**
Inumin	ee·*noo*·meen	**Drinks**
Alak	*a*·lak	**Spirits**
Serbesa	ser·*be*·sa	**Beers**

at the table

sa mesa

Please bring a/the...	*Pakidalá ang ...*	pa·kee·da·*la* ang ...
bill	*tsit*	tseet
cloth	*mantél*	man·*tel*
glass	*glas*	glas
serviette	*napkin*	*nap*·keen
wineglass	*waynglas*	wainglas

ashtray
ustray
as·tray

spoon
kutsara
koot·*sa*·ra

fork
tinidór
tee·nee·*dor*

plate
plato
pla·to

knife
kutsilyo
kut·*seel*·yo

wineglass
wayn glas
wain glas

glass
baso
ba·so

table
mesa
me·sa

eating out

163

talking food

This is …	*Itó ay …*	ee·to ai …
(too) cold	*(masyadong)*	(mas·*ya*·dong)
	malamíg	ma·la·*meeg*
spicy	*maangháng*	ma·ang·*hang*
superb	*napakagalíng*	na·pa·ka·ga·*leeng*

I love this dish.
   Gustó ko ng lutong itó.   goos·*to* ko nang *loo*·tong ee·*to*

I love the local cuisine.
   Gustó ko ng lutong   goos·*to* ko nang *loo*·tong
   Pilipino.   pee·lee·*pee*·no

That was delicious!
  Masaráp!   ma·sa·*rap*

My compliments to the chef.
  Ang galíng ng naglutò.   ang ga·*leeng* nang nag·*loo*·to'

I'm full.
  Busog na akó.   boo·*sog* na a·*ko*

---

from hand to mouth

In some regions of the Philippines people eat with their
hands instead of cutlery. If you're going to attempt this,
there are certain rules of etiquette to abide by. Firstly, you
can only touch the food with your fingers (up to the second
knuckle) – the food shouldn't touch your palm at all. Once
you have the food between your fingers you push it into
your mouth with your thumb. Well, there's a challenge!

---

methods of preparation

pamamaraán ng paghahandâ

I'd like it ...	*Gustó ko na*	goos·*to* ko na
	itó ay ...	ee·*to* ai ...
I don't want it ...	*Ayoko na itó ay ...*	a·*yo*·ko na ee·*to* ai ...
boiled	*pinakuluán*	pee·na·koo·loo·*an*
broiled	*binunlián*	bee·nan·lee·*an*
fried	*pinirito*	pee·nee·*ree*·to
grilled	*inihaw*	ee·*nee*·how
mashed	*minasa*	mee·*na*·sa
medium	*bahagyâ*	ba·hag·*ya*'
rare	*medyo hindí*	*med*·yo heen·*dee*
	lutô	loo·to'
reheated	*pinainitan*	pee·na·ee·*nee*·tan
steamed	*inistím*	ee·nees·*teem*
well-done	*lutúng-lutô*	loo·*toong*·loo·to'
with the dressing	*ang sows ay*	ang sohs ai
on the side	*nasa tabí*	*na*·sa ta·*bee*
without ...	*waláng ...*	wa·*lang* ...

You'll find street vendors thoughout the Philippines, not only on the footpath, but also on the road with their produce strung over their shoulders. It's common for vendors to knock on your car window to sell you their wares.

Here are a few tasty treats you can find walking down the street or possibly in a traffic jam.

savoury

Balut ba·*loot* is not for the weak of stomach. It's a cooked duck's egg containing a half-formed embryo. If eating semi-formed animals is not your thing, try a *penoy* pe·noy – a cooked duck's egg with no surprises inside.

balut	ba·*loot*	duck's egg with embryo
litsón sa kawalì	leet·son sa ka·*wa*·lee'	refried roast pork
penoy	pe·noy	duck's egg
maís	ma·*ees*	corn
manê	ma·ne'	peanuts

sweet

banana cue	ba·*na*·na kyoo	skewered banana with caramelised sugar
buko (juice)	boo·ko (jus)	coconut (juice)
tubó	too·bo	sugar can
pápsikel	pap·see·kel	popsicles
prutas	proo·tas	fruit
puto	poo·to	sweet bread/cake
sagó gulaman	sa·go goo·*la*·man	jelly & tapioca drink
sorbetes	sor·be·tes	ice-cream

Discover other Filipino specialities in the **menu decoder**, page 175.

nonalcoholic drinks

waláng alak na inumin

... mineral water	... míneral water	... mee·ne·ral wa·ter
sparkling	isparkling	ees·park·leng
still	istíl	ees·teel
buko juice	buko juice	boo·ko joos
calamansi cordial	kalamansí juice	ka·la·man·see joos
guyabano juice	guyabano juice	goo·ya·ba·no joos
orange juice	orens juice	o·rens joos
halu-halo (iced dessert)	halu-halo	ha·loo·ha·lo
soft drink	sopdrink	sop·dreenk
(hot) water	(mainit na) tubig	(ma·ee·neet na) too·beeg
(cup of) tea	isáng tsaá	ee·sang tsa·a
(cup of) coffee	isáng kapé	ee·sang ka·pe
... with (milk)	... may (gatas)	... mai (ga·tas)
... without (sugar)	... waláng (asukal)	... wa·lang (a·soo·kal)

coffee

black	walang gatas	wa·lang ga·tas
decaffeinated	dikap	dee·kap
iced	iced	ais
strong	matapang	ma·ta·pang
weak	di matapang	dee ma·ta·pang
white	may gatas	mai ga·tas

alcoholic drinks

beer	*serbesa*	ser·*be*·sa
brandy	*brandi*	*bran*·dee
champagne	*tsampán*	tsam·*payn*
cocktail	*kakteyl*	*kak*·tayl

a bottle/glass	*isáng bote/baso*	ee·*sang* bo·te/*ba*·so
of ... wine	*ng ... alak*	nang ... na *a*·lak
dessert	*pangmatamís*	pang·ma·ta·*mees*
red	*red*	red
rosé	*rosey*	ro·*say*
sparkling	*isparkling*	ees·*park*·leeng
white	*white*	wait
wine	*wayn*	wain
a shot of ...	*isáng shot ng ...*	ee·*sang* shat nang ...
basi	*basì*	*ba*·see'
(local wine)		
gin	*gin*	jeen
lambanog	*lambanóg*	lam·ba·*nog*
rum	*rum*	ram
Tanduay rum	*Tanduáy rum*	tan·doo·*ai* ram
tequila	*tekila*	te·*kee*·la
tuba	*tubâ*	too·*ba'*
vodka	*bodka*	*bod*·ka
whisky	*wiski*	*wees*·kee
a ... of beer	*isáng ...*	ee·*sang* ...
	ng serbesa	nang ser·*be*·sa
glass	*baso*	*ba*·so
jug	*pitsél*	peet·*sel*
small bottle	*maliít na bote*	ma·lee·*eet* na bo·te
large bottle	*malakíng bote*	ma·la·*keeng* bo·te

in the bar

I'm next.
  Akó ang súsunód.   a·ko ang soo·soo·nod

I'll have …
  Gustó ko ng …   goos·to ko nang …

Same again, please.
  Ganitó rin, pakí lang.   ga·nee·to reen pa·kee lang

No ice, thanks.
  Waláng yelo, salamat.   wa·lang ye·lo sa·la·mat

I'll buy you a drink.
  Ibíbilí kitá ng   ee·bee·bee·lee kee·ta nang
  inumin.   ee·noo·meen

What would you like?
  Anó ang gustó mo?   a·no ang goos·to mo

I don't drink alcohol.
  Hindî akó umíinóm   heen·dee' a·ko oo·mee·ee·nom
  ng alak.   nang a·lak

It's my round.
  Sagót ko itó.   sa·got ko ee·to

How much is that?
  Magkano?   mag·ka·no

Do you serve meals here?
  Nagsisilbí ba kayó ng   nag·see·seel·bee ba ka·yo nang
  pagkain dito?   pag·ka·een dee·to

---

listen for …

Anó ang gustó mo? a·no ang goos·to mo	**What are you having?**
Tamá na! ta·ma' na	**That's enough!**
Hulíng order na. hoo·leeng or·der na	**Last orders.**

eating out

169

drinking up

Cheers!
Tagayan tayo.
ta·*ga*·yan ta·yo

This is hitting the spot.
Itó ang tunay.
ee·*to* ang *too*·nai

I think I've had one too many.
Sobra na yata ang nainóm ko.
so·bra na *ya*·ta ang na·*ee*·nom ko

I'm feeling drunk.
Lasíng na ang pakiramdám ko.
la·*seeng* na ang pa·kee·ram·*dam* ko

I feel ill.
Masamâ ang pakiramdám ko.
ma·sa·*ma'* ang pa·kee·ram·*dam* ko

Where's the toilet?
Násaán ang kubeta?
na·sa·*an* ang koo·*be*·ta

I'm tired, I'd better go home.
Pagód na akó, makauwí na.
pa·*god* na a·*ko* ma·ka·oo·*wee* na

Can you call a taxi for me?
Pakitawag mo akó ng taksi.
pa·kee·*ta*·wag mo a·*ko* nang *tak*·see

local drinks		
basì	*ba*·see'	sweet wine from fermented sugarcane
tubâ	*too*·ba'	alcoholic drink made from palm juice

buying food

pagbilí ng pagkain

What's the local speciality?
Anó ang espesyalidád dito?   a·no ang es·pes·ya·lee·*dad* dee·to

What's that?
Anó iyán?   a·no ee·*yan*

Can I taste it?
Pakitikmán ko nga?   pa·kee·teek·*man* ko nga

How much (is a kilo of cheese)?
Magkano (ang isáng kilo ng keso)?   mag·*ka*·no (ang ee·*sang* kee·lo nang *ke*·so)

Where can I find the ... section?	Saán ang seksyón ng ...?	sa·*an* ang seks·*yon* nang ...
dairy	gatas at keso	*ga*·tas at *ke*·so
fish	isdâ	ees·*da'*
frozen goods	mga bagay na frozen	ma·*nga* ba·gai na *pro*·sen
fruit and vegetable	prutas at gulay	*proo*·tas at *goo*·lai
meat	karné	kar·*ne*
poultry	manók	ma·*nok*

listen for ...

Anó ang gustó mo? a·no ang goos·*to* mo	**What would you like?**
May ibá pa ba? mai ee·*ba* pa ba	**Anything else?**
May maitutulong ba akó? mai ma·ee·too·*too*·long ba a·*ko*	**Can I help you?**
Ubós na. oo·*bos* na	**There's no more.**

I'd like ...	Pagbilán ng ...	pag·bee·lan nang ...
(200) grams	(200) gramo	(200) gra·mo
(half) a dozen	(kalahating) dosena	ka·la·ha·teeng do·se·na
(two) kilos	(dalawáng) kilo	(da·la·wang) kee·lo
a bottle	isáng bote	ee·sang bo·te
a packet	isáng pakete	ee·sang pa·ke·te
(three) pieces	(tatlóng) piraso	(tat·long) pee·ra·so
(six) slices	(anim na) hiwà	(a·neem na) hee·wa'
a tin	isáng lata	ee·sang la·ta
(just) a little	kauntí (lang)	ka·oon·tee (lang)
more	dágdagán pa	dag·da·gan pa
that/this one	iyán/itó	ee·yan/ee·to

Less.	Bawasan.	ba·wa·san
A bit more.	Dágdagán pa.	dag·da·gan pa
Enough.	Tama na.	ta·ma na

cooking utensils

I need a/an ...	Kailangan ko ng ...	ka·ee·la·ngan ko nang ...
chopping board	sangkalan	sang·ka·lan
frying pan	kawalì	ka·wa·lee'
knife	kutsilyo	koot·seel·yo
saucepan	saucepan	sohs·pan

For more cooking implements, see the **dictionary**.

food stuff		
cooked	lutô	loo·to'
cured	binabad	bee·na·bad
dried	pinatuyô	pee·na·too·yo'
fresh	sariwà	sa·ree·wa'
frozen	pinagyelo	pee·nag·ye·lo
smoked	pináusukan	pee·na·oo·soo·kan
raw	hindí lutô	heen·dee loo·to'

ordering food

Do you have (vegetarian) food?
Mayroón ba kayóng   mai·ro·*on* ba ka·*yong*
(bedyetaryan) na pagkain?   (bed·ye·*tar*·yan) na pag·*ka*·een

Is there a (halal/kosher) restaurant near here?
Mayroón bang   mai·ro·*on* bang
(halál/kosyer) na restoran   (ha·*lal/kos*·yer) na res·*to*·ran
na malapit dito?   na ma·*la*·peet *dee*·to

I don't eat (red meat).
Hindî akó kumakain   heen·*dee'* a·ko koo·ma·*ka*·een
ng (karné).   nang (kar·*ne*)

Is it cooked with (pork)?
Niluto ba iyán na may   nee·*loo*·to ba ee·*yan* na mai
(karnéng baboy)?   (kar·*neng ba*·boy)

Is it cooked in (oil)?
Niluto ba iyán sa   nee·*loo*·to ba ee·*yan* sa
(mantikà)?   (man·*tee*·ka')

Is this ...?	*Itó ba uy ...?*	ee·to ba ai ...
decaffeinated	*dikap*	*dec*·kap
free of animal	*waláng halong*	wa·*lang ha*·long
produce	*mulá sa hayop*	moo·*la* sa *ha*·yop
free-range	*malayang*	ma·*la*·yang
chicken	*manók*	ma·*nok*
genetically	*binago ang*	bee·*na*·go ang
modified	*kaanyuán*	ka·an·yoo·*an*
gluten-free	*waláng gluten*	wa·*lang gloo*·ten
low-fat	*lo-fat*	*lo*·pat
low in sugar	*mababa sa asúkal*	ma·*ba*·ba sa a·*soo*·kal
organic	*organik*	or·*ga*·neek
salt-free	*waláng asín*	wa·*lang* a·*seen*

Could you prepare a meal without …?	Puwede ka bang magluto ng waláng …?	poo-we-de ka bang mag-loo-to nang wa-lang …
butter	mantekilya	man-te-keel-ya
eggs	itlóg	eet-log
fish	isdâ	ees-da'
fish stock	panlasang isdâ	pan-la-sang ees-da'
meat stock	panlasang karné	pan-la-sang kar-ne
MSG	betsin	bet-seen
pork	karnéng baboy	kar-neng ba-boy
poultry	manók	ma-nok

special diets & allergies

espesyál na pagkain at mga alerhiyá

I'm on a special diet.

May espesyál na diyeta akó. mai es-pes-yal na dee-ye-ta a-ko

I'm (a) …	Akó ay …	a-ko ai …
Buddhist	Budista	boo-dees-ta
Hindu	Hindu	heen-doo
Jewish	Hudyó	hood-yo
Muslim	Muslim	moos-leem
vegan	bedyan	bed-yan
vegetarian	bedyetaryan	bed-ye-tar-yan

I'm allergic to …	Allergic akó sa …	a-ler-jeek a-ko sa …
dairy produce	keso at gatas	ke-so at ga-tas
eggs	itlóg	eet-log
gelatine	gulaman	goo-la-man
gluten	gluten	gloo-ten
honey	pulótpukyutan	poo-lot-pook-yoo-tan
MSG	betsin	bet-seen
nuts	nuwés	noo-wes
peanuts	manê	ma-ne'
seafood	pagkaing-dagat	pag-ka-eeng-da-gat
shellfish	isdáng may talukap	ees-dang mai ta-loo-kap

menu decoder
babasahín sa paglulutò

This miniguide to Filipino cuisine lists dishes and ingredients in Filipino alphabetical order. It's designed to help you get the most out of your gastronomic experience by providing you with food terms that you may see on menus. For certain dishes we've marked the region or city where they're most popular. If you see a word on the menu that starts with a 'c', also have a look under 'k', as many words are spelled with both letters.

A

abokado a-bo-*ka*-do *avocado*
— **juice** a-bo-*ka*-do joos *avocado drink*
achara at-*sa*-ra *see atsara*
achuete at-soo-we-te *see atsuete*
adobo a-*do*-bo *the national dish of the Philippines – any dish stewed in vinegar, garlic, salt, peppercorns, bay leaves & soy sauce, usually served with rice • meat, fish or vegetables cooked in garlic & vinegar (cooking method)*
— **baboy** *ba*-boy *pork adobo*
— **Batangas** ba-*tang*-gas *adobo from Batangas - a mixture of beef, ox heart, liver & pork adobo*
— **hipon** hee-pon *shrimp adobo*
— **isdâ** ees-*da'* *fish adobo*
— **manók** ma-*nok chicken adobo*
— **manók at baboy** ma-*nok* at *ba*-boy *chicken & pork adobo*
— **palós** pa-*lus eel adobo*
— **pusít** poo-*seet squid in a mixture of vinegar, garlic, salt, peppercorns, bay leaves & soy sauce, served with rice*
— **sugpô** soog-*po' prawn adobo*
agahan a-*ga*-han *breakfast (also called almusál)*
agre dulce/agre dulce *ag*-re dool-se *sweet & sour sauce*
alimango a-lee-*ma*-ngo *variety of large crab with thick dark shell*
alimasag a-lee-*ma*-sag *variety of crab with spotted thin shell & large pincers*
almóndigas al-mon-dee-gas *pork meat balls*
— **na karné at atay** na kar-*ne* at a-*tai meat balls with liver*
— **na may hipon/sugpô** na mai hee-pon/soog-*po' meat balls with shrimp/prawn*
almusál al-moo-*sal breakfast*
alugbati a-loog-*ba*-*tee' Malabar spinach*
amargoso a-mar-*go*-so *see ampalayá*
ampalayá am-pa-la-*ya bitter melon (also called amargoso)*

apol juice *a*-pol joos *apple cider*
apritada ap-ree-*ta*-da *pork, chicken or beef stewed in a tomato-based sauce*
apritadang baboy ap-ree-*ta*-dang *ba*-boy *pork stewed in a tomato-based sauce*
apritadang baka ap-ree-*ta*-dang *ba*-ka *beef stewed in a tomato-based sauce*
apritadang manók ap-ree-*ta*-dang ma-*nok chicken stewed in a tomato-based sauce*
apulid a-poo-leed *water chestnuts*
arina a-*ree*-na *flour*
arróz a-ros *rice*
— **a la cubana** a la koo-*ba*-na *Cuban-style rice with plantains & fried eggs*
— **caldo (con pollo)** *kal*-do (con *pol*-yo) *thick rice soup with chicken pieces & ginger*
asado a-*sa*-do *pot roast*
asadong baboy a-*sa*-dong *ba*-boy *pork rump simmered in water, soy sauce, sugar, salt, garlic & seasoning*
asín a-*seen salt*
asukal a-*soo*-kal *sugar*
atáy a-*tai liver*
atis a-tees *custard apple*
atsara at-*sa*-ra *Philippine sauerkraut – side dish made from grated green papaya pickled in vinegar, Spanish onions, salt, sugar & ginger (also called achara)*
atsuete at-soo-we-te *seeds (from the annatto tree) used for food colouring*

B

baboy *ba*-boy *pork • pig*
bagkát bag-*net* see binagkát*
bagnét bag-*net* see bagnít*
bagnít bag-*neet dried pork belly deep-fried with bagoong (Iloko); also called bagnét*
bagoong ba-*go*-ong *salty paste made from fermented salted fish or shrimp paste*
— **alamáng** a-la-*mang bagoong made from very small shrimp*

175

menu decoder

— **Balayan** Ba-*la*-yan *anchovy bagoong from Balayan*

baka ba-ka *cow • beef*

bakahan at manukan ba-*ka*-han at ma-*nuo*-kan *cattle ranch & poultry yard*

balimbíng ba-leem-*beeng* *'five-corner fruit' • star fruit • carambola*

balút ba-*loot* *boiled fertilised duck eggs (with formed embryo), best eaten warm with salt*

banana cue ba-*na*-na kyoo *sabá bananas, fried & rolled in sugar, skewered on thin bamboo sticks*

bangús ba-*ngoos* *milkfish (national fish)*

basì ba-*see'* *a sweet port-like wine made from sugarcane juice*

bataw ba-*tow* *hyacinth beans*

bater ba-ter *batter*

batsoy bat-soy *pork kidney, liver, heart & pork meat sautéed with onions, ginger & fish sauce*

bawang ba-wang *garlic*

bayabas ba-ya-bas *guava*

berdeng bélpeper ber-deng bel-pe-per *green capsicum • green bell pepper*

bibingka bee-*beeng*-ka *ground glutinous rice flour with sugar & coconut baked in the oven & topped with some cheese and/or grated coconut*

Bicol exprés bee-kol eks-*pres* *a fiery pork dish with seeded green peppers cooked in coconut milk (Bicol)*

bigás bee-*gas* *uncooked rice*

bihon bee-hon *dried vermicelli noodles*

biko bee-ko *glutinous rice cooked in gatâ, water & sugar and sprinkled with latík*

binagkát bee-nag-*kat* *sweet potato sliced & cooked with brown sugar which forms a crisp crust (also called bagkát)*

binagoongang baboy bee-na-go-o-ngang ba-boy *pork with shrimp paste*

binakól bee-na-*kol* *chicken soup with buko (Iloilo City & Bacolod)*

binatíng itlóg bee-na-*teeng* eet-*log* *scrambled egg*

binatóg bee-na-tog *corn kernels boiled with grated coconut & salt (popular in farming areas)*

binuro bee-*noo*-ro *method of salting foods*

binusáng manè bee-*noo-sang* ma-*ne'* *roasted peanuts*

bisték/bistík (ng Maynílà) bees-*tek* (nang mai-*nee*-la') *Philippine-style beef steak, ie beef & onion rings braised in soy sauce*

bitswelas/bitsuwelas beet-*swee*-las *see puting abítsuwelas*

biyá bee-*ya'* *goby (fish)*

braso ni Mercedes *bra*-so nee mer-*se*-des *'the arm of Mercedes' – log cake filled with cream (also called brazo de Mercedes)*

brazo de Mercedes *bra*-so dee mer-se-des *see braso ni Mercedes*

bringhé breeng-*he* *rice dish made with coconut milk (Pampanga)*

bukayò boo-ka-*yo'* *coconut caramel or toffee*

buko boo-ko *young coconut*

— **juice** joos *juice of the young coconut, good for staving off dehydration*

— **pie** pai *baked crust pie using sweetened & thickened slivers of young coconut meat & milk*

bulaló boo-la-*lo* *oxtail soup with bone marrow (Batangas)*

bulangláng boo-lang-*lang* *vegetable stew & beancurd*

bulíg boo-*leeg* *young or medium-sized mudfish*

buntót ng baka boon-*tot* nang ba-ka *oxtail*

buro boo-ro *fermented rice (Pampanga)*

butóng-pakwán boo-tong-pak-*wan* *dried, salted watermelon seeds*

C

calamansi ka-la-man-*see'* *see kalamansí*

caldereta kal-de-re-ta *see kaldereta*

callos kal-yos *see kamiás/kalyos*

camaron rebosada ka-ma-ron re-bo-sa-do *see kamarón rebosado*

camias kam-yas *see kamyás*

carabao ka-ra-bow *see kalabaw*

carinderia ka-reen-der-ya *see karinderyá*

cocido ko-see-do *see kosido*

curacha koo-*rat*-sa *see kuratsa*

Ch

chicharó seet-sa-ro *see sitsaró*

chicharón seet-sa-ron *see sitsarón*

chorizo so-ree-so *see soriso*

— **de bilbáo** de bel-*bow* *see sorisong bilbáw*

K

kabuté ka-boo-te *mushroom (also spelled kabutí)*

kabuténg butones ka-boo-teng boo-to-nes *button mushrooms*

kabutí ka-boo-tee *see kabuté*

kaimitó kai-mee-to' *star apple*

kalabasa ka-la-ba-sa *squash • pumpkin*

kalabaw ka-la-bow *water buffalo*

kalamansí ka-la-man-see' *cumquat • sweet, little native lime used to make cordial, added to black tea or mixed with soy sauce as dipping sauce (also spelled calamansi)*

kaldereta kal-de-re-ta *a goat's meat stew of Spanish origin, also prepared using beef, pork or chicken (also spelled caldereta)*

kalyós kal-yos *stew of ox tripe with chickpeas & sorisong bilbao pieces (also spelled callos)*

kamarón rebosado ka-ma-ron re-bo-sa-do *shelled shrimps/prawns in batter & deep-fried with tails intact (also spelled camaron rebosado)*

kamatis ka-ma-tees *tomato*

kamayan ka-ma-yan *restaurants where you eat food with your fingers instead of cutlery, sometimes food is served on banana leaves*

kamiás/kamyás kam-yas *small, cylindrical yellow-green sour fruit related to star fruit (also spelled camiás)*

kamote ka-mo-te *sweet potato*
— **cue** kyoo *sliced kamote, fried & rolled in sugar & skewered on bamboo sticks*

kamoteng kahoy ka-mo-teng ka-hoy *cassava • manioc*

kandulí kan-doo-lee *type of catfish*

kangkóng kang-kong *water spinach*

kanin ka-neen *steamed rice*

kantón kan-ton *fresh or dried egg noodles*

kaong ka-ong *palm nut, sweetened & served as a dessert*

kapé ka-pe *coffee*

karé-karé ka-re-ka-re *oxtail with vegetables stewed in peanut sauce*

karinderyá ka-reen-der-ya *diner (also spelled carindería)*

karné kar-ne *meat*

karnéng baboy kar-neng ba-boy *pork*

karnéng baka kar-neng ba-ka *beef*

karnéng kambing kar-neng kam-beeng *goat meat*

karnéng usá kar-neng oo-sa *venison*

karot ka-rot *carrot*

karpa kar-pa *carp*

kasabá cake ka-sa-ba kayk *cassava cake*

kasubhâ ka-soob-ha *saffron*

kawalî ka-wa-lee *frying pan • wok*

keso ke-so *cheese*

kilawín kee-la-ween *see kiniláw*

kinadkád na niyóg kee-nad-kad na nee-yog *grated coconut (also spelled ginadgád na niyóg)*

kiniláw kee-nee-low *any fish & seafood marinated in vinegar or kalamansi juice & often spiced with other ingredients & eaten raw (also spelled kilawín)*
— **na talabá** na ta-la-ba *kiniláw of oysters*
— **na tangginggì** na tang-geeng-gee *mackerel in vinegar & ginger, served with onions, hot peppers & sometimes coconut milk*

kintsáy keen-tsai *coriander (also called wansóy)*

kondensada kon-den-sa-da *condensed milk*

kosido ko-see-do *platter with sausage, pork, sweet potatoes, corn & bananas (Zamboanga) • Spanish-influenced cooking using pork, beef or chicken with leeks, sorisong bilbao, bok choy, carrots, bacon, potatoes, carrots & snake beans (also spelled cocido)*

kuratsa koo-rat-sa *sweet-flavoured type of crab (Zamboanga); also spelled curacha*

kutsáy koot-sai *leek*

kutsintá koot-seen-ta *glutinous ground rice flour with sugar, coconut milk & lye solution, steamed & served with freshly grated coconut*

D

dahon ng pandán da-hon nang pan-dan *pandanus leaf (screwpine) used for flavouring & colouring*

dahon ng saging da-hon nang sa-geeng *banana leaves*

dalág da-lag *mudfish*

dalandán da-lan-dan *orange*

dalanghíta da-lang-hee-ta *mandarine*

dayap da-yap *lime*

dílaw dee-low *turmeric*

dilis dee-lees *long-jawed anchovy*

dinaing dee-na-eeng *fish first cut at the back, then opened like a butterfly & sun-dried*

dinuguán dee-noo-goo-an *stew of pork offal & fresh pig blood seasoned with vinegar & hot peppers served with puto as a meryenda or as a main meal with rice*

dugó ng baboy doo-go nang ba-boy *pig's blood*

duhat doo-hat *Java plum*

durián door-yan *durian*

E

ebaporada e-ba-po-ra-da *evaporated milk*

embutido em-boo-tee-do *seasoned mince meat wrapped like a sausage in cheesecloth or foil, then baked– meat mixture may include chopped sorisong bilbao, hard-boiled egg & raisins*

ensaimada/ensaymada en-sai-ma-da *buttery bun sprinkled with sugar & cheese - a variation contains red eggs in the bun mixture (Pampanga)*

ensalada en-sa-la-da *salad (also called salad)*

escabeche es-ka-bet-se *sweet & sour fish dish*

estopado/estofado es-to-pa-do *stew • meat stewed in vinegar & other spices*

G

gabi ga-bee *taro*

galantina ga-lan-tee-na *stuffed chicken roll*

galapóng ga-la-pong *ground rice flour*

galunggóng ga-loong-gong *scad (fish)*

garbansos/garbanzos gar-ban-sos *chickpeas*

gatâ ga-ta *coconut milk or cream (of mature coconut), a very popular ingredient in the Bicol region*
— **ng niyóg** nang nee-yog *coconut cream or milk*

gatas ga-tas *milk*
— **ng kalabáw** ga-tas nang ka-la-bow *water buffalo milk*

gawgáw gow-gow *cornflour (used as a thickening agent for sauces)*

ginadgád na niyóg gee-nad-*gad* na nee-*yog* see **kinadkád na niyóg**

ginataán gee-na-ta-*an* cooked in coconut milk

ginataáng alimango gee-na-ta-*ang* a-lee-*ma*-ngo crab cooked in coconut cream/milk

ginataáng langká gee-na-ta-*ang* lang-*ka'* jackfruit stewed in coconut milk with **bagoóng**

ginatán gee-na-*tan* a dessert of **sabá**, tapioca, sweet potato, taro & jackfruit cooked in coconut milk & sugar, sometimes with **galapóng** rolled into balls

ginisá gee-nee-*sa* sautéed in oil with garlic & onions or ginger

ginisang munggó gee-nee-*sang* moong-go sautéed mung beans

gisado gee-*sa*-do sautéed (cooking method)

gisadong gulay gee-*sa*-dong goo-lai sautéed vegetables (but often with prawns, pork or chicken)

gisantes gee-*san*-tes peas

goto *go*-to Filipino congee – thick rice soup cooked with ginger, garlic & tripe, sprinkled with crisply fried garlic pieces & fish sauce

guava jelly goo-*wa*-ba je-lee jelly made from the juice of boiled guavas & apples thickened with sugar & lemon juice

gulaman goo-la-*man* agar-agar • sweetened fruit set in agar-agar or gelatine

gulay goo-lai vegetables

guyabano goo-ya-*ba*-no soursop (fruit which looks like a small jackfruit but with a taste similar to custard apple)

— **juice** joos sweet & refreshing juice made from soursop

H

halaán ha-la-*an* sea clams

halabós ha-la-*bos* cooked with salt & little water (cooking method)

halayá ha-la-*ya* dessert made from **ubi**, milk, coconut milk & sugar

halayáng ubi ha-la-*yang* oo-bee see **halayá**

halu-halò ha-loo-ha-lo' 'mix-mix' – dessert made from an exotic sweetened fruit mix in a tall glass, topped with crushed ice & milk; the mix may include bananas, beans, mung beans, **ubi**, jackfruit, palm seeds, cubed gelatine & **buko**

hamón ha-*mon* ham

hapunan ha-poo-nan dinner

hiláw na sampalok hee-low na sam-*pa*-lok green tamarind

hipon hee-pon shrimp

hipong halabós hee-pong ha-la-bos shrimp cooked in a little water & salt

hitô hee-to' catfish

humba hoom-ba Chinese-style dish of ham or pork rump cooked until tender with garlic, water, soy sauce, brown sugar, oregano, bay leaves & **tausì**

I

ihaw ee-how see **inihaw)**

ihaw-ihaw ee-how-ee-how see **inihaw**

inadobo ee-na-do-bo see **adobo**

inasál ee-na-*sal* barbecued chicken marinated in citrus & annatto (Bacolod)

inasnán ee-nas-*nan* refers to food preserved with salt

inasnáng hipon ee-nas-*nang* hee-pon salted shrimp

inihaw ee-nee-how grilled meat or seafood (also called **ihaw/ihaw-ihaw**)

— **na baboy** na ba-boy grilled pork

— **na bangús** na ba-ngoos milkfish stuffed with onions, sprinkled with lemon, then wrapped in banana leaf or foil & grilled, roasted or baked

— **na hamonadong manók** na ha-mo-na-dong ma-nok roast or grilled chicken marinated in honey, soy sauce, lemon, salt & pepper

— **na hita ng manók** na hee-ta nang ma-nok roast or grilled chicken legs

— **na lapu-lapu** na la-poo-la-poo grilled grouper seasoned with salt, pepper, garlic & sauce

— **na maís** na ma-ees roasted corn on the cob

— **na paá ng manók** na pa-a nang ma-nok roast or grilled chicken feet (also playfully called 'adidas')

— **na sugpô** na soog-po' grilled tiger prawns

itlóg eet-log egg(s)

— **na maalat** na ma-a-lat salted duck egg with the shell dyed red and served as a condiment or side dish

— **ng pugò** eet-log nang poo-go' quail eggs

L

labanós la-ba-nos white radish

labóng la-bong bamboo shoots

labuyò la-boo-yo' small hot chilli peppers • bird's eye chillies

laing *la*-eeng young taro leaves simmered in spiced coconut milk, may also include shrimps, chopped onions & hot chilli peppers (Bicol)

lamáng-dagat na may talukap la-*mang-da*-gat na may ta-loo-kap shellfish

lamáng-loób la-mang-lo-ob offal

— **ng baboy** la-mang-lo-ob nang ba-boy pork offal

lambanóg lam-ba-nog a very strong alcoholic drink of roughly distilled palm juice (see **tubâ**)

langís panlutò la-ngees pan-loo-to' cooking oil (also called **mantikà**)

lansones/lanzones lan-so-nes small yellow-skinned fruits with sweet lychee-like flesh

lapu-lapu la-poo-la-poo grouper (fish)

latik la-teek edible dregs of coconut milk left over after cooking & extracting the oil – it's sprinkled on top of rice cakes to enhance look & taste

laurél low-rel bay leaves

leche flan let-se plan see **letseplán**

lechón let-son see **litsón**

lengua leng-gwa cow's tongue

letseplán let-se-plan crème caramel (steamed or baked) – the Pampanga version is made with water buffalo milk (also spelled leche flan)

letsugas let-soo-gas lettuce

lihiyá lee-hee-ya lye

limón lee-mon lemon

limonada lee-mo-na-da lemonade

lingá lee-nga sesame seeds

litsón leet-son roasted suckling pig served with thick liver sauce – a popular fiesta dish (also spelled lechón)

— sa kawali sa ka-wa-lee' deep-fried pork

lomo lo-mo beef loin • pork liver & kidney soup (Ilocano)

longganisa/longanisa long-ga-nee-sa Chinese sausage made from fatty pork mince (Pampanga)

longsilóg long-see-log coined word for breakfast consisting of **longanisa**, **sinangág** & **piniritong itlóg**

lumpiyá loom-pya Philippine-style filled spring rolls which come in many meat and vegetarian varieties

lumpiyáng sariwà loom-pyang sa-ree-wa' spring rolls filled with chopped coconut, chickpeas & shrimps & served with a slightly sweet sauce

lumpiyáng shanghái loom-pyang shang-hai local version of the Chinese minispring rolls, stuffed with meat, shellfish or vegetables

lumpiyáng ubod loom-pyang oo-bod crepes or spring rolls filled with palm hearts (specialty of Iloilo City)

luya loo-ya ginger

M

maalat ma-a-lat salty

maanghíng ma-ang-hang hot (peppery or with chilli)

maasim ma-a-seem sour

mahablangka ma-ha-blang-ka coconut & cornstarch cake (also spelled maja blanca)

maja blanca ma-ha blang-ka see **mahablangka**

makapunô/macapunô ma-ka-poo-no' variety of coconut that produces fruit with very soft meat, often served as small sweetened balls or strands

manê ma-ne' see **mani**

manggá mang-ga mango

manggáng hiláw mang-gang hee-low green mango

manggáng manibaláng mang-gang ma-nee-ba-lang semi-ripe mango

mango juice man-go joos mango drink

mángosteen man-goos-teen mangosteen

mani ma-nee' peanuts – primary ingredient for **karé karé** sauce & often used as a garnish (also spelled manê)

manók ma-nok chicken

mantikà man-tee-ka' lard • cooking oil

mantikilya man-tee-keel-ya butter

mapaít ma-pa-eet bitter

margarina mar-ga-ree-na margarine

mársipan mar-see-pan marzipan

maruyà ma-roo-ya' deep-fried mixture of plain flour, baking powder, eggs, evaporated milk & sliced **sabá** bananas

matamís ma-ta-mees sweet

may yelong mango juice mai ye-long man-go joos ice-based mango shake

maya-maya ma-ya-ma-ya red snapper

mechado met-sa-do see **mitsado**

membrillo mem-breel-yo fruit sweetmeat using guava paste made from guava pulp, sugar & lemon

menudo me-noo-do 'tiny' – stew with pieces of meat or offal and potatoes or other vegetables

meringge me-reeng-ge meringue

meriyenda/meryenda mer-yen-da snack

miki mee-kee rice noodles

milón mee-lon cantaloupe • rockmelon

míneral water mee-ne-ral wa-ter mineral water

miswa/misua mees-wa thin wheat noodles or vermicelli

mitsado meet-sa-do braised beef • also spelled mechado

morisqueta tostada mo-rees-ke-ta tos-ta-da fried rice

morkón/morcón mor-kon stuffed beef rolls

munggó moong-go mung beans

murang sibuyas moo-rang see-boo-yas spring onions

mustasa moos-ta-sa mustard greens

N

nata de coco na-ta de ko-ko coconut gelatine

nilagà nee-la-ga' boiled in water

nilagàng mais nee-la-gang ma-ees boiled corn on the cob

niyóg nee-yog mature coconut, grated & squeezed with water to make **gatâ**

O

okra ok-ra okra • lady's finger

orégano o-re-ga-no oregano

P

pabo *pa-bo* turkey

paella *pa-el-ya* rice dish with pork, chicken, seafood, ham, sausages & vegetables

pakbét *pak-bet* see **pinakbét**

paksiw *pak-sew* fish or meat cooked in vinegar, ginger, garlic, salt & soy sauce that has a slightly sweet taste (cooking method); also called *pinaksiw*)
— **na pata** *na pa-ta* pork hock cooked in vinegar, ginger, garlic, salt & soy sauce

pakwán *pak-wan* watermelon

palitáw *pa-lee-tow* little balls of sweetened ground rice, flattened & boiled in water, then rolled in sugar, *lingá* & freshly grated coconut

palós *pa-los* eel

pambalot ng lumpiá *pam-ba-lot nang loom-pya* egg roll wrappers

pamintá *pa-meen-ta* pepper • black peppercorns

pandán ice tea *pan-dan ais tee* pandanus ice tea

pangát *pa-ngat* method of cooking fish in water with vinegar & salt added (also called *pinangát*)

pansit/pancit *pan-seet* noodles – may be made from rice, wheat flour or mung beans
— **bihon** *bee-hon* sautéed dish using fried rice vermicelli noodles
— **cantón** *kan-ton* popular noodle dish with meat & vegetables, but you won't find it in Canton!
— **gisado/guisado** *gee-sa-do* sautéed fried noodles with meat & vegetables
— **habháb** *hab-hab* noodles served in a banana leaf (Quezon)
— **luglóg** *loog-log* noodle dish garnished with seafood
— **Malabón** *ma-la-bon* noodles with oysters & squid (Malabon speciality)
— **Mariláo** *ma-ree-low* noodles with rice crisps (Marilao speciality)
— **molo** *mo-lo* Philippine-style dumpling noodle soup (Iloilo City)

papaya *pa-pa-ya* papaya • pawpaw
— **salad** *sa-lad* papaya salad

paprika *pa-pree-ka* paprika (spice)

pápsikel *pap-see-kel* popsicle

pasingáw *pa-see-ngow* see **pinasingawán**

pastillas *pas-teel-yas* little bar-shaped sweets of milk & sugar, sometimes with nuts

pata *pa-ta* pork hocks
— **ng baka** *nang ba-ka* ox leg

patani *pa-ta-nee* lima beans

patís *pa-tees* fish sauce

pato *pa-to* duck

patola *pa-to-la* sponge gourd

penoy *pe-noy* hard-boiled duck eggs

pesà *pe-sa* stew of meat or fish with vegetables simmered with ginger

pesang dalág *pe-sang da-lug* mudfish stew cooked with garlic, onion, ginger, peppercorn, cabbage, **sayote** & **petsay**

petsay *pet-sai* Chinese cabbage • bok choy

píkadilyo/picadillo *pee-ka-deel-yo* beef mince soup or stew

pimiento *peem-yen-to* pimento

pinais *pee-na-ees* fish or shrimp dish wrapped in banana leaves & steamed with tomatoes, onions & coconut (Bicol)

pinakbét *pee-nak-bet* a combination of vegetables in bagoong (also called *pakbét*)

pinaksíw *pee-nak-sew* see **paksiw**

pinangát *pee-na-ngat* see **pangát**

pinasingawán *pee-na-see-nga-wan* steamed (cooking method)

pinausukan *pee-na-oo-soo-kan* cooking method consisting of smoking foods just before eating • a restaurant specialising in smoked foods

piniritong itlóg *pee-nee-ree-tong eet-log* fried egg(s)

pinyá/piña *peen-ya* pineapple

pipino *pee-pee-no* cucumber

pitisó *pee-tee-so* cream puffs

pitsi-pitsi/pichi-pichi *pee-tsee-pee-tsee* cassava patties rolled in freshly grated coconut, sometimes topped with grated cheese

potsero/pochero *pot-se-ro* dish similar to the Spanish-style **kosido** (contains boiled meat or mudfish & vegetables)

prito *pree-to* fried

prutas *proo-tas* fruit

puláng bélpeper *poo-lang bel-pe-per* red capsicum • red bell pepper

pulutan *poo-loo-tan* small snacks served with alcohol • finger foods

pulút-pukyutan *poo-loot-pook-yoo-tan* honey

pusít *poo-seet* squid

puso ng saging *poo-so nang sa-geeng* banana heart • banana blossom

puting abitsuwelas *poo-teeng a-beet-soo-we-las* white beans (also called *bitswelas/bitsuwelas*)

puto *poo-to* generic term for cake or sweet bread
— **bumbóng** *boom-bong* sweet purple-coloured rice cake steamed in a bamboo tube & served topped with brown sugar & grated coconut
— **kutsintâ** *koot-seen-ta* **puto** & **kutsintâ** eaten as a combination, both served with freshly grated coconut

putong malagkít *poo-tong ma-lag-keet* sticky rice cakes

R

relyeno/relleno *rel-ye-no* any stuffed food

relyenong isda *rel-ye-nong ees-da* stuffed fish baked or fried

relyenong pato *rel-ye-nong pa-to* stuffed duck

relyenong talóng *rel-ye-nong ta-long* stuffed aubergine

repolyo *re-pol-yo* cabbage

S

sabá sa-ba' *variety of banana used primarily for cooking*

sabáw sa-bow *broth*

saging sa-geeng *banana*

saging na sabá sa-geeng na sa-ba *plantains • cooking bananas*

saging sa gulaman sa-geeng sa goo-la-man *bananas in jelly*

sagó sa-go *tapioca*
— at nata de coco at na-ta de ko-ko *a drink mix of sago & cubed coconut gelatine served cold in a glass*

sagó-gulaman sa-go-goo-la-man *red or green coloured jelly cut into small cubes boiled with tapioca seeds, then mixed in sweetened iced water & served as a refreshing drink*

salabát sa-la-bat *Filipino ginger tea served hot*

salitre sa-leet-re *saltpetre*

saluyot sa-loo-yot *ramie (jute) leaves*

sampalok sam-pa-lok *tamarind*

santól san-tol *santol*

sapín-sapín sa-peen-sa-peen *'layer upon layer' – layers of glutinous rice cake cooked with coconut milk & sugar*

sardinas sar-dee-nas *sardines*

sariwà sa-ree-wa' *fresh*

sariwang gatas sa-ree-wang ga-tas *fresh milk*

sarsa sar-sa *sauce*
— ng litsón nang leet-son *liver sauce for litsón*
— ng lumpiá nang loom-pya' *sauce served with spring rolls*

sarsang misó sar-sang mee-so *miso sauce*

sarsang talóng sar-sang ta-long *aubergine sauce • eggplant sauce*

sarsiyado/sarsiado sar-see-ya-do *pork, beef or chicken sautéed in ginger, garlic, onion, tomatoes & peppercorns*

sawsawan sow-sa-wan *dipping sauce*

sawsawang manggá sow-sa-wang mang-ga *mango relish*

sawsawang suka sow-sa-wang soo-ka' *vinegar dipping sauce*

sayote sa-yo-te *chayote • chokoes*

sibuyas see-boo-yas *onions*
— na murà na moo-ra' *spring onions • shallots*
— Tagalog ta-ga-log *small reddish native onions*

sili see-lee *chilli*

siling habà see-leeng ha-ba' *long green variety of chilli peppers*

siling labuyò see-leeng la-boo-yo' *small, very hot peppers • bird's eye chillies*

sinabawáng hipon at gulay see-na-ba-wang hee-pon at goo-lai *vegetable soup with shrimp*

sinabawáng sugpó at gulay see-na-ba-wang soog-po' at goo-lai *vegetable soup with prawns*

sinámpalukang manók see-nam-pa-loo-kang ma-nok *chicken pieces stewed in water, tamarind juice & tamarind leaves with garlic & ginger, has a salty-sour taste (Bulacan)*

sinangág see-na-ngag *fried rice*

singkamás seeng-ka-mas *yam bean • native turnip*

sinigáng see-nee-gang *soup slightly soured with acidic fruits such as sampalok or kamyás*
— na baboy na ba-boy *sinigáng of pork & vegetables*
— na baka na ba-ka *sinigáng of beef & vegetables*
— na hipon na hee-pon *tamarind or kamyás-flavoured sinigáng of big-sized shrimps with kangkóng*
— na isdá na ees-da' *sinigáng of fish (often bangús)*
— na sugpó na soug-po' *a tamarind or kamyás-flavoured sinigáng of prawns & vegetables*

sinigwélas see-neeg-we-las *Spanish plum*

sinuám/sinuwám see-noo-wam *sautéing fish or shellfish, then boiling it with ginger & garlic (cooking method)*

siomai syo-mai *steamed dumplings*

siopao syo-pow *Chinese-style steamed dough bun with pork or chicken filling*

sitaw see-tow *string beans • snake beans*

sitsaró seet-sa-ro *sweet pea (also spelled chicharó)*

sitsarón seet-sa-ron *pork crackling (also spelled chicharón)*

sorbetes sor-be-tes *ice-cream*

soriso so-ree-so *any dried Spanish-style pork sausage (also spelled chorizo)*

sorisong bilháw so-ree-song beel-bow *spicy blood sausage packed in a paprika flavoured lard (also called chorizo de bilbdo)*

sótanghon so-tang-hon *Chinese-style dish of translucent vermicelli mung-bean noodles with, often, chicken*

sukà soo-ka' *(palm-wine) vinegar*

sukà at bawang na sawsawan soo-ka' at ba-wang na sow-sa-wan *vinegar & garlic dipping sauce*

suám na tulyá soo-wam na tool-ya *clam soup cooked with ginger & garlic*

sugpó soog-po' *prawns*

suhà soo-ha' *grapefruit*

suman soo-man *glutinous rice boiled with coconut & sugar wrapped in banana leaves and steamed*

T

tadyáng tad-yang spare ribs
— **ng baboy** ng ba-boy
pork spare ribs marinated in soy sauce, sugar & salt, then baked or broiled
tahóng ta-hong mussels
táhure ta-hoo-re beancurd made from salted, fermented black & yellow soy beans
talabá ta-la-ba oysters
talangkà ta-lang-ka' small freshwater crabs
talóng ta-long aubergine • eggplant
tamales ta-ma-les packets of ground rice flour with a sweet or savoury filling wrapped in banana leaves
tangginggì tang-geeng-gee' mackerel (also called tanigi)
tanghalian tang-ha-lee-an lunch
tanglád tang-lad lemongrass
tanigi ta-nee-gee' see **tangginggì**
tapa ta-pa thinly sliced dried beef
tapsilóg tap-see-log a combination of tapa (dried beef), sinangág (fried rice) & itlóg (fried egg) – usually eaten for breakfast
tatos ta-tos type of crab dish with a coconut taste (Zamboanga)
tausì tow-see' fermented black soya beans
tengang daga te-ngang da-ga' curly black wood-fungus • dried black Chinese mushrooms
tibúk-tibók tee-book-tee-bok water buffalo milk blended with corn (Pampanga)
tilapyà tee-lap-ya' tilapia (fish)
tinapá tee-na-pa smoked fish
tinapay tee-na-pai bread
tinola tee-no-la soup of meat or fish pieces flavoured with ginger & vegetables
tinolang manók tee-no-lang ma-nok boiled chicken pieces with ginger & vegetables
tocino to-see-no see **tusino**
togè to-ge' bean sprouts
tokwa tok-wa beancurd • tofu
torta tor-ta omelette
tortang giniling na baboy tor-tang gee-nee-leeng na ba-boy omelette stuffed with pork mince
tortang patatas tor-tang pa-ta-tas omelette stuffed with fried potato strips

tortang sibuyas tor-tang see-boo-yas omelette stuffed with fried onions
toyò to-yo' dark soy sauce
— **at kalamansi** at ka-la-man-see' soy sauce with **kalamansi**
tsaá tsa-a tea
tsokolate tso-ko-la-te chocolate • hot chocolate (drink)
tubâ too-ba' alcoholic drink made from palm or sugar cane juice
tubig too-beeg water
tubó juice too-bo joos sugarcane juice
tulyá tool-ya freshwater clams
turón too-ron fruit fritters in lumpia wrappers
turrones too-ro-nes ground sweetened nuts, often peanuts, in a rice-paper wrapper (Pampanga)
— **de casoy** de ka-soy turrones made from cashews
turu-turò too-roo-too-ro' 'point point' – restaurants where you point at selections on display
tusino too-see-no honey-cured pork (province of Pampanga); also spelled tocino

U

ubi oo-bee purple yam
ubod oo-bod palm hearts
ukoy oo-koy appetiser made from small shrimps or bean sprouts fried in batter then served with vinegar & garlic sauce
uláng oo-lang lobster
upo oo-po bottle gourd • winter melon

W

wansoy wan-soy see **kintsáy**

Y

yelo ye-lo ice
yema ye-ma sweets made with egg yolk, condensed milk & sugar

emergencies

mga emerhénsiyá

Help!	Saklolo!	sak·lo·lo
Stop!	Hintô!	heen·to'
Go away!	Umalís ka!	oo·ma·lees ka
Thief!	Magnanakaw!	mag·na·na·kow
Fire!	Sunog!	soo·nog
Watch out!	Abatan mo!	a·ba·tan mo

Call an/the ...	Tumawag ka ng ...	too·ma·wag ka nang ...
police	pulís	poo·lees
doctor	doktór	dok·tor
ambulance	ambulánsiya	am·boo·lan·see·ya

Is it safe ...?	Ligtás ba ...?	leeg·tas ba ...
at night	sa gabí	sa ga·bee
for gay people	para sa mga baklâ	pa·ra sa ma·nga bak·la'
for travellers	para sa naglálakbáy	pa·ra sa nag·la·lak·bai
for women	para sa mga babae	pa·ra sa ma·nga ba·ba·e
on your own	ang nag-íisá ka	ang nag·ee·ee·sa ka

It's an emergency.
Emérdyensí itó. e·mer·jen·see ee·to

There's been an accident.
May aksidente. mai ak·see·den·te

Could you please help?
Puwede ka bang tumulong? poo·we·de ka bang too·moo·long

Can I use your phone?
    Pakigamit ng telépono?   pa·kee·*ga*·meet nang te·*le*·po·no

I'm lost.
    Nawawulâ akó.   na·wa·wa·*la'* a·ko

Where are the toilets?
    Násaán ang kubeta?   na·sa·an ang koo·*be*·ta

police

Where's the police station?
    Násaán ang istasyón ng   na·sa·an ang ees·tas·*yon* nang
    pulís?   poo·*lees*

Please telephone the police.
    Pakitawagan ang pulís.   pa·kee·ta·*wa*·gan ang poo·*lees*

I want to report an offence.
    Gustó kong irepórt ang   goos·*to* kong ee·re·*port* ang
    nangyari.   nang·*ya*·ree

My ... was/were stolen.	*Ang aking ... ay nánakaw.*	ang *a*·keeng ... ai na·*na*·kow
I've lost my ...	*Nawalâ ang aking ...*	na·wa·*la'* ang *a*·keeng ...
backpack	*backpack*	*bak*·pak
bags	*mga bag*	ma·*nga* bag
credit card	*krédit kard*	*kre*·deet kard
handbag	*hanbag*	*han*·bag
jewellery	*alahas*	a·*la*·has
money	*pera*	*pe*·ra
papers	*papeles*	pa·*pe*·les
travellers cheques	*travellers checks*	*tra*·be·lers tsek
passport	*pasaporte*	pa·sa·*por*·te
wallet	*wallet*	*wa*·let

I've been …	*Akó ay …*	a·*ko* ai …
He/She has been …	*Siyá ay …*	see·*ya* ai …
assaulted	*sinalakay*	see·na·*la*·kai
raped	*ginahasà*	gee·na·*ha*·sa'
robbed	*ninakawan*	nee·na·*ka*·wan

He/She tried	*Tinangká niyá*	tee·nang·*ka* nee·*ya*
to … me.	*akóng …*	a·*kong* …
assault	*salakayin*	sa·la·*ka*·yeen
rape	*gahasain*	ga·ha·*sa*·een
rob	*nakawan*	na·*ka*·wan

I have insurance.
Mayroón akóng seguro. — mai·ro·on a·*kong* se·*goo*·ro

It was him/her.
Siyá iyón. — see·*ya* ee·*yon*

What am I accused of?
Anó ang paratang laban — a·*no* ang pa·*ra*·tang *la*·ban
sa akin? — sa *a*·keen

I didn't realise I was doing anything wrong.
Hindí ko alám na malî — heen·*dee* ko a·*lam* na ma·*lee*'
ang aking ginagawà. — ang *a*·keeng gee·na·ga·*wa*'

I didn't do it.
Hindí ko ginawâ iyón. — heen·*dee* ko gee·na·*wa*' ee·*yon*

Can I pay an on-the-spot fine?
Puwede ba akóng — poo·*we*·de ba a·*kong*
magbayad ng multáng — mag·*ba*·yad nang mool·*tang*
'on-the-spot'? — on·da·ees·*pat*

I want to contact my embassy/consulate.
Gustó kong tawagan ang — goos·*to* kong ta·*wa*·gan ang
aking émbasi/konsulado. — a·keeng *em*·ba·see/kon·soo·*la*·do

Can I make a phone call?
Puwede ba akóng — poo·*we*·de ba a·*kong*
tumelépono? — too·me·*le*·po·no

Can I have a lawyer (who speaks English)?
Mayroón bang atorni na — mai·ro·*on* bang a·*tor*·nee na
(marunong ng Inglés)? — (ma·*roo*·nong nang eeng·*gles*)

This drug is for personal use.

Ang drogang itó ay pansariling gamit.

ang *dro*·gang ee·*to* ai pan·sa·*ree*·leeng *ga*·meet

I have a prescription for this drug.

May reseta akó para sa drogang itó.

mai re·*se*·ta a·*ko* pa·ra sa *dro*·gang ee·*to*

doctor

doktór

Where's the nearest ...?	Násaán ang pinakamalapit na ...?	na·sa·an ang pee·na·ka·ma·la·peet na ...
dentist	dentista	den·tees·ta
doctor	doktór	dok·tor
emergency department	emérdyensi department	e·mer·jen·see de·part·ment
hospital	ospitál	os·pee·tal
optometrist	óptiko	op·tee·ko
(night) pharmacist	botika (na bukás sa gabí)	bo·tee·ka (na boo·kas sa ga·bee)

I need a doctor (who speaks English).
Kailangan ko ng doktór (namarunong ng Inglés).
ka·ee·la·ngan ko nang dok·tor (na ma·roo·nong nang eeng·gles)

Could I see a female doctor?
May doktór bang babae?
mai dok·tor bang ba·ba·e

Could the doctor come here?
Puwede bang magpuntá dito ang doktór?
poo·we·de bang mag·poon·ta dee·to ang dok·tor

Is there an after-hours emergency number?
May telépono bang pang emérdyensi sa labás ng normál na oras?
mai te·le·po·no bang pang e·mer·jen·see sa la·bas nang nor·mal na o·ras

I've run out of my medication.
Ubós na ang aking medikasyón.
oo·bos na ang a·keeng me·dee·kas·yon

This is my usual medicine.
Itó ang aking karaniwang gamót.
ee·to ang a·keeng ka·ra·nee·wang ga·mot

My child weighs (20 kilos).
 (Beynte kilo) ang timbáng (*bayn*·te *kee*·lo) ang teem·*bang*
 ng anák ko. nang a·*nak* ko

What's the correct dosage?
 Anó ang tamang dosis? a·*no* ang *ta*·mang *do*·sees

My prescription is …
 Ang reseta ko ay … ang re·*se*·ta ko ai …

How much will it cost?
 Magkano? mag·*ka*·no

Can I have a receipt for my insurance?
 Pakibigyán mo akó ng pa·kee·beeg·*yan* mo a·*ko* nang
 resibo para sa aking re·*see*·bo *pa*·ra sa *a*·keeng
 seguro. se·*goo*·ro

I don't want a blood transfusion.
 Ayokong masalinan a·*yo*·kong ma·sa·*lee*·nan
 ng dugô. nang doo·*go'*

Please use a new syringe.
 Pakigamit lang ng pa·kee·*ga*·meet lang nang
 bagong heringgilya. *ba*·gong he·reeng·*geel*·ya

I have my own syringe.
 May sarili akóng mai sa·*ree*·lee a·*kong*
 heringgilya. he·reeng·*geel*·ya

I've been	*May bakuna*	mai ba·*koo*·na
vaccinated	*na akó*	na a·*ko*
against …	*laban sa …*	*la*·ban sa …
He/She has been	*May bakuna na*	mai ba·*koo*·na na
vaccinated	*siyá laban sa …*	*see*·ya la·ban sa …
against …		
tetanus	*tétano*	*te*·ta·no
typhoid	*tipus*	*tee*·poos
hepatitis	*hepataytis*	he·pa·*tai*·tees
A/B/C	*A/B/C*	ay/bee/see

I need new …	*Kailangan ko*	ka·ee·*la*·ngan ko
	ng bagong …	nang *ba*·gong …
contact lenses	*kontak lens*	*kon*·tak lens
glasses	*salamín sa matá*	sa·la·*meen* sa ma·*ta*

the doctor may say ...

Anó ang problema?		What's the problem?
a·*no* ang pro·*ble*·ma		
Saán masakít?		Where does it hurt?
sa·*an* ma·sa·*keet*		
May lagnát ka ba?		Do you have a temperature?
mai lag·*nat* ka ba		
Gaano katagál ka nang ganitó?		How long have you been like this?
ga·*a*·no ka·ta·*gal* ka nang ga·nee·*to*		
Nagkaroón ka na ba nitó?		Have you had this before?
nag·ka·ro·*on* ka na ba nee·*to*		
Gaano katagál ang paglálakbáy mo?		How long are you travelling for?
ga·*a*·no ka·ta·*gal* ang pag·la·lak·*bai* mo		
Ikáw ba ay nakíkipagtalik?		Are you sexually active?
ee·*kow* ba ai na·kee·*kee*·pag·*ta*·leek		
Nagkaroón ka ba ng di-protektadong seks?		Have you had unprotected sex?
nag·ka·ro·*on* ka ba nang dee·pro·tek·*ta*·dong seks		

Ikáw ba ay ...?	ee·*kow* ba ai ...	Do you ...?
umíinóm	oo·*mee*·ee·*nom*	drink
nanínigarilyó	na·*nee*·nee·ga·reel·*yo*	smoke
nagdodroga	nag·do·*dro*·ga	take drugs

Ikáw ba ay ...?	ee·*kow* ba ai ...	Are you ...?
allergic sa	a·*ler*·jeek sa	allergic to
kahit anó	*ka*·heet a·*no*	anything
may medikasyón	mai me·dee·kas·*yon*	on medication
sa kasalukuyan	sa ka·sa·loo·*koo*·yan	

189

the doctor may say ...

Kailangan kang ipasok sa ospitál.
    ka·ee·*la*·ngan kang
    ee·*pa*·sok sa os·pee·*tal*
	You need to be admitted to hospital.

Dapat itóng ipatsek pag-uwî mo.
    da·pat ee·*tong* ee·pa·*tsek*
    pag·oo·*wee* mo
	You should have it checked when you go home.

Kailangang umuwí ka para magpagamót.
    ka·ee·*la*·ngang oo·moo·*wee*
    ka *pa*·ra mag·pa·ga·*mot*
	You should return home for treatment.

symptoms & conditions

mga sintomás at kalagayan

I'm sick.
> *May sakít akó.* mai sa·*keet* a·ko

My friend/child is (very) sick.
> *Ang aking kaibigan/* ang *a*·keeng ka·ee·*bee*·gan/
> *anák ay (napakalubhâ)* a·*nak* ai (na·pa·ka·loob·*ha'*)
> *ang sakít.* ang sa·*keet*

She's about to have a baby.
> *Manganganak na siya.* ma·nga·nga·*nak* na see·*ya*

He/She is having a/an ...	*Siyá ay nagkákaroón ng ...*	see·*ya* ai nag·*ka*·ka·ro·*on* nang ...
allergic reaction	*allergic na reaksiyón*	a·*ler*·jeek na re·ak·see·*yon*
asthma attack	*atake ng hikà*	a·*ta*·ke nang *hee*·ka'
epileptic fit	*atakeng epileptik*	a·*ta*·keng e·pee·*lep*·teek
heart attack	*atake sa pusò*	a·*ta*·ke sa *poo*·so'

I've been bitten by an animal.
Nákagát akó ng hayop.   na·ka·*gat* a·ko nang *ha*·yop

It hurts here.
Masakít dito.   ma·sa·*keet dee*·to

I'm dehydrated.
Nanunuyót akó.   na·noo·noo·*yot* a·ko

I've been ...	*Akó ay ...*	a·ko ai ...
He/She has been ...	*Siyá ay ...*	see·*ya* ai ...
injured	*nasugatan*	na·soo·*ga*·tan
vomiting	*nagsúsuká*	nag·*soo*·soo·ka

I feel ...	*Akó ay ...*	a·ko ai ...
anxious	*balisá*	ba·lee·*sa*
better	*mas mabuti na*	mas ma·*boo*·tee na
depressed	*malungkót*	ma·loong·*kot*
dizzy	*nahihilo*	na·hee·*hee*·lo
hot and cold	*naíinitan at*	na·*ee*·ee·*nee*·tan at
	nalálamigán	na·*la*·la·mee·*gan*
nauseous	*naliliyó*	na·lee·lee·*yo*
shivery	*nangingiki*	na·ngee·*ngee*·kee
strange	*kakáibá*	ka·ka·*ee*·ba
weak	*nanghihinà*	nang·hee·*hee*·na'
worse	*mas grabe*	mas *gra*·be

---

the doctor may say ...

Gumagamit ka ba ng kontrasepsiyón? goo·ma·*ga*·meet ka ba nang kon·tra·sep·see·*yon*	**Are you using contraception?**
May regla ka ba? mai *reg*·la ka ba	**Are you menstruating?**
Buntís ka ba? boon·*tees* ka ba	**Are you pregnant?**
Kailán ka hulíng niregla? ka·ee·*lan* ka hoo·*leeng* nee·*reg*·la	**When was your last period?**
Buntís ka. boon·*tees* ka	**You're pregnant.**

I can't sleep.
Hindî akó makatulog.   heen·*dee*' a·ko ma·ka·*too*·log

I'm on medication for …
Nakámedikasyón akó   na·*ka*·me·dee·kas·*yon* a·ko
para sa …   *pa*·ra sa …

He/She is on medication for …
Nakámedikasyón   na·*ka*·me·dee·kas·*yon*
siyá para sa …   see·*ya pa*·ra sa …

I have (a/an) …
Akó ay mayroóng …   a·ko ai mai·ro·*ong* …

He/She has (a/an) …
Siyá ay mayroóng …   see·*ya* ai mai·ro·*ong* …

I've recently had (a/an) …
Kailán lang, akó ay   ka·ee·*lan* lang a·ko ai
nagkaroón ng …   nag·ka·ro·*on* nang …

He/She has recently had (a/an) …
Kailán lang, siyá ay   ka·ee·*lan* lang see·*ya* ai
nagkaroón ng …   nag·ka·ro·*on* nang …

asthma	*hikà*	*hee*·ka'
bilharzia	*bilharsya*	beel·*hars*·ya
cholera	*kólera*	*ko*·le·ra
cold n	*sipón*	see·*pon*
constipation	*tibí*	tee·*bee*
cough n	*ubó*	oo·*bo*
diabetes	*diyabetis*	dee·ya·*be*·tees
diarrhoea	*pagtataé*	pag·ta·ta·*e*
dysentery	*disinteryá*	dee·seen·ter·*ya*
fever	*lagnát*	lag·*nat*
giardiasis	*giyárdiyasis*	gee·yar·dee·*ya*·sees
headache	*sakít ng ulo*	sa·*keet* nang oo·lo
malaria	*malarya*	ma·*lar*·ya
nausea	*pagkaliyó*	pag·ka·lee·*yo*
pain	*sakít*	sa·*keet*
rabies	*rabis*	*ra*·bees
sore throat	*masakít na*	ma·sa·*keet* na
	lalamunan	la·la·*moo*·nan
worms	*bulate*	boo·*la*·te

women's health

(I think) I'm pregnant.
(Palagay ko) Akó ay buntís.   (pa·la·*gai* ko) a·*ko* ai boon·*tees*

I'm on the pill.
Nagpipíls akó.   nag·pee·*peels* a·*ko*

I haven't had my period for (six) weeks.
Hindî akó dinatnán ng   heen·*dee'* a·*ko* dee·nat·*nan* nang
regla ng (anim na) linggó.   *reg*·la nang (*a*·neem na) leeng·*go*

I've noticed a lump here.
May nápansin akóng   mai *na*·pan·seen a·*kong*
umbók dito.   oom·*bok* dee·to

Do you have something for (period pain)?
May maibíbigáy ka ba   mai ma·ee·*bee*·bee·*gai* ka ba
para sa (dismenorya)?   *pa*·ra sa (dees·me·nor·*ya*)

I think it's the medication I'm on.
Palagáy ko itó ay   pa·la·*gai* ko ee·*to* ai
dahil sa medikasyón.   *da*·heel sa me·dee·kas·*yon*

I have a ...	*Mayroón akóng ...*	mai·ro·*on* a·*kong* ...
urinary tract infection	*impeksiyón sa daluyan ng ihì*	eem·pek·see·*yon* sa da·*loo*·yan nang ee·*hee'*
yeast infection	*impeksiyóng yeast*	eem·pek·see·*yong* yeest

I need ...	*Kailangan ko ng ...*	ka·ee·*la*·ngan ko nang ...
contraception	*kontrasepsiyón*	kon·tra·sep·see·*yon*
the morning-after pill	*morning-after pill*	mor·neeng·*ap*·ter peel
a pregnancy test	*pambuntís na tes*	pam·boon·*tees* na tes

parts of the body

My ... hurts.
masakít ang aking ... — ma·sa·*keet* ang a·*keeng* ...

I can't move my ...
Hindí ko maikilos — heen·*dee* ko ma·ee·*kee*·los
ang aking ... — ang *a*·keeng ...

I have a cramp in my ...
May pulikat akó sa — mai poo·*lee*·kat a·*ko* sa
aking ... — *a*·keeng ...

My ... is swollen.
Ang ... ko ay magâ. — ang ... ko ai ma·*ga'*

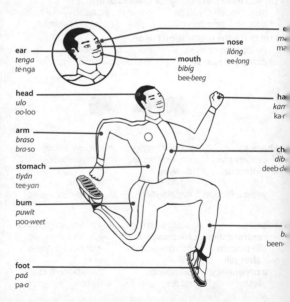

ear
tenga
te·nga

nose
ilóng
ee·*long*

mouth
bibíg
bee·*beeg*

head
ulo
oo·loo

arm
braso
bra·so

stomach
tiyán
tee·*yan*

bum
puwít
poo·*weet*

foot
paá
pa·*a*

alternative treatments

I don't use (Western medicine).
Hindî akó gumagamit   heen·*dee*′a·ko goo·ma·*ga*·meet
ng (kanluraning gamót).   nang (kan·loo·*ra*·neeng ga·*mot*)

I prefer ...	*Mas gustó ko ng ...*	mas goos·to ko nang ...
Can I see	*Puwede ba akóng*	poo·*we*·de ba a·*kong*
someone who	*magpatingín sa*	mag·pa·tee·*ngeen* sa
practises ...?	*isáng nag-*	ee·*sang* nag·
	papraktis ng ...?	pa·*prak*·tees nang ...
acupuncture	*akyupangtiyúr*	ak·yoo·pang·tee·*yoor*
naturopathy	*nátuyoropatí*	na·too·yo·ro·pa·*tee*
reflexology	*repleksólodyi*	re·plek·*so*·lo·jee

allergies

I'm allergic to ...	*Allergic akó sa ...*	a·*ler*·jeek a·ko sa ...
He/She is	*Siyá ay allergic*	see·*ya* ai a·*ler*·jeek
allergic to ...	*sa ...*	sa ...
antibiotics	*antibayótikó*	an·tee·ba·yo·tee·ko
anti-	*gamót laban sa*	ga·*mot la*·ban sa
inflammatories	*pamamagâ*	pa·ma·ma·*ga*′
aspirin	*áspirin*	*as*·pee·reen
bees	*bubuyog*	boo·*boo*·yog
codeine	*kodéyn*	ko·*dayn*
penicillin	*penisilín*	pe·nee·see·*leen*
pollen	*polen*	*po*·len
sulphur-	*mga droga na*	ma·*nga* dro·ga na
based drugs	*may sulpur*	may *sool*·poor

I have a skin allergy.
  Mayroón akóng alerhiya   mai·ro·*on* a·*kong* a·ler·*hee*·ya
  sa balát.   sa ba·*lat*

inhaler	*sinísinghót*	see·nee·seeng·*hot*
injection	*iniksiyón*	ee·neek·see·*yon*
antihistamines	*antihístamin*	an·tee·*hees*·ta·meen

For food-related allergies, see **vegetarian & special meals**, page 173.

pharmacist

parmasyótiko

I need something for (a headache).
  Kailangan ko ng para sa   ka·ee·*la*·ngan ko nang *pa*·ra sa
  (sakít ng ulo).   (sa·*keet* nang *oo*·lo)

Do I need a prescription for (antihistamines)?
  Kailangan ko ba ng   ka·ee·*la*·ngan ko ba nang
  reseta para sa   re·*se*·ta *pa*·ra sa
  (antihístamin)?   (an·tee·*hees*·ta·meen)

I have a prescription.
  Mayroón akóng reseta.   mai·ro·*on* a·*kong* re·*se*·ta

the pharmacist may say ...	
Dalawáng beses isáng araw (kasabáy ng pagkain). da·la·*wang* be·ses ee·*sang* a·row (ka·sa·*bai* nang pag·*ka*·een)	**Twice a day (with food).**
Nakáinóm ka na ba nitó? na·*ka*·ee·*nom* ka na ba nee·*to*	**Have you taken this before?**
Kailangang tapusin mo ang kurso. ka·ee·*la*·ngang ta·*poo*·seen mo ang *koor*·so	**You must complete the course.**

antimalarials	laban sa malarya	la·ban sa ma·lar·ya
antiseptic n	antiséptiko	an·tee·sep·tee·ko
contraceptives	kontrasepsiyón	kon·tra·sep·see·yon
gut blockers (for diarrhoea)	panlaban sa pagtataé	pan·la·ban sa pag·ta·ta·e
painkillers	pang-alís ng sakít	pang·a·lees nang sa·keet
thermometer	termometro	ter·mo·met·ro
rehydration salts	mga salitreng panlaban sa panunuyót	ma·nga sa·lee·treng pan·la·ban sa pa·noo·noo·yot
water purification tablets	mga tabletas na pampapuro ng tubig	ma·nga tab·le·tas na pam·pa·poo·ro nang too·beeg

How many times a day?
Ilán̄g beses isán̄g araw?   ee·lang be·ses ee·sang a·row

Will it make me drowsy?
Áantukín ba akó dahil dito?   a·an·too·keen ba a·ko da·heel dee·to

dentist

dentista

I have a …	Mayroón akóng …	mai·ro·on a·kong …
broken tooth	siráng ngipin	see·rang ngee·peen
cavity	butas sa ngipin	boo·tas sa ngee·peen
toothache	sakít ng ngipin	sa·keet nang ngee·peen

I've lost a filling.
Natanggál ang aking pasta.   na·tang·gal ang a·keeng pas·ta

My dentures are broken.
Nasira ang aking pustiso.   na·see·ra ang a·keeng poos·tee·so

My gums hurt.
Masakít ang aking gilagid.   ma·sa·keet ang a·keeng gee·la·geed

I don't want it extracted.
Ayokong ipabunot itó.   a·yo·kong ee·pa·boo·not ee·to

Ouch!
Arúy!   a·rooy

I need (a/an) ... Kailangan ko ng ... ka·ee·la·ngan ko nang ...
anaesthetic pampamanhíd pam·pa·man·heed
filling pasta pas·ta

---

the dentist may say ...

Ngangáng mabuti. nga·ngang ma·boo·tee	Open wide.
Hindî ito sásakít man lang. heen·dee' ee·to sa·sa·keet man lang	This won't hurt a bit.
Kagatín mo itó. ka·ga·teen mo ee·to	Bite down on this.
Huwág kang gágalaw. hoo·wag kang ga·ga·low	Don't move.
Magmumog ka. mag·moo·mog ka	Rinse!
Bumalík ka, hindí pa akó tapós. boo·ma·leek ka, heen·dee pa a·ko ta·pos	Come back, I haven't finished.

SUSTAINABLE TRAVEL

As the climate change debate heats up, the matter of sustainability becomes an important part of the travel vernacular. In practical terms, this means assessing our impact on the environment and local cultures and economies – and acting to make that impact as positive as possible. Here are some basic phrases to get you on your way …

communication & cultural differences

I'd like to learn some of your local dialects.
> *Gustó kong matuto ng iyóng mga wikà.*
> goos·*to* kong ma·*too*·to nang ee·*yong* ma·*nga wee*·ka'

Would you like me to teach you some English?
> *Gustó mo bang turuan kitá ng kaunting Inglés?*
> goos·*to* mo bang too·*roo*·an kee·*ta* nang ka·*oon*·teeng eeng·*gles*

Is this a local or national custom?
> *Itó ba ay kaugalián dito o sa buóng bansâ?*
> ee·*to* ba ai ka·oo·ga·lee·*an dee*·to o sa boo·*ong* ban·*sa'*

community benefit & involvement

I'd like to volunteer my skills.
> *Gustó kong magboluntaryo ng aking mga kasanayán.*
> goos·*to* kong mag·bo·loon·*tar*·yo nang a·keeng ma·*nga* ka·sa·na·*yan*

Are there any volunteer programs available in the area?
> *May mga boluntaryong programa ba dito?*
> mai ma·*nga* bo·loon·*tar*·yong prog·*ra*·ma ba *dee*·to

What sorts of issues is this community facing?

Anu-anóng mga isyu	a·noo·a·*nong* ma·*nga ees*·yoo	
ang hinaharáp ng	ang hee·na·ha·*rap* nang	
komunidád na itó?	ko·moo·nee·*dad* na ee·*to*	

ecotourism	*turismong*	too·*rees*·mong
	nakaayon sa	na·ka·a·yon sa
	kalikasan	ka·lee·*ka*·san
education crisis	*krisis sa*	*kree*·sees sa
	edukasyón	e·doo·kas·*yon*
environmental	*pamamahalà*	pa·ma·ma·ha·*la'*
management	*sa kapaligirán*	sa ka·pa·lee·gee·*ran*
media control	*pagkontról sa*	pag·kon·*trol* sa
	midya	*meed*·ya
military unrest	*kaguluhan sa*	ka·goo·*loo*·han sa
	militár	mee·lee·*tar*
natural disasters	*mga*	ma·*nga*
	kapinsalaang	ka·peen·sa·*la*·ang
	likhâ ng	leek·*ha'* nang
	kalikasan	ka·lee·*ka*·san
religious conflict	*hidwaang*	heed·*wa*·ang
	pangrelihiyón	pang·re·lee·hee·*yon*

environment

Where can I recycle this?

Saán ko itó puwedeng	sa·*an* ko ee·*to* poo·*we*·deng
i-recycle?	ee·re·*sai*·kel

transport

Can we get there by public transport?

Puwede ba tayong	poo·*we*·de ba ta·*yong*
sumakáy ng	soo·ma·*kai* nang
pampublikong	pam·poob·lee·*kong*
sasakyán	sa·sak·*yan*
papuntá doón?	pa·poon·*ta* do·*on*

Can we get there by bike?

Puwede ba tayong   poo·*we*·de ba *ta*·yong
magbisikleta papunta   mag·bee·seek·*le*·ta pa·poon·ta
doon?   do·*on*

I'd prefer to walk there.

Mas gustó kong   mas goos·to kong
maglakád   mag·la·*kad*
papuntá doon.   pa·poon·ta do·*on*

accommodation

I'd like to stay at a locally run hotel.

Gustó kong tumulóy sa   goos·to kong too·moo·*loy* sa
isáng lokal na otél.   ee·*sang* lo·kal na o·*tel*

Can I turn the air conditioning off and open the window?

Puwede ko bang   poo·*we*·de ko bang
patayín ang erkon   pa·ta·*yeen* ang *er*·kon
at buksán   at book·*san*
ang bintanà?   ang been·*ta*·na'

There's no need to change my sheets.

Hindi kailangang   heen·dee ka·ee·*la*·ngang
palitán ang aking sapín   pa·lee·*tan* ang *a*·keeng sa·*peen*
sa kama.   sa *ka*·ma

shopping

Where can I buy locally produced goods/souvenirs?

Saán akó makabíbilí   sa·*an a*·ko ma·ka·*bee*·bee·lee
ng mga   nang ma·*nga*
bagay/subenír   ba·gai/soo·be·*neer*
na dito ginawâ?   na *dee*·to gee·na·*wa*'

Do you sell Fair Trade products?

Nagtitindá ba   nag·tee·teen·*da* ba
kayó ng mga   ka·*yo* nang ma·*nga*
produktong   pro·*dook*·tong
Fair Trade?   *fe*·a trayd

food

Do you sell ...?	Nagtítindá	nag·tee·teen·da
	ka ba ng ...?	ka ba nang ...
locally produced	mga pagkaing	ma·nga pag·ka·eeng
food	ani dito	a·nee dee·to
organic	produktong	pro·dook·tong
produce	orgánik	or·ga·neek

Which Filipino foods should I try?

Alíng mga pagkaing	a·leeng ma·nga pag·ka·eeng
Pilipino ang dapat kong	pee·lee·pee·no ang da·pat kong
tikmán?	teek·man

sightseeing

Does your	Ang kompanyá	ang kom·pan·ya
company ...?	mo ba ay ...?	mo ba ai ...
donate money	nagbíbigáy	nag·bee·bee·gai
to charity	ng donasyón sa	nang do·nas·yon sa
	káwanggawà	ka·wang·ga·wa'
hire local guides	umuupa ng	oo·moo·oo·pa nang
	mga giyang	ma·nga gee·yang
	tagarito	ta·ga·ree·to

Are cultural tours available?

| Mayroón bang mga | mai·ro·on bang ma·nga |
| tur na pangkultura? | toor na pang·kool·too·ra |

Does the guide speak local dialects?

| Nagsásalitá ba ang giya | nag·sa·sa·lee·ta ba ang gee·ya |
| ng lokal na wikà? | nang lo·kal na wee·ka' |

Kinaray-a	Kinaráy-a	kee·na·rai·a
Maguindanao	Maquíndanao	ma·geen·da·now
Maranao	Maranao	ma·ra·now
Tagalog	Tagalog	ta·ga·log
Tausug	Tausúg	ta·oo·soog

See pp 117–120 for more local dialects.

Unless otherwise specified, the verbs listed have three forms organised in the following way: patient voice (pv), then actor voice (av) followed by the root verb in brackets. For example the verb for 'cook' is *ilutò/maglutò (lutò)*. If only one form of the verb is given then this is the most commonly used form and is marked either as a patient or actor voice verb. See the **phrasebuilder** for explanations on verbs. You'll also find words marked as adjective ⓐ, noun ⓝ, verb ⓥ, preposition ⓟ, singular sg, plural pl, masculine ⓜ and feminine ⓕ where necessary.

A

aboard *nakasakáy* na-ka-sa-*kai*
abortion *aborsyón* a-bors-*yon*
about *tungkól sa* toong-*kol* sa
above *sa itaás ng* sa ee-ta-*as* nang
abroad *nasa ibáng bansá*
　na-sa ee-*bang* ban-*sa'*
accident *aksidente* ak-se-*den*-te
accommodation *akomodasyón*
　a-ko-mo-das-*yon*
account (bank) ⓝ *akáwnt* a-*kawnt*
across *sa kabilà* sa ka-bee-*la'*
activist *aktibista* ak-tee-*bees*-ta
actor *artista* ar-*tees*-ta
acupuncture *akupangtiyúr*
　a-koo-pang-tee-*yoor*
adaptor *adaptor* a-*dap*-tor
addiction *adiksyón* a-deeks-*yon*
address ⓝ *tirahan* tee-*ra*-han
administration *administrasyón*
　ad-mee-nees-tras-*yon*
admission (price) *halagá ng pagpasok*
　ha-la-*ga* nang pag-*pa*-sok
admit (into a place)
　papasukin/magpapasok (pasok)
　pa-pa-soo-keen/mag-pa-*pa*-sok (*pa*-sok)
adult ⓐ *nasa edád* na-sa e-*dad*
advertisement *anúnsiyo* a-*noon*-see-yo
advice *payo* pa-*yo*
aerobics *erobiks* e-*ro*-beeks
aeroplane *eruplano* e-roo-*pla*-no
Africa *Áprica* ap-ree-ka
after *makalipas* ma-ka-*lee*-pas
afternoon *hapon* ha-*pon*

aftershave *pangmatapos mag-ahit*
　pang-ma-*ta*-pos mag-a-*heet*
again *uli* oo-*lee'*
age ⓝ *edád* e-*dad*
agree ⓥ *umayon* av oo-*ma*-yon
agriculture *agrikultura* ag-ree-kool-*too*-ra
ahead *nasa unahán* na-sa oo-na-*han*
AIDS *AIDS* ayds
air *hangin* ha-ngeen
airconditioned *may erkon* mai er-kon
airconditioning *erkon* er-kon
airline *eruplano* e-roo-*pla*-no
airmail *ermeyl* er-mayl
airplane *eruplano* e-roo-*pla*-no
airport *erport* er-port
airport tax *buwís sa erport*
　boo-*wees* sa er-port
aisle (on plane) *daanan* da-*a*-nan
alarm clock *alárm klak* a-*larm* klak
alcohol *alak* a-lak
all *lahát* la-*hat*
allergy *alerhiya* a-ler-*hee*-ya
almond *pili* pee-*lee'*
almost *halos* ha-los
alone *nag-íisá* nag-ee-ee-sa
already *na* na
also *rin/din* reen/deen
altar *altár* al-tar
altitude *taás* ta-*as*
always *palagì* pa-*la*-gee'
ambassador *embahadór* em-ba-ha-*dor*
ambulance *ambulansiya*
　am-boo-*lan*-see-ya
amphetamines *ampetamin* am-pe-ta-*meen*
anaemia *anemya* a-*nem*-ya
anarchist *anárkista* a-*nar*-*kees*-ta
ancient *napakatandá na* na-pa-ka-tan-*da* na

and *at* at
angry *galit* ga·*leet*
animal *hayop* ha·yop
ankle *bukung-bukong* boo·koong·*boo*·kong
another *ibá* ee·ba
answer ⓝ *sagót* sa·got
ant *langgám* lang·gam
antibiotics *antibayótiko* an·tee·ba·yo·tee·ko
antinuclear *antinúkliyar* an·tee·nook·lee·yar
antique ⓐ *antigo* an·tee·go
antiseptic ⓐ *antiséptiko* an·tee·sep·tee·ko
any *anumán* a·noo·man
apartment *apartment* a·part·ment
appendix (body) *apendiks* a·pen·deeks
apple *mansanas* man·sa·nas
appointment *tipanan* tee·pa·nan
apricot *aprikota* ap·ree·ko·ta
April *Abríl* ab·reel
archaeological *arkeolóhikal*
  ar·ke·ho·lo·hee·kal
architect *arkitekto/a* ⓜ/ⓕ ar·kee·tek·to/a
architecture *arkitektura* ar·kee·tek·too·ra
argue *magtalo* av mag·ta·lo
arm *bisig* bee·seeg
aromatherapy *aromatérapi*
  a·ro·ma·te·ra·pee
arrest ⓥ *arestuhin/umaresto (aresto)*
  a·res·too·hin/oo·ma·res·to (a·res·to)
arrivals *datingan* da·tee·ngan
arrive *dumating* av doo·ma·teeng
art *arte* ar·te
art gallery *galeriyang pang-arte*
  ga·le·ree·yang pang·ar·te
artist *artista* ar·tees·ta
ashtray *sinisero* see·nee·se·ro
Asia *Asya* as·ya
ask (a question) *magtanóng* av
  mag·ta·nong
ask (for something) *humingî* av
  hoo·mee·ngee'
asparagus *aspáragus* as·pa·ra·goos
aspirin *áspirin* as·pee·reen
asthma *hikà* hee·ka'
at *sa* sa
athletics *atletiks* at·le·teeks
atmosphere *atmóspera* at·mos·pe·ra
aubergine *talóng* ta·long
August *Agosto* a·gos·to
aunt *tiyá* tee·ya
Australia *Australya* ows·tral·ya
automated teller machine (ATM)
  ÁTM ay·tee·em
autumn *taglagás* tag·la·gas
avenue *abenida* a·be·nee·da
avocado *abukado* a·boo·ka·do
awful *kakilákilabot* ka·kee·la·kee·la·bot

204

B

B&W (film) *blak en wayt* blak en wait
baby *beybi* *bata* bay·bee
baby food *pagkain ng beybi*
  pag·ka·een nang bay·bee
baby powder *pulbós ng beybi*
  pool·bos nang bay·bee
babysitter *tagapag-alaga ng beybi*
  ta·ga·pag·a·la·ga nang bay·bee
back (body) *likód* lee·kod
back (position) *sa likód* sa lee·kod
backpack *backpack* back·pack
bacon *bekon* be·kon
bad *masamâ* ma·sa·ma'
bag *bag* bag
baggage *bagahe* ba·ga·he
baggage allowance
  takdáng bigát ng bagahe
  tak·dang bee·gat nang ba·ga·he
baggage claim *kuhanán ng bagahe*
  koo·ha·nan nang ba·ga·he
bakery *panederyá* pa·ne·der·ya
balance (account) *balanse ng akáwnt*
  ba·lan·se nang a·kownt
balcony *bálkoni* bal·ko·nee
ball (sport) *bola* bo·la
ballet *baléy* ba·lay
banana *saging* sa·geeng
band (music) *banda* ban·da
bandage ⓝ *bendahe* ben·da·he
Band-Aid *band-eyd* band·ayd
bank ⓝ *bangko* bang·ko
bank account *bank akáwnt* bank a·kownt
banknote *perang papél* pe·rang pa·pel
baptism *binyág* been·yag
bar *bar* bar
bar work *trabaho sa bar* tra·ba·ho sa bar
barber *barbero* bar·be·ro
baseball *beisbol* bays·bol
basket *basket* bas·ket
basketball *básketbol* bas·ket·bol
bath ⓝ *banyera* ban·ye·ra
bathing suit *damít pampaligò*
  da·meet pam·pa·lee·go'
bathroom *banyo* ban·yo
battery *bateryá* ba·ter·ya
become *maging* av ma·geeng
beach *tabíng-dagat* ta·beeng da·gat
beach volleyball *bólibol sa bits*
  bo·lee·bol sa beets
bean *bin* been
beansprout *togè* to·ge'
beautiful *magandá* ma·gan·da
beauty salon *pakulutan* pa·koo·loo·tan

because *dahil* da-heel
bed *kama* ka-ma
bed linen *kumot sa kama* koo-mot sa ka-ma
bedding *kagamitán para sa kama*
  ka-ga-mee-tan pa-ra sa ka-ma
bedroom *kuwartong tulugán* kwar-tong
  too-loo-gan
bee *bubuyog* boo-boo-yog
beef *karné* kar-ne
beer *serbesa* ser-be-sa
beetroot *bitrut* beet-root
before *bago* ba-go
beggar *pulubi* poo-loo-bee
behind *sa likurán* sa lee-koo-ran
Belgium *Bélhika* bel-hee-ka
below *sa ibabâ* sa ee-ba-ba'
beside *sa tabí* sa ta-bee
best *pinakamagaling* pee-na-ka-ma-ga-leeng
bet ⓝ *pustá* poos-ta
better *mas magaling* mas ma-ga-leeng
between *sa pagitan* sa pa-gee-tan
Bible *Bíbliya* beeb-lee-ya
bicycle *bisikleta* bee-seek-le-ta
big *malakí* ma-la-kee
bigger *mas malakí* mas ma-la-kee
biggest *pinakamalakí*
  pee-na-ka-ma-la-kee
bike *bisikleta* bee-seek-le-ta
bike chain *kadena ng bisikleta*
  ka-de-na nang bee-seek-le-ta
bike lock *kandado ng bisikleta*
  kan-da-do nang bee-seek-le-ta
bike path *daanán ng bisikleta*
  da-a-nan nang bee-seek-le-ta
bike shop *tindahan ng bisikleta*
  teen-da-han ng bee-seek-le-ta
bill (restaurant) *tsit* tseet
binoculars *largabista* lar-ga-bees-ta
bird *ibon* ee-bon
birth certificate *bert sertípiket*
  bert ser-tee-pee-ket
birth control *bert kontról* bert kon-trol
birthday *kapangánákan* ka-pa-nga-na-kan
biscuit *biskwít* bees-kweet
bite (dog/insect) ⓝ *kagát* ka-gat
bitter *mapaklá* ma-pak-la
black *maitím* ma-ee-teem
bladder *pantóg* pan-tog
blanket *blangket* blang-ket
blind *bulág* boo-lag
blister ⓝ *paltós* pal-tos
blocked *barado* ba-ra-do
blood *dugô* doo-go'
blood group *grupo ng dugó*
  groo-po nang doo-go'

blood pressure *presyón ng dugó*
  pres-yon nang doo-go'
blood test *pagsusuri sa dugó*
  pag-soo-soo-ree sa doo-go'
blue *asúl* a-sool
board (plane, ship) *isakáy/sumakáy (sakáy)*
  ee-sa-kai/soo-ma-kai (sa-kai)
boarding house *bording haus*
  bor-deeng hows
boarding pass *bording pas* bor-deeng pas
boat *bapór* ba-por
body *katawán* ka-ta-wan
boiled *kumulô* koo-moo-lo'
bone *butó* boo-to
book ⓝ *libró* lee-bro
book ⓥ *ibúk/magbúk (búk)*
  ee-book/mag-book (book)
booked out *punó na* poo-no na
bookshop *tindahan ng libró*
  teen-da-han nang lee-bro
boots (footwear) *mga bota* ma-nga bo-ta
border *hangganan* hang-ga-nan
bored *bagót* ba-got
boring *nakabábagót* na-ka-ba-ba-got
borrow *ipahiram/humirám (hiram)*
  ee-pa-hee-ram/hoo-mee-ram (hee-ram)
botanic garden *harding botánika*
  har-deeng bo-ta-nee-ka
both *pareho* pa-re-ho
bottle ⓝ *bote* bo-te
bottle opener *pambukás ng bote*
  pam-boo-kas nang bo-te
bottle shop *tindahan ng inumin*
  teen-da-han nang ee-noo-meen
bottom (body) *puwít* poo-weet
bottom (position) *sa ilalim* sa ee-la-leem
bowl *mangkók* mang-kok
box ⓝ *kahón* ka-hon
boxer shorts *bakser syorts* bak-ser syorts
boxing *boksing* bok-seeng
boy *batang lalaki* ba-tang la-la-kee
boyfriend *boypren* boi-pren
bra *bra* bra
brakes *preno* pre-no
brandy *brandi* bran-dee
brave ⓐ *matapang* ma-ta-pang
bread *tinapay* tee-na-pai
bread rolls *pan de sal* pan de sal
break ⓥ *sirain* see-ra-een
break down *nasirà* na-see-ra'
breakfast *agahan* a-ga-han
breast (body) *suso* soo-so
breathe *humingá* ⓐⓥ hoo-mee-nga
bribe ⓝ *suhol* soo-hol
bridge ⓝ *tuldy* tool-lal
briefcase *portpolyo* port-pol-yo

brilliant *magalíng* ma-ga-*leeng*
bring *dalhín/magdalá (dalá)*
dal-*heen*/mag-da-*la* (da-*la*)
broccoli *brokoli* bro-ko-lee
brochure *polyeto* pol-ye-to
broken *sirâ* see-ra'
broken down *nasirà* na-see-ra'
bronchitis *brongkitis* brong-kee-tees
brother *kapatíd na lalaki*
ka-pa-*teed* na la-*la*-kee
brown *kulay lupà* koo-lai *loo*-pa
bruise ⊙ *pasâ* pa-sa'
brush *iskoba* ees-ko-ba
bucket *timbâ* teem-ba'
Buddhist *Budisto* boo-*dees*-to
budget *badyet* bad-yet
buffet *bupéy* boo-*pay*
bug ⊙ *insekto* een-sek-to
build *itayô/magtayô (itayô)*
ee-ta-yo'/mag-ta-yo' (ee-ta-yo')
builder *karpintero* kar-peen-*te*-ro
building *gusali* goo-sa-lee'
bumbag *bambag* bam-bag
burn ⊙ *pasô* pa-so'
burnt *sunóg* soo-nog
bus (city) *bus* boos
bus station *istasyón ng bus*
ees-tas-*yon* nang boos
bus stop *hintuan ng bus*
heen-*too*-an nang boos
business *negosyo* ne-gos-yo
business class *bisnis klas* bees-nees klas
business person *negosyante* ne-gos-yan-te
business trip *biyaheng pangnegosyo*
bee-ya-heng pang-ne-gos-yo
busker *basker* bas-ker
busy *bisi* bee-see
but (however) *pero* pe-ro
butcher *magkakarné* mag-ka-kar-ne
butcher's shop *tindahan ng magkakarné*
teen-*da*-han nang mag-ka-kar-ne
butter *mantekilya* man-te-*keel*-ya
butterfly *paruparó* pa-roo-pa-ro
button *butones* boo-to-nes
buy *bilí* bee-*lee*

C

cabbage *repolyo* re-*pol*-yo
cable car *kebol kar* ke-bol kar
café *kapihan* ka-*pee*-han
cake *keyk* kayk
cake shop *tindahan ng keyk*
teen-*da*-han nang kayk
calculator *kalkuletor* kal-koo-*le*-tor

calendar *kalendaryo* ka-len-*dar*-yo
call ⊙ *tawagan/tumawag (tawag)*
ta-*wag*-an/too-ma-wag (ta-wag)
camera *kámera* *ka*-me-ra
camera shop *tindahan ng kámera*
teen-*da*-han nang *ka*-me-ra
camp ⊙ *magkamping* av *mag-kam*-peeng
camping ground *kampingan*
kam-*pee*-ngan
camping store
tindahan ng pangkamping
teen-*da*-han nang pang-*kam*-peeng
camp site *kampingan* kam-*pee*-ngan
can (be able) *maáarì* av ma-*a*-a-ree
can (have permission) *puwede ba* av
poo-*we*-de ba
can (tin) *lata* *la*-ta
can opener *abrelata* ab-re-*la*-ta
Canada *Kánada* *ka*-na-da
cancel *ikanseló/magkanselá*
(kanselahín) ee-kan-se-*la*/mag-kan-se-la
(kan-se-la-*heen*)
cancer *kanser* kan-ser
candle *kandilà* kan-*dee*-la
candy *kendi* ken-dee
cantaloupe *milón* mee-*lon*
capsicum *bel peper* bel *pe*-per
car *kotse* kot-se
car ferry *kar peri* kar *pe*-ree
car hire *arkilahán ng kotse*
ar-kee-la-*han* nang kot-se
car owner's title *katunayan ng*
pagmamay-ari ng kotse ka-too-*na*-yan
nang pag-ma-mai-a-ree nang kot-se
car park *páradahán ng sasakyán*
pa-ra-da-han nang sa-sak-*yan*
car registration *rehistrasyón ng kotse*
re-hees-tras-*yon* nang kot-se
caravan *káraban* ka-ra-ban
cardiac arrest *atake sa pusò*
a-*ta*-ke sa *poo*-so'
cards (playing) *baraha* ba-ra-ha
care for *magmahál sa* av mag-ma-*hal*
carpark *páradahán ng sasakyán*
pa-ra-da-han nang sa-sak-*yan*
carpenter *karpintero* kar-peen-*te*-ro
carriage (horse-drawn) *kalesa* ka-*le*-sa
carrot *karot* ka-rot
carry *dalhín/magdalá (dalá)*
dal-*heen*/mag-da-*la* (da-*la*)
carton *kartón* kar-ton
cash ⊙ *pera* pe-ra
cash (a cheque) *ipalít/magpalít (palit)*
ee-pa-*leet*/mag-pa-*leet* (pa-*leet*)
cash register *kaha* *ka*-ha
cashew *kasóy* ka-soy

cashier *kahero/a* ⓜ/ⓕ ka-*he*-ro/a
casino *kasino* ka-*si*-no
cassette *kasét* ka-*set*
castle *kastilyo* kas-*teel*-yo
casual work *trabahong kaswal*
  tra-*ba*-hong *kas*-wal
cat *pusà* poo-*sa*'
cathedral *katedrál* ka-ted-*ral*
Catholic *Katóliko* ka-to-lee-ko
Catholicism *Katólisismo* ka-to-lee-*sees*-mo
cauliflower *koliplawer* ko-lee-*pla*-wer
cave *kuweba* koo-*we*-ba
CD *CD* see-dee
celebration *pagdiriwang* pag-dee-*ree*-wang
cemetery *sementeryo* se-men-*ter*-yo
cent *séntimo* *sen*-tee-mo
centimetre *sentimetro* sen-tee-*me*-tro
centre *sentro* *sen*-tro
ceramics *serámika* se-*ra*-mee-ko
cereal *siriyál* see-ree-*yal*
certificate *katunayan* ka-too-*na*-yan
chain ⓝ *kadena* ka-*de*-na
chair *upuan* oo-*poo*-an
champagne *tsampán* sam-*pan*
championships *kampeonato*
  kam-pe-yo-*na*-to
chance *pagkakátaon* pag-ka-*ka*-ta-on
change (coins) ⓝ *suklî* sook-*lee*'
change (money) ⓥ *ipalít/magpalít (palit)*
  ee-pa-*leet*/mag-pa-*leet* (pa-*leet*)
changing room (in shop) *bihisán*
  bee-hee-*san*
charming *kaakit-akit* ka-a-*keet*-a-keet
chat up *makipagkilala* av
  ma-kee-pag-kee-*la*-la
cheap *mura* *moo*-ra
cheat *manloloko* man-lo-*lo*-ko
check (look for) *tingnán* pv teeng-*nan*
check (banking) *tseke* *tse*-ke
check (bill) *tsit* tseet
check-in (desk) *tsek-in* tsek-een
checkpoint *tsekpoynt* tsek-point
cheese *keso* *ke*-so
cheese shop *tindahan ng keso*
  teen-*da*-han nang *ke*-so
chef *shep* shep
chemist (pharmacist) *parmasyótiko/a* ⓜ/ⓕ
  par-mas-*yo*-tee-ko/a
chemist (pharmacy) *botika* bo-*tee*-ka
cheque (banking) *tseke* *tse*-ke
cheque (bill) *tsit* tseet
cherry *tseri* *tse*-ree
chess *tses* tses
chessboard *tses bord* tses bord
chest (body) *dibdib* deeb-*deeb*
chestnut *kastanyas* kas-*tan*-yas

chewing gum *bábolgam* ba-*bol*-gam
chicken *manók* ma-*nok*
chicken pox *bulutong-tubig*
  boo-*loo*-tong too-*beeg*
chickpea *garbansos* gar-*ban*-sos
child *batà* ba-*ta*'
child seat *upuan ng batà*
  oo-*poo*-an nang ba-*ta*'
childminding *pag-aalaga ng batà*
  pag-a-*la*-ga nang ba-*ta*'
children *mga batà* ma-*nga* ba-ta
chilli *sili* *see*-lee
chilli sauce *sili sows* *see*-lee sohs
China *Tsina* *tsee*-na
chiropractor *kiropraktor*
  kee-ro-*prak*-tor
chocolate *tsokolate* tso-ko-*la*-te
choose *piliin/pumilì (pilì)*
  pee-lee-*een*/poo-*mee*-lee' (pee-*lee*)
chopping board *sangkalan* sang-*ka*-lan
chopsticks *tsop istík* tsop ees-*teek*
Christian *Kristiyano* krees-tee-*ya*-no
Christian name *pangalan* pa-*nga*-lan
Christmas *Paskó* pas-ko
Christmas Day *araw ng Paskó*
  a-row nang pas-ko
Christmas Eve *Bisperás ng Paskó*
  bees-pe-*ras* nang pas-ko
church *simbahan* seem-*ba*-han
cider *sayder* *sai*-der
cigar *tabako* ta-*ba*-ko
cigarette *sigarilyo* see-ga-*reel*-yo
cigarette lighter *layter* *lai*-ter
cinema *sinehán* see-ne-*han*
circus *sirko* *seer*-ko
citizenship *pagkamámamayán*
  pag-ka-*ma*-ma-ma-yan
city *siyudád* see-yoo-*dad*
city centre *sentro ng siyudád*
  sen-tro nang see-yoo-*dad*
civil rights *karapatáng sibíl*
  ka-ra-pa-*tang* see-*beel*
class (category) *klase* *i*-se
class system *sistema ng klase*
  sees-*te*-ma nang *kla*-se
classical *klasikál* kla-see-*kal*
clean ⓐ *malinis* ma-*lee*-nees
clean ⓥ *linisin/maglinis (linis)*
  lee-nee-*seen*/mag-*lee*-nees (lee-*nees*)
cleaning *kalinisan* ka-lee-*nee*-san
client *kliyente* klee-*yen*-te
cliff *bangín* ba-*ngeen*
climb ⓥ *umakyát* av oo-mak-*yat*
cloakroom *lagakan ng mga balabal*
  la-*ga*-kan nang ma-*nga* ba-*la* bal
clock *orasán* o-ra-*san*

close ⊙ *isará/magsará (isará)*
ee-sa-ra/mag-sa-ra (ee-sa-ra)
close ⓐ *malapit* ma-la-peet
closed *sarado* sa-ra-do
clothesline *sampayan* sam-pa-yan
clothing *damít* da-meet
clothing store *tindahan ng damít*
teen-da-han nang da-meet
cloud *ulap* oo-lap
cloudy *maulap* ma-oo-lap
clutch (car) *kámbiyo* kam-bee-yo
coach (trainer) *kowts* kohts
coast *baybayin* bai-ba-yeen
coat *kapa* ka-pa
cocaine *kokéyn* ko-kayn
cock *tandáng* tan-dang
cockfighting *sabong* sa-bong
cockroach *ipis* ee-pees
cocktail *kaktéyl* kak-tayl
cocoa *kokwa* kok-wa
coconut *niyóg* nee-yog
coffee *kapé* ka-pe
coins *baryá* bar-ya
cold ⓝ *lamíg* la-meeg
cold ⓐ *malamíg* ma-la-meeg
colleague *katrabaho* ka-tra-ba-ho
collect call *kolék kol* ko-lek kol
college *koléhiyo* ko-le-hee-yo
colour *kulay* koo-lai
comb ⓝ *sukláy* sook-lai
come *dumatíng* av doo-ma-teeng
comedy *komedya* ko-med-ya
comfortable *komportable* kom-por-tab-le
commission *komisyón* ko-mees-yon
communications (profession)
komunikasyón ko-moo-nee-kas-yon
communion *komunyón* ko-moon-yon
communist *komunista* ko-moo-nees-ta
companion *kasama* ka-sa-ma
company (firm) *kompanyá* kom-pan-ya
compass *kompas* kom-pas
complain *magreklamo* av mag-rek-la-mo
complaint *reklamo* rek-la-mo
complimentary (free) *libre* lee-bre
computer *kompyuter* komp-yoo-ter
computer game *kompyuter geym*
komp-yoo-ter gaym
concert *konsiyerto* kon-see-yer-to
concussion *pagkakalóg na utak*
pag-ka-ka-log nang oo-tak
conditioner (hair) *kondísyoner*
kon-dees-yo-ner
condom *kondom* kon-dom
conference *kompirénsiya*
kom-pee-ren-see-ya
confession *kumpisál* koom-pee-sal

confirm (a booking)
tiyakín/tumiyak (tiyakín)
tee-ya-keen/too-mee-yak (tee-ya-keen)
congratulations *maligayang batì*
ma-lee-ga-yang ba-tee'
conjunctivitis *kondyángtibaytis*
kon-jang-tee-bai-tees
connection *koneksiyón* ko-nek-see-yon
conservative *konserbatibo*
kon-ser-ba-tee-bo
constipation *tibí* tee-bee
consulate *konsulado* kon-soo-la-do
contact lens solution *panlinis sa kontak
lens* pan-lee-nees sa kon-tak lens
contact lenses *kontak lens* kon-tak lens
contraceptives *kontrasepsiyón*
kon-tra-sep-see-yon
contract *kontrata* kon-tra-ta
convenience store *tindahang sari-sarì*
teen-da-hang sa-ree-sa-ree'
convent *kumbento* koom-ben-to
cook ⓝ *tagalutò* ta-ga-loo-to'
cook ⓥ *ilutò/maglutò (lutò)*
ee-loo-to'/mag-loo-to' (loo-to')
cookie *biskwít* bees-kweet
cooking *paglulutò* pag-loo-loo-to'
cool (temperature) *malamíg* ma-la-meeg
corkscrew *tribusón* tree-boo-son
corn *maís* ma-ees
corner *kanto* kan-to
cornflakes *kornpleks* korn-pleks
corrupt ⓐ *may katiwalián*
mai ka-tee-wa-lee-an
cost ⓝ *presyuhán* pres-yoo-han
cotton (fabric) *koton* ko-ton
cotton (thread) *sinulad* see-noo-lad
cotton balls *bulak* boo-lak
cotton buds *koton bad* ko-ton bad
cough ⓥ *umubó* av oo-moo-bo
cough ⓝ *ubó* oo-bo
cough medicine *gamót sa ubó*
ga-mot sa oo-bo
count ⓥ *bilangin* pv bee-la-ngeen
counter (at bar) *kawnter* kown-ter
country *bansâ* ban-sa'
countryside *sa probínsiya* sa pro-been-see-ya
coupon *kupón* koo-pon
courgette *sukini* soo-kee-nee
court (legal) *korte* kor-te
court (tennis) *tenis kort* te-nees kort
couscous *kuskus* koos-koos
cover charge *kaber tsards* ka-ber tsarj
cow *baka* ba-ka
cracker (fireworks) *paputók* pa-poo-tok
crafts *sining* see-neeng
crash ⓝ *banggaan* bang-ga-an

crazy *lukúlukó* loo·koo·loo·ko
cream *krema* kre·ma
crèche *álagán ng batà* a·la·ga·an nang ba·ta'
credit *kredit* kre·deet
credit card *kredit kard* kre·deet kard
cricket (sport) *larong kriket* la·rong kree·ket
crop *paltik* pal·teek
cross (religious) ⓝ *krus* kroos
crowded *siksikan* seek·see·kan
cucumber *pipino* pee·pee·no
cup *tasa* ta·sa
cupboard *aparadór* a·pa·ra·dor
currency exchange *palitan ng pera*
   pa·lee·tan nang pe·ra
current (electricity) *koryente* kor·yen·te
current affairs *pangkasalukuyang*
   pangyayari pang·ka·sa·loo·koo·yang
   pang·ya·ya·ree
curry *kari* ka·ree
custard apple *atis* a·tees
custom *kostumbre* kos·toom·hre
customs *adwana* ad·wa·na
cut ⓥ *hiwain* pv hee·wa·een
cutlery *kutsara at tinidór*
   koot·sa·ra at tee·nee·dor
CV *CV* see·bee
cycle ⓥ *magbisikleta* av mag·bee·seek·le·ta
cycling *pagbibisikleta* pag·bee·bee·seek·le·ta
cyclist *siklista* seek·lees·ta
cystitis *sistaytis* sees·tai·tees

D

dad *tatay/dadi* ta·tai/da·dee
daily *araw-araw* a·row·a·row
dance ⓥ *sumayáw* av soo·ma·yow
dancing *sayawan* sa·ya·wan
dangerous *peligroso* pe·lee·gro·so
dark *madilím* ma·dee·leem
dark (of colour) *maitím* ma·ee·teem
date (appointment) *tipanan* tee·pa·nan
date (go out with) *dinéyt/magdéyt (déyt)*
   dee·nayt/mag·dayt (dayt)
date (day) *petsa* pet·sa
date (fruit) *dátiles* da·tee·les
date of birth *petsa ng kapanganakan*
   pet·sa nang ka·pa·nga·na·kan
daughter *anák na babae* a·nak na ba·ba·e
dawn *bukáng liwaywáy*
   boo·kang lee·wai·wai
day *araw* a·row
(the) day after tomorrow
   samakalawá sa·ma·ka·la·wa
(the) day before yesterday
   kamakalawá ka·ma·ka·la·wa

dead *patáy* pa·tai
deaf *bingí* bee·ngee
deal (cards) *ipamigáy* pv ee·pa·mee·gai
December *Disyembre* dees·yem·bre
decide *magdesisyón* av mag·de·sees·yon
deep *malalim* ma·la·leem
deforestation *pagkaubos ng gubat*
   pag·ka·oo·bos nang goo·bat
degrees (temperature) *digrí* dee·gree
delay *pagkaantala* pag·ka·an·ta·la
delicatessen *groseryá* gro·ser·ya
deliver *ihatíd* pv ee·ha·teed
democracy *demokrasya* de·mo·kras·ya
demonstration *demonstrasyón*
   de·mons·tras·yon
Denmark *Denmark* den·mark
dental floss *dental plos* den·tal plos
dentist *dentista* den·tees·ta
deodorant *deyódorant* de·yo·do·rant
depart *umalís* av oo·ma·lees
department store *department istór*
   de·part·ment ees·tor
departure *pag-alís* pag·a·lees
departure gate *departyur geyt*
   de·part·yoor gayt
deposit (bank) *depósito* de·po·see·to
derailleur *diskaríl* dees·ka·reel
descendant *inapó* ee·na·po
desert *disyerto* dees·yer·to
design *disenyo* dee·sen·yo
dessert *matamís* ma·ta·mees
destination *púpuntahán* poo·poon·ta·han
details *mga detalye* ma·nga de·tal·ye
diabetes *diyabetis* dee·ya·be·tees
dial tone *dayal ton* da·yal ton
diaper *lampín* lam·peen
diaphragm *dáyapram* da·ya·pram
diarrhoea *pagtataé* pag·ta·ta·e
diary *dáyari* da·ya·ree
dice *days* dais
dictionary *diksiyunaryn*
   deek·see·yoo·nar·yo
die *mamatáy* av ma·ma·tai
diet *diyeta* dee·ye·ta
different *kakaibá* ka·ka·ee·ba
difficult *mahirap* ma·hee·rap
dining car *kainán* ka·ee·nan
dinner *hapunan* ha·poo·nan
direct *diretso* dee·ret·so
direct-dial *dirék-dayal* dee·rek·da·yal
direction *adrés* a·dres
director *direktór* dee·rek·tor
dirty *marumí* ma·roo·mee
disabled *may disabilidád*
   mai dees·a·bee·lee·dad
disco *disko* dees·ko

discount *diskuwento* dees-koo-*wen*-to

discrimination *diskriminasyón*
dees-kree-mee-nas-*yon*

disease *sakít* sa-*keet*

dish (food) *putahe* poo-*ta*-he

disk (CD-ROM) *disk* deesk

disk (floppy) *plopi disk* plo-pee deesk

diving *daybing* dai-beeng

diving equipment
kagamitáng pangdaybing
ka-ga-mee-*tang* pang-*dai*-beeng

divorced *diborsiyado* dee-bor-see-*ya*-do

dizzy *hiló* hee-*lo*

do *gawín/gumawâ (gawín)*
ga-*ween*/goo-ma-*wa* (ga-*ween*)

doctor *doktór* dok-*tor*

documentary *dokumentaryo*
do-koo-men-*tar*-yo

dog *aso* a-so

dole *dol* dol

doll *manika* ma-*nee*-ka

dollar *dolyár* dol-*yar*

door *pintô* peen-*to'*

double *doble* *dob*-le

double bed *dobol bed* do-bol bed

double room *kuwartong pandalawahan*
koo-*war*-tong pan-da-la-*wa*-han

down (location) *sa ibabâ* sa ee-ba-*ba'*

downhill *pababâ* pa-ba-*ba'*

dozen *dosena* do-*se*-na

drama *drama* dra-ma

dream ⓝ *panaginip* pa-na-gee-neep

dress ⓝ *damít* da-*meet*

dried *tuyó* too-*yo'*

dried fruit *tuyóng prutas*
too-*yong* proo-tas

drink *inumin* ee-noo-meen

drink (alcoholic) ⓝ *alak* a-lak

drink ⓥ *inumín/umínom (inóm)*
ee-noo-*meen*/oo-*mee*-nom (ee-*nom*)

drive ⓥ *manehohin/magmaneho (maneho)*
ma-ne-ho-heen/mag-ma-*ne*-ho (ma-*ne*-ho)

drivers licence *lisensiyá sa pagmamaneho*
lee-sen-see-*ya* sa pag-ma-ma-*ne*-ho

drug addiction *adiksiyón sa droga*
a-deek-see-*yon* sa *dro*-ga

drug dealer *diler ng droga*
dee-ler nang *dro*-ga

drug(s) (illicit) *droga* dro-ga

drug trafficking *trápiker ng droga*
tra-pee-ker nang *dro*-ga

drug user *gumagamit ng droga*
goo-ma-*ga*-meet nang *dro*-ga

drugs (illicit) *mga droga* ma-*nga* dro-ga

drum *dram* dram

drunk *lasíng* la-*seeng*

dry ⓐ *tuyô* too-*yo'*

dry (clothes) ⓥ *pinatuyô/magpatuyó
(tuyúin)* pee-na-too-*yo*/mag-pa-too-*yo*
(too-*yoo*-een)

duck *bibi* bee-bee

dummy (pacifier) *dami* da-mee

DVD *DVD* dee-bee-*dee*

E

each *kada* ka-da

ear *tenga* te-nga

early *maaga* ma-*a*-ga

earn *kumita* av koo-*mee*-ta

earplugs *pamasak sa tenga*
pa-*ma*-sak sa *te*-nga

earrings *hikaw* hee-kow

Earth *mundó* moon-*do*

earthquake *lindól* leen-*dol*

east *silangan* see-*la*-ngan

Easter *Semana Santa* se-*ma*-na *san*-ta

easy *madalî* ma-da-*lee'*

eat *kainin/kumain (kain)*
ka-ee-neen/koo-ma-een (ka-*een*)

economy class *ekónomi klas*
e-*ko*-no-mee klas

ecstacy (drug) *ékstasi* eks-ta-see

eczema *eksema* ek-se-ma

education *edukasyón* e-doo-kas-*yon*

egg *itlóg* eet-*log*

eggplant *talóng* ta-*long*

election *eleksiyón* e-lek-see-yon

electrical store *eléktrikal istór*
e-*lek*-tree-kal ees-*tor*

electricity *eléktrisidád* e-lek-tree-see-*dad*

elevator *elebeytor* e-le-*bay*-tor

email *émeyl* e-mayl

embarrassed *nahihiyâ* na-hee-hee-*ya'*

embassy *émbasi* em-ba-see

emergency *emérdyensi* e-mer-jen-see

emotional *emosyonál* e-mos-yo-*nal*

employee *kawaní* ka-wa-*nee*

employer *pinaglílingkurán*
pee-nag-*lee*-leeng-koo-*ran*

empty ⓐ *waláng lamán* wa-*lang* la-man

end ⓝ *katapúsan* ka-ta-*poo*-san

endangered species *nanganganib na urì*
na-nga-*nga*-neeb na oo-*ree'*

engaged *may kásunduang pakákasál*
mai ka-soon-*doo*-ang pa-*ka*-ka-sal

engagement *kásunduang pakákasál*
ka-soon-*doo*-ang pa-*ka*-ka-sal

engine *mákina* *ma*-kee-na

engineer *inhinyero* een-heen-*ye*-ro

engineering *indyiniring* een-jee-*nee*-reeng

England *Inglatera* eeng-gla-*te*-ra
English *Inglés* eeng-*gles*
enjoy (oneself) *magsayá* av mag-sa-*ya*
enough *hustó* hoos-*to*
enter *pinasok/pumasok (pasukin)*
  pee-*na*-sok/poo-*ma*-sok (pa-soo-keen)
entertainment guide
  giya tungkól sa libangan
  gee-ya toong-*kol* sa lee-*ba*-ngan
entry *pasukán* pa-soo-*kan*
envelope *sobre* so-bre
environment *kapaligirán* ka-pa-lee-gee-*ran*
epilepsy *epilepsi* e-pee-*lep*-see
equal opportunity
  pantáy-pantáy na oportunidád
  pan-*tai*-pan-*tai* na o-por-too-nee-*dad*
equality *pagkakápantáy-pantáy*
  pag-ka-ka-pan-*tai*-pan-*tai*
equipment *kagamitán* ka-ga-mee-*tan*
eruption (volcanic) *pagsabog* pag-*sa*-bog
escalator *eskaleytor* es-ka-*luy*-tor
estate agency *ahensiyá ng mga lupaín*
  a-hen-see-ya nang ma-*nga* loo-pa-*een*
euro *yuro* yoo-ro
Europe *Europa* yoo-ro-pa
euthanasia *yutanasya* yoo-ta-*nas*-ya
evening *gabí* ga-bee
every *bawa't* ba-wat
everyone *lahát* la-hat
everything *lahát* la-*hat*
exactly *eksakto* ek-*sak*-to
example *halimbawà* ha-leem-*ba*-wa
excellent *nápakagaling* na-pa-ka-ga-*leeng*
excess (baggage) *sobra* sob-ra
exchange ⓝ *palít* pa-*leet*
exchange ⓥ *ipalit/magpalít (palit)*
  ee-pa-*leet*/mag-pa-*leet* (pa-*leet*)
exchange rate *palitan* pa-*lee*-tan
excluded *di-kasali* dee-ka-sa-lee
exhaust (car) *tambutso* tam-*boot*-so
exhibition *iksibisyón* eek-see-bees-*yon*
exit ⓝ *labasan* la-*ba*-san
expensive *mahál* ma-*hal*
experience ⓝ *karanasán* ka-ra-na-*san*
exploitation *pagsasamantalá*
  pag-sa-sa-man-ta-*la*
express ⓐ *eksprés* eks-pres
(by) express mail *eksprés meyl*
  eks-pres mayl
extension (visa) *ekstensyón*
  eks-tens-yon
eye *matá* ma-ta
eye drops *pampaták sa matá*
  pam-pa-*tak* sa ma-ta
eyes *mga matá* ma-nga ma-*tá*

F

fabric *tela* te-la
face ⓝ *mukhá* mook-*ha'*
face cloth *bimpo* beem-po
factory *pábrika* pab-ree-ka
factory worker *manggagawa sa pábrika*
  mang-ga-ga-wa sa *pab*-ree-ka
fall (autumn) ⓝ *taglagás* tag-la-*gas*
fall (down) ⓥ *nalaglág* pv na-lag-*lag*
family *pamilya* pa-*meel*-ya
family name *apelyido* a-pel-*yee*-do
famous *bantóg* ban-*tog*
fan (machine) *bentiladór* ben-tee-la-*dor*
fan (sport) *mánghahangà*
  mang-ha-ha-nga'
fanbelt *panbelt* pan-belt
far *malayò* ma-*la*-yo'
fare *bayad* ba-yad
farm *sakahán* sa-ka-*han*
farmer *magsasaká* mag-sa-sa-*ka*
fashion *moda* mo-da
fast ⓐ *mabilís* ma-bee-*lees*
fat ⓐ *matabá* ma-ta-*ba'*
father *amá* a-ma
father-in-law *biyanáng lalaki*
  bee-ya-nang la-*la*-kee
faucet *gripo* gree-po
(someone's) fault *kasalanan* ka-sa-*la*-nan
faulty *may sirà* mai see-ra'
fax machine *paks* paks
February *Pebrero* peb-*re*-ro
feed ⓥ *pakainin* pv pa-ka-ee-neen
feel (touch) *hipuin/humipò (hipò)*
  hee-poo-een/hoo-mee-po (hee-po)
feeling (physical) *pakiramdám*
  pa-kee-ram-*dam*
feelings ⓝ *mga pakiramdám*
  ma-*nga* pa-kee-ram-*dam*
female *babae* ba-ba-e
fence *bakod* ba-kod
fencing (sport) *eskrima* es-*kree*-ma
ferry *peri* pe-ree
festival *píyesta* pee-*yes*-ta
fever *lagnát* lag-*nat*
few *ilán* ee-*lan*
fiance *nobyo* nob-yo
fiancee *nobya* nob-ya
fiction *kathá* kat-*ha'*
fig *igos* ee-gos
fight ⓝ *laban* la-ban
Filipino expatriate
  Filipino/a Balik Bayan ⓜ/ⓕ
  pee-lee-*pee*-no/a ba-*leek* bal-yan
Filipino (language) *Filipino* pee-lee-*pee*-no

Filipino (person) *Filipino/a* ⓜ/ⓕ
pee-lee-*pee*-no/a

fill *punuín* pv poo-*noo*-een

fillet *hiwà* *hee*-wa'

film (cinema) *pelíkula* pe-*lee*-koo-la

film (for camera) *pilm* peelm

film speed *ispíd ng pilm*
ees-*peed* nang peelm

filtered *piltrado* peel-*tra*-do

find *hanapin/maghanap (hanapin)*
ha-*na*-peen/mag-*ha*-nap (ha-na-peen)

fine *mabuti* ma-*boo*-tee

fine (penalty) *multá* mool-*ta*

finger *dalirì* da-*lee*-ree'

finish (end) ⓝ *katapusán* ka-ta-poo-*san*

finish ⓥ *tapusin* pv ta-*poo*-seen

Finland *Pinlándiya* peen-*lan*-dee-ya

fire *apóy* a-*poy*

firewood *panggatong* pang-*ga*-tong

first *una* oo-na

first class *pers klas* pers klas

first-aid kit *first aid* pers ayd

fish *isdâ* ees-*da*'

fish monger *mag-iisdâ* mag-ee-ees-*da*'

fishing *pangingisdâ* pa-nge-ngees-*da*'

fish shop *tindahan ng isdâ*
teen-*da*-han nang ees-*da*'

flag ⓝ *bandera* ban-*de*-ra

flannel *pranela* pra-*ne*-la

flashlight *plaslayt* plas-lait

flat ⓐ *plat* plat

flat (apartment) *apartment* a-*part*-ment

flea *pulgás* pool-*gas*

fleamarket *plímarket/palengke*
plee-mar-ket/palengke

flight *playt* plait

flood *bahâ* ba-*ha*'

floor *sahíg* sa-*heeg*

floor (storey) *palapág* pa-la-*pag*

florist *magtitindâ ng bulaklák*
mag-tee-teen-*da* nang boo-lak-*lak*

flour *arina* a-*ree*-na

flower *bulaklák* boo-lak-*lak*

flu *plu trangkaso* ploo

fly ⓥ *lumipád* av loo-mee-*pad*

foggy *maulap* ma-oo-lap

follow *sumundâ* av soo-moo-*nod*

food *pagkain* pag-*ka*-een

food supplies *panustós na pagkain*
pa-noos-*tos* na pag-*ka*-een

foot *paá* pa-*a*

football (soccer) *football* poot-bol

footpath *daanán ng tao*
da-a-*nan* nang ta-*o*

foreign *banyagà* ban-ya-*ga*'

forest *gubat* goo-bat

forever *magpakailanmán*
mag-pa-ka-ee-lan-*man*

forget *kalimutan* pv ka-lee-*moo*-tan

forgive *patawarin* pv pa-ta-*wa*-reen

fork *tinidór* tee-nee-*dor*

fortnight *dalawáng linggó*
da-la-*wang* leeng-go

fortune teller *manghuhulà*
mang-hoo-*hoo*-la'

foul (sport) *foul* powl

foyer *labi* la-*bee*

fragile *delikado* de-lee-*ka*-do

France *Pránsiya* pran-see-ya

free (available) *libre* *lee*-bre

free (gratis) *libre* lee-bre

free (not bound) *malayà* ma-la-ya'

freeze (up) *magyelo* av mag-ye-lo

freeze (something) *pinagyeluhin* pv
pee-nag-ye-lo-heen

fresh *sariwà* sa-*ree*-wa

Friday *Biyernes* bee-yer-nes

fridge *rep repridyeretor* rep

fried *pinirito* pee-nee-*ree*-to

friend *kaibigan* ka-ee-bee-gan

from *mulâ* moo-*la*'

frost *namuóng hamóg* na-moo-*ong* ha-*mog*

frozen *nagyelo* nag-ye-lo

fruit *prutas* proo-tas

fruit picking *pamimitás ng prutas*
pa-mee-mee-*tas* nang *proo*-tas

fry ⓥ *iprito/pumiríto (prito)*
ee-*pree*-to/poo-mee-*ree*-to (*pree*-to)

frying pan *kawalî* ka-wa-lee'

full *punô* poo-no'

full-time *full-time* pool-taim

fun *masayá* ma-sa-ya

funeral *libing* lee-beeng

funny *nakatátawá* na-ka-*ta*-ta-wa

furniture *muwebles* moo-*web*-les

future *kinabukasan* kee-na-boo-*ka*-san

G

game (match) *geym* gaym

game (sport) *larô* la-*ro*'

garage *garahe* ga-*ra*-he

garbage *basura* ba-soo-ra

garbage can *básurahán* ba-soo-ra-han

garden *garden* gar-den

gardener *hardinero* har-dee-*ne*-ro

gardening *paggagarden* pag-ga-*gar*-den

garlic *bawang* ba-wang

gas (for cooking) *gas* gas

gas (petrol) *gasolina* ga-so-*lee*-na

gas cartridge *tangké ng gaás*
tang-*ke* nang gas

gastroenteritis *pagtataé* pag·ta·ta·*e*
gate (airport, etc) *geyt* gayt
gauze *gasa* ga·sa
gay *baklâ* bak·*la*
Germany *Alemanya* a·le·*man*·ya
get *kinuha/kumuha (kunin)*
  kee·*noo*·ha/koo·*moo*·ha (*koo*·neen)
get off (a train) *bumabâ* av boo·ma·*ba'*
gift *regalo* re·ga·lo
gig *palabás* pa·la·*bas*
gin *dyin* jeen
girl *batang babae* ba·tang ba·ba·e
girlfriend *nobya* nob·ya
give *ibigay/magbigáy (bigyan)*
  ee·bee·*gai*/mag·bee·*gai* (*beeg*·yan)
glandular fever *glándiyular piber*
  glan·dee·yoo·lar pee·ber
glass ⓝ *baso* ba·so
glasses (spectacles) *salamín* sa·la·*min*
glove(s) *guwantes* goo·*wan*·tes
glue *pandikit* pan·dee·*keet*
go *umalís* av oo·ma·*lees*
goal *gol* gol
goalkeeper *golkiper* gol·*kee*·per
goat *kambing* kam·*beeng*
god (general) *diyós* dee·*yos*
godfather *ninong* nee·nong
godmother *ninang* nee·nang
goggles *mga gogel* ma·*nga* go·gel
gold *gintô* geen·*to'*
golf ball *golp bol* golp bol
golf course *golp kors* golp kors
good *mabuti* ma·*boo*·tee
Good Friday *Biyernes Santo*
  bee·*yer*·nes *san*·to
goodbye *babay* ba·bai
go out *lumabás* av loo·ma·*bas*
go out with *makipag-déyt* av
  ma·kee·pag·*dayt*
go shopping *mamilí* av ma·mee·*lee*
government *gobyerno* gob·*yer*·no
gram *gramo* gra·mo
grandchild *apó* a·*po*
grandfather *lolo* lo·lo
grandmother *lola* lo·la
grapefruit *suhà* soo·*ha'*
grapes *ubas* oo·bas
grass *damó* da·*mo*
grateful *nagpapasalamat*
  nag·pa·pa·sa·*la*·mat
grave ⓝ *puntód* poon·*tod*
gray *kulay abó* koo·lai a·bo
great (fantastic) *magaling* ma·ga·*leeng*
green *berde* ber·de
greengrocer *tindera/o* ⓜ/ⓕ teen·*de*·ra/o
grey *kulay abó* koo·lai a·bo

grocery *groseryá* gro·ser·ya
groundnut *nuwés* noo·wes
grow *tumubò* av too·moo·bo'
g-string *g-istríng* jee·ees·treeng
guaranteed *garántisado* ga·ran·tee·sa·do
guess ⓥ *hulaan/humulà (hulaan)*
  hoo·*la*·an/hoo·moo·*la* (hoo·*la*·an)
guesthouse *bahay-bisita* ba·hai bee·*see*·ta
guide *giya* gee·ya
guide dog *asong taga-akay ng bulág*
  a·song ta·ga·*a*·kai nang boo·*lag*
guidebook *giyang libró* gee·yang lee·bro
guided tour *may giyang tur*
  mai *gee*·yang toor
guilty *maysala* mai·sa·la
guitar *gitara* gee·*ta*·ra
gum *gilagid* gee·*la*·geed
gun *baríl* ba·*reel*
gym (place) *dyim* jeem
gymnastics *dyimnastiks* jeem·*nas*·teeks
gynaecologist *ginokolohista*
  gee·no·ko·lo·*hees*·ta

H

hair *buhók* boo·hok
hairbrush *bras ng buhók* bras nang boo·*hok*
haircut *gupít* goo·*peet*
hairdresser *mangungulot*
  ma·ngoo·ngoo·lot
halal *halál* ha·*lal*
half *kalahatì* ka·la·*ha*·tee'
hallucination *guniguní* goo·nee·goo·*nee*
ham *hamón* ha·mon
hammer *martilyo* mar·*teel*·yo
hammock *duyan* doo·yan
hand *kamáy* ka·mai
handbag *hanbag* han·bag
handball *hanbol* han·bol
handicrafts *mga yaring-kamáy*
  ma·*nga* ya·reeng ka·*mai*
handkerchief *panyó* pan·*yo'*
handlebars *hawakán* ha·wa·*kan*
handmade *yaring-kamáy* ya·reeng ka·*mai*
handsome *guwapo* goo·*wa*·po
happy *masayá* ma·sa·ya
harassment *panliligalig* pan·lee·lee·*ga*·leeg
harbour *puwerto* poo·*wer*·to
hard (not soft) *matigás* ma·tee·*gas*
hard-boiled *nilagâ* nee·la·ga'
hardware store *hardwer istór*
  hard·wer ees·*tor*
hash *has* has
hat *sombrero* som·*bre*·ro
have *mayroón* av mai·ro·*on*

have a cold *may sipón* av mai see·pon
have fun *magsayá* av mag·sa·ya
hay fever *sipón* see·pon
hazelnut *héyselnat* hay·sel·nat
he *siyá* see·ya
head ⓝ *ulo* oo·lo
headache *sakit ng ulo* sa·keet nang oo·lo
headlights *ilaw sa unahán*
ee·low sa oo·na·han
health *kalusugan* ka·loo·soo·gan
hear *márinig* pv ma·ree·neeg
hearing aid *hiring eyd* hee·reeng ayd
heart *pusô* poo·so'
heart attack *atake sa pusô* a·ta·ke sa poo·so'
heart condition *kondisyón sa pusô*
kon·dees·yon sa poo·so'
heat *init* ee·neet
heated *pinainitan* pee·na·ee·nee·tan
heater *pampainit* pam·pa·ee·neet
heating *pampainit* pam·pa·ee·neet
heavy *mabigát* ma·bee·gat
helmet *helmet* hel·met
help ⓝ *tulong* too·long
help ⓥ *tulungan/tumulong (tulong)*
too·loo·ngan/too·moo·long
(too·loong)
Help! *saklolo* sak·lo·lo
hepatitis *hepataytis* he·pa·tai·tees
her *siyá* see·ya
herb *damó* da·mo
herbalist *albularyo* al·boo·lar·yo
here *dito* dee·to
heroin *héroin* he·ro·ween
herring *hering* he·reeng
hers *kanyá* kan·ya
high *mataás* ma·ta·as
high school *mataás na páaralán*
ma·ta·as na pa·a·ra·lan
highchair *silyang pambatà*
seel·yang pam·ba·ta'
highway *haywey* hai·way
hike *maglakád nang mahabà* av
mag·la·kad nang ma·ha·ba'
hiking *paglalakád nang mahabà*
pag·la·la·kad nang ma·ha·ba'
hiking boots
botang panlakad nang mahabà
bo·tang pan·la·kad nang ma·ha·ba'
hiking route
daán sa paglalakád nang mahabà
da·an sa pag·la·la·kad nang ma·ha·ba'
hill *buról* boo·rol
him *siyá* see·ya
Hindu *Hindu* heen·doo
hire *arkilahín/umarkilá (arkilá)*
ar·kee·la·heen/oo·mar·kee·la (ar·kee·la)

his *kanyá* kan·ya
historical *istóriko* ees·to·ree·ko
history *istorya* ees·tor·ya
hitchhike *umangkás* av oo·mang·kas
HIV *HIV* ayts·ai·bee
hockey *haki* ha·kee
holiday *hálidey* ha·lee·day
holidays *bakasyón* ba·kas·yon
Holy Week *Semana Santa*
se·ma·na san·ta
home *tahanan* ta·ha·nan
homeless *waláng tahanan*
wa·lang ta·ha·nan
homemaker *maybahay* mai·ba·hai
homeopathy *homeópati*
ho·me·yo·pa·tee
homosexual *baklâ* bak·la'
honey *pulót-pukyutan*
poo·lot pook·yoo·tan
honeymoon *pulót-gatâ* poo·lot·ga·ta'
horoscope *hóroskop* ho·ros·kop
horse *kabayo* ka·ba·yo
horse riding *pangangabayo*
pa·nga·nga·ba·yo
hospital *ospitál* os·pee·tal
hospitality *kagandahang-loób*
ka·gan·da·hang·lo·ob
hostage *bihag* bee·hag
hot *mainit* ma·ee·neet
hot water *mainit na tubig*
ma·ee·neet na too·beeg
hotel *otél* o·tel
hour *oras* o·ras
house *bahay* ba·hai
housework *gawaing bahay*
ga·wa·eeng ba·hai
how *paano* pa·a·no
how much *magkano* mag·ka·no
hug ⓥ *yakapin/yumakap (yakapin)*
ya·ka·peen/yoo·ma·kap (ya·kap)
huge *malakí* ma·la·kee
human resources *mga manggagawa*
ma·nga mang·ga·ga·wa
human rights *karapatáng pantao*
ka·ra·pa·tang pan·ta·o
humanities *hiyumánitis*
hee·yoo·ma·nee·tees
hundred *sandáán* san·da·an
hungry (to be) *magutom* ma·goo·tom
hunting *pamamaríl* pa·ma·ma·reel
hurt (someone) *saktan/masaktan (saktan)*
sak·tan/ma·sak·tan (sak·tan)
hurt (feel pain) *masakit* ma·sa·keet
husband *asawa* a·sa·wa

I

I *akó* a-ko
ice *yelo* ye-lo
ice axe *ayspik* ais-peek
ice cream *sorbetes* sor-be-tes
ice hockey *ays haki* ais ha-kee
ice-cream parlour *tindahan ng sorbetes*
teen-da-han nang sor-be-tes
identification *ID* ai-dee
identification card (ID) *ID* ai-dee
idiot *tangá* ta-nga
if *kung* koong
ill *maysakit* mai-sa-keet
immigration *imigrasyón* ee-mee-gras-yon
important *importante* eem-por-tan-te
impossible *di-maáari* dee-ma-a-a-ree
in *sa* sa
in a hurry *nagmámadalî* nag-ma-ma-da-lee'
in front of *sa harapán ng*
sa ha-ra-pan nang
included *kasali* ka-sa-lee
income tax *buwís* boo-wees
India *Índiya* een-dee-ya
indicator *nagpapakita* nag-pa-pa-kee-ta
indigestion *masamáng sikmurà*
ma-sa-mang seek-moo-ra'
Indonesia *Indonesia* een-do-ne-sya
indoor *sa loób* sa lo-ob
industry *indústriya* een-doos-tree-ya
infection *impeksiyón* eem-pek-see-yon
inflammation *pamamagâ* pa-ma-ma-ga'
influenza *plu/trangkaso* ploo/trang-ka-so
information *impormasyón*
eem-por-mas-yon
ingredient *halò* ha-lo'
inject *iniksiyunán/mag-iniksiyun*
(iniksiyunán) ee-neek-see-yoo-nan/
mag-ee-neek-see-yon
(ee-neek-see-yoo-nan)
injection *iniksiyón* ee-neek-see-yon
injured *nasaktán* na-sak-tan
injury *nasugatan* na-soo-ga-tan
inner tube *panloób na tubo*
pan-lo-ob na too-bo
innocent *inosente* ee-no-sen-te
inside *sa loób* sa lo-ob
instructor *titser* teet-ser
insurance *seguro* se-goo-ro
interesting *kawili-wili* ka-wee-lee-wee-lee
intermission *intermisyon* een-ter-mees-yon
international *internasyonál*
een-ter-nas-yo-nal
Internet *ínternet* een-ter-net
Internet café *ínternet kapé* een-ter-net ka-pe

interpreter *tagapagsalin sa wikà*
taga-pag-sa-leen sa wee-ka'
interview *ínterbyu* een-ter-byoo
invite *imbitahín* pv eem-bee-ta-heen
Ireland *Irlándiya* eer-lan-dee-ya
iron (for clothes) *plantsa* plant-sa
island *ísla* ees-la
Israel *Ísrael* ees-ra-el
it (that) *iyón* ee-yon
IT *IT* ai-tee
Italy *Italya* ee-tal-ya
itch *katí* ka-tee
itemised *nakalistá* na-ka-lees-ta
itinerary *taymteybol* taim-te-bol
IUD *IUD* ai-yoo-dee

J

jacket *dyaket* ja-ket
jail *preso* pre-so
jam *diyam* jam
January *Enero* e-ne-ro
Japan *Hapón* ha-pon
jar *garapón* ga-ra-pon
jaw *pangá* pa-nga
jealous *seloso/a* ⑩/① se-lo-so/a
jeans *dyins* jeens
jeep *dyip* jeep
jet lag *dyet lag* jet lag
jewellery *alahas* a-la-has
Jewish *Hudyó* hood-yo
job *trabaho* tra-ba-ho
jogging *dyaging* ja-geeng
joke *birò* bee-ro'
journalist *diyornalista* jor-na-lees-ta
journey *paglalakbáy* pag-la-lak-bai
judge *hukóm* hoo-kom
juice *katás* ka-tas
July *Hulyo* hool-yo
jump ⑦ *lundagín/lumundág (lundág)*
loon-dag-een/loo-moon-dag
(loon-dag)
jumper (sweater) *suwíter* soo-wee-ter
jumper leads *dyamper lids* jam-per leeds
June *Hunyo* hoon-yo

K

ketchup *ketsap* ket-sap
key *susì* soo-see'
keyboard *kíbord* kee-bord
kick *sipà* see-pa'
kidnap *kidnap* keed-nap
kidnapping *kídnaping* keed-na-peeng

kidney *batô* ba·to
kilo *kilo* kee·lo
kilogram *kilo* kee·lo
kilometre *kilometro* kee·lo·me·tro
kind (nice) *mabaít* ma·ba·eet
kindergarten *kinder* keen·der
king *harí* ha·ree'
kiosk *tindahan* teen·da·han
kiss ⓝ *halík* ha·leek
kiss ⓥ *halikán* ha·lee·kan
kitchen *kusinà* koo·see·na'
kiwifruit *kíwiprut* kee·wee·proot
knee *tuhod* too·hod
knife *kutsilyo* koot·seel·yo
know *alám* pv a·lam
kosher *kosyer* kos·yer

L

labourer *trabahadór* tra·ba·ha·dor
lace *leys* lays
lake *lawà* la·wa'
lamb *tupa* too·pa
land ⓝ *lupà* loo·pa'
landlady *kasera* ka·se·ra
landlord *kasero* ka·se·ro
language *wikà* wee·ka'
laptop *laptap* lap·tap
large *malakí* ma·la·kee
last (previous) *nakaraán* na·ka·ra·an
last (week) *nakaraán* na·ka·ra·an
late *hulí* hoo·lee
later *mámayâ* ma·ma·ya'
laugh *halakhakán/humalakhák (halakhák)* ha·lak·ha·kan/hoo·ma·lak·hak (ha·lak·hak)
launderette *londri* lon·dree
laundry (clothes) *lálabhan* la·lab·han
laundry (place) *londri* lon·dree
laundry (room) *pálabahan* pa·la·ba·han
lava *laba* la·ba
law *batás* ba·tas
law (field) *abogasyá* a·bo·gas·ya
lawyer *abogado* a·bo·ga·do
laxative *pampalusaw* pam·pa·loo·saw
lazy *tamád* ta·mad
leader *lider* lee·der
leaf *dahon* da·hon
learn *matuto* av ma·too·to
leather *katad* ka·tad
lecturer *titser* teet·ser
ledge *pasimano* pa·see·ma·no
leek *lik* leek
left (direction) *kaliwâ* ka·lee·wa'
left luggage *naiwang bagahe* na·ee·wang ba·ga·he

left luggage (office) *upisina ng naiwang bagahe* oo·pee·see·na nang na·ee·wang ba·ga·he
left-wing *lepwing* lepweeng
leg *bintí* been·tee'
legal *legál* le·gal
legislation *batás* ba·tas
legume *gulay na butó* goo·lai na boo·to
lemon *limón* lee·mon
lemonade *limonada* lee·mo·na·da
lens *lens* lens
lentil *lentil* len·teel
lesbian *tomboy* tom·boy
less *kakauntí* ka·ka·oon·tee'
letter (mail) *sulat* soo·lat
lettuce *letsugas* let·soo·gas
liar *sinungaling* see·noo·nga·leeng
library *aklatan* ak·la·tan
lice *kuto* koo·to
licence *lisénsiya* lee·sen·see·ya
license plate number *número ng lisensiya* noo·me·ro nang lee·sen·see·ya
lie (not stand) *humigâ* av hoo·mee·ga'
life *buhay* boo·hai
life jacket *layp dyaket* laip ja·ket
lift (elevator) *elebeytor* e·le·bay·tor
light *ilaw* ee·low
light (not heavy) *magaán* ma·ga·an
light (of colour) *murà* moo·ra'
light bulb *bombilya* bom·beel·ya
light meter *layt miter* lait mee·ter
lighter *pansindí* pan·seen·dee
lighter (cigarette) *layter* lai·ter
like ⓥ *gustó/magustuhán (gustó)* goos·to/ma·goos·too·han (goos·to)
lime (fruit) *dayap* da·yap
linen (material) *linen* lee·nen
linen (sheets) *mga kumot* ma·nga koo·mot
lip balm *lip bam* leep bam
lips *labì* la·bee'
lipstick *lipistik* lee·pees·teek
liquor store *tindahan ng alak* teen·da·han nang a·lak
listen (to) *makinig (sa)* av ma·kee·neeg (sa)
little *maliít* ma·lee·eet
little (not much) *kauntí* ka·oon·tee'
live (somewhere) *tumirá* av too·mee·ra
liver *atáy* a·tai
lizard *butikí* boo·tee·kee'
local *lokal* lo·kal
lock ⓝ *kandado* kan·da·do
lock ⓥ *kandaduhan/magkandado (kandado)* kan·da·doo·han/ mag·kan·da·do (kan·da·do)
locked *nakakandado* na·ka·kan·da·do
lollies *kendi* ken·dee
long *mahabà* ma·ha·ba'

look *tingnán* pv teeng·*nan*
look after *alagaan* pv a·la·*ga*·an
look for *hanapin* pv ha·*na*·peen
lookout ⓝ *tanawan* ta·*na*·wan
loose *maluwág* ma·loo·*wag*
loose change *baryá* bar·*ya*
lose ⓥ *mawalá* ma·wa·*la'*
lost *nawalá* na·wa·*la'*
lost property office *upisina ng nawaláng ari-arian* oo·pee·*see*·na nang na·wa·*lang* a·ree·a·*ree*·an
a lot (ang) *dami* (ang) *da*·mee
loud *malakás* ma·la·*kas*
love ⓝ *pagmamahál* pag·ma·ma·*hal*
love ⓥ *mahál/magmahál (mahál)* ma·*hal*/mag·ma·*hal* (ma·*hal*)
lover *nagmamahál* nag·ma·ma·*hal*
low *mababà* ma·ba·*ba'*
lubricant *lubrikante* loo·bree·*kan*·te
luck *suwerte* soo·*wer*·te
lucky *masuwerte* ma·soo·*wer*·te
luggage *bagahe* ba·*ga*·he
luggage lockers *mga laker ng bagahe* ma·*nga* la·ker nang ba·*ga*·he
luggage tag *tag ng bagahe* tag nang ba·*ga*·he
lump *umbók* oom·*bok*
lunch *tanghalian* tang·ha·*lee*·an
lung *bagá* ba·*ga'*
luxury ⓝ *pang-mayaman* pang·ma·*ya*·man

M

machine *mákina* ma·*kee*·na
magazine *mágasin* ma·ga·seen
mail (letters) *sulat* soo·lat
mail (postal system) *koreó* ko·re·o
mailbox *hulugán ng sulat* hoo·loo·*gan* nang soo·lat
main *pinakaimportante* pee·na·ka·eem·por·*tan*·te
main road *haywey* hai·way
make-up *meyk ap* mayk ap
Malaysia *Malaysia* ma·*lays*·ya
mammogram *mámogram* ma·mo·gram
man (male) *lalaki* la·*la*·kee
manager *mánedyer* ma·ned·yer
manager (restaurant, hotel) *mánedyer* ma·ned·yer
mandarin *dalandán* da·lan·*dan*
mango *manggá* mang·*ga*
manual worker *manwál na trabahadór* man·*wal* na tra·ba·ha·*dor*
many *marami* ma·*ra*·mee
map *mapa* ma·pa

March *Marso* mar·so
margarine *mantekilya* man·te·*keel*·ya
marijuana *marihuwana* ma·ree·hoo·*wa*·na
marital status *estado* es·*ta*·do
market *palengke* pa·*leng*·ke
marmalade *mármaleyd* mar·ma·layd
marriage *kasál* ka·*sal*
married *kasál* ka·*sal*
marry *ikasál* ee·ka·*sal*
martial arts *marsyal art* mars·yal art
mass (Catholic) *misa* *mee*·sa
massage *masahe* ma·*sa*·he
masseur/masseuse *masahista* ma·sa·*hees*·ta
mat *baníg* ba·*neeg*
match (sports) *geym* gaym
matches (for lighting) *póspóro* *pos*·po·ro
mattress *kutsón* koot·*son*
May *Mayo* *ma*·yo
maybe *bakâ* ba·*ka'*
mayonnaise *mayonesa* ma·yo·*ne*·sa
mayor *meyor* me·yor
me *ako* a·*ko*
meal *pagkain* pag·*ka*·een
measles *tigdás* teeg·*das*
meat *karné* kar·*ne*
mechanic *mekániko* me·*ka*·nee·ko
media *midya* *meed*·ya
medicine (medication) *medikasyón* me·dee·kas·*yon*
medicine (study, profession) *medisina* me·*dee*·see·na
meditation *meditasyón* me·dee·tas·*yon*
meet *magkita* mag·*kee*·ta
melon *milón* mee·*lon*
member *miyembro* mee·*yem*·bro
menstruation *regla* *reg*·la
menu *menú* me·*noo*
message *mensahe* men·*sa*·he
metal ⓐ *metál* me·*tal*
metre *metro* *met*·ro
metro (train) *metro tren* *met*·ro tren
metro station *istasyón ng metro* ees·tas·*yon* nang *met*·ro
microwave (oven) *máykroweyb* mai·kro·wayb
midday *tanghaling tapát* tang·ha·leeng ta·*pat*
midnight *hatinggabí* ha·teeng·ga·*bee*
migraine *maygreyn* mai·grayn
military ⓝ *militár* mee·lee·*tar*
military base *himpilan ng militár* heem·*pee*·lan nang mee·lee·*tar*
military service *serbisyong militár* ser·*bees*·yong mee·lee·*tar*
milk *gatas* *ga*·tas
millimetre *milimetro* mee·lee·*met*·ro

million *milyón* meel·*yon*
mince ⓝ *giniling* gee·nee·leeng
mine *akin* a·keen
mineral water *míneral water*
　mee·ne·ral wo·ter
minute *minuto* mee·noo·to
mirror *salamín* sa·la·*meen*
miscarriage *pagkakunan* pag·ka·koo·nan
miss (feel absence of) pv *namí-miss*
　na·*mee*·mees
mistake *pagkakámalì* pag·ka·ka·ma·*lee'*
mix ⓝ *halò* ha·lo'
mobile phone *mobayl pon* mo·bail pon
modem *modem* mo·dem
modern *moderno* mo·der·no
moisturiser *pampalambót* pam·pa·lam·bot
monastery *monasteryo* mo·nas·*ter*·yo
Monday *Lunes* loo·nes
money *pera* pe·ra
monk *monghe* mong·he
month *buwán* boo·wan
monument *monumento* mo·noo·men·to
moon *buwán* boo·wan
more *higit pa* hee·geet pa
morning *umaga* oo·ma·ga
morning sickness *pagsusuká*
　pag·soo·soo·ka
mosque *mosk* mosk
mosquito *lamók* la·mok
mosquito coil *katól* ka·tol
mosquito net *kulambô* koo·lam·bo'
motel *motél* mo·tel
mother *iná* ee·na
mother-in-law *biyanáng babae*
　bee·ya·*nang* ba·ba·e
motorbike *motorsiklo* mo·tor·seek·lo
motorboat *mótorbowt* mo·tor·boht
motorcycle *motorsiklo* mo·tor·seek·lo
motorway (tollway) *mótorway* mo·tor·way
mountain *bundók* boon·dok
mountain bike *bisikletang pambundók*
　bee·seek·le·tang pam·boon·dok
mountain path *landás sa bundók*
　lan·das sa boon·dok
mountain range *mga bundók*
　ma·nga boon·dok
mountaineering *pamumundók*
　pa·moo·moon·dok
mouse *bubuwít* boo·boo·weet
mouth *bibíg* bee·beeg
movie *pelíkula* pe·lee·koo·la
Mr *Ginoó* gee·no·o
Mrs *Ginang* gee·nang
Ms; Miss *Binibini* bee·nee·bee·nee
mud *putik* poo·teek
mudslide *agos ng putik* a·gos nang poo·teek

muesli *musli* moos·lee
mum *iná* ee·na
mumps *bekè* be·ke'
murder ⓝ *pagpatáy sa tao* pag·pa·*tai* sa ta·o
muscle *masel* ma·sel
museum *museo* moo·se·o
mushroom *kabuté* ka·boo·te
music *músika* moo·see·ka
music shop *tindahan ng músika*
　teen·da·han nang moo·see·ka
musician *musikero* moo·see·ke·ro
Muslim *Muslím* moos·leem
mussel *paros* pa·ros
mustard *mustasa* moos·ta·sa
mute *pipi* pee·pee
my *akin* a·keen

N

nail clippers *panggupít ng kukó*
　pang·goo·peet nang koo·ko
name *pangalan* pa·nga·lan
napkin *napkin* nap·keen
nappy *lampín* lam·peen
nappy rash *singáw dahil sa lampín*
　see·ngow da·heel sa lam·peen
national park *parkeng nasyonál*
　par·keng nas·yo·nal
nationality *nasyonalidád* nas·yo·na·lee·dad
nature *kalikasan* ka·lee·ka·san
naturopathy *natuyoropatí*
　na·too·yo·ro·pa·tee
nausea *pagkaliyó* pag·ka·lee·yo
near *malapit* ma·la·peet
nearby *malapit* ma·la·peet
nearest *pinakamalapit*
　pee·na·ka·ma·la·peet
necessary *kailangan* ka·ee·la·ngan
necklace *kuwintás* koo·ween·tas
nectarine *néktarin* nek·ta·reen
need *kailangan* pv ka·ee·la·ngan
needle (sewing) *karayom* ka·ra·yom
needle (syringe) *heringgilya*
　he·reeng·geel·ya
negative *negatibo* ne·ga·i·bo
neither *alinmán ay hindî* a·leen·man ai
　heen·dee'
net *net* net
Netherlands *Olanda* o·lan·da
never *hindî kailanmán* heen·dee
　ka·ee·lan·man
new *bago* ba·go
New Year's Day *Bagong Taón* ba·gong ta·on
New Year's Eve *Bisperás ng Bagong Taón*
　bees·pe·ras nang ba·gong ta·on

New Zealand *New Zealand* nyoo see-land
news *balità* ba-lee-ta'
newsagency *tindahan ng páhayagán*
  teen-*da*-han nang pa-ha-ya-gan
newspaper *diyaryo* dee-yar-yo
newsstand *tindahan ng páhayagán*
  teen-*da*-han nang pa-ha-ya-gan
next *sa súsunód na* soo-soo-nod na
next to *katabí ng* ka-ta-bee nang
nice *mabuti* ma-boo-tee
nickname *palayaw* pa-la-yow
night *gabí* ga-bee
night out *paglabás sa gabí*
  pag-la-bas sa ga-bee
nightclub *naytklab* nait-klab
no *walâ* wa-la'
no vacancy *waláng bakante*
  wa-lang ba-kan-te
noisy *maingay* ma-ee-ngai
none *walâ* wa-la'
non-smoking *waláng manínigarilyó*
  wa-lang ma-nee-nee-ga-reel-yo
noodles *nudels* noo-dels
noon *tanghali* tang-ha-lee'
north *hilagà* hee-la-ga'
Norway *Norway* nor-way
nose *ilóng* ee-long
not *hindî* heen-dee'
notebook *notbuk* not-book
nothing *walâ* wa-la'
November *Nobyembre* nob-yem-bre
now *ngayón* nga-yon
nuclear energy *enerhiyáng nukliyár*
  e-ner-hee-yang nook-lee-yar
nuclear testing *na nukliyár* tes-teeng
  na nook-lee-yar
nuclear waste *aksayáng nukliyár* ak-sa-yang
  nook-lee-yar
number *número* noo-me-ro
numberplate *número ng plaka*
  noo-me-ro nang pla-ka
nun *madre* ma-dre
nurse *nars* nars
nut *nuwés* noo-wes

O

oats *owts* ohts
ocean *dagat* da-gat
October *Oktubre* ok-too-bre
off (spoiled) *paní s* pa-nees
office *upisina* oo-pee-see-na
office worker *kawaní sa upisina*
  ka-wa-nee sa oo-pee-see-na
often *madalás* ma-da-las

oil (cooking) *mantikà* man-tee-ka
oil (petrol) *langís* la-ngees
old *matandâ* ma-tan-da'
olive *oliba* o-lee-ba
olive oil *langís ng oliba*
  la-ngees nang o-lee-ba
Olympic Games *Olimpik Geyms*
  o-leem-peek gayms
omelette *torta* tor-ta
on *sa ibabaw* sa ee-ba-bow
on time *nasa oras* na-sa o-ras
once *minsan* meen-san
one *isá* ee-sa
one-way (ticket) *wanwey* wan-way
onion *sibuyas* see-boo-yas
only *lang* lang
open ⓥ *ibukás* pv ee-boo-kas
open ⓐ *bukás* boo-kas
opening hours *oras ng bukasan*
  o-ras nang boo-ka-san
opera *ópera* o-pe-ra
opera house *ópera haus* o-pe-ra hows
operation *operasyón* o-pe-ras-yon
operator *opereytor* o-pe-ray-tor
opinion *opinyón* o-peen-yon
opposite *katapát* ka-ta-pat
optometrist *óptiko* op-tee-ko
or *o* o
orange (fruit) *kahél* ka-hel
orange (colour) *orens* o-rens
orange juice *orens juice* o-rens joos
orchestra *órkestra* or-kes-tra
order ⓝ *order* or-der
order ⓥ *order/magorder (order)*
  or-der/mag-or-der (or-der)
ordinary *ordinaryo* or-dee-nar-yo
orgasm *orgasmo* or-gas-mo
original *orihinál* o-ree-hee-nal
other *ibá* ee-ba
our *namin* na-meen
ours *amin* a-meen
out of order *sirâ* see-ra'
outside *sa labás* sa la-bas
ovarian cyst *sis sa obaryo* sees sa o-bar-yo
ovary *obaryo* o-bar-yo
oven *pugón* poo-gon
overcoat *óberkot* o-ber-kot
overdose *sobrang dosis* sob-rang do-sees
overnight *magdamág* mag-da-mag
overseas *ibáng bansâ* ee-bang ban-sa'
owe *utang* oo-tang
owner *may-arì* mai-a-ree
oxygen *oksiheno* ok-see-he-no
oyster *talabá* ta-la-ba
ozone layer *oson leyer* o-son le-yer

P

pacemaker *péysmeyker* pays·may·ker
pacifier (dummy) *pasipayer* pa·see·pa·yer
package *pakete* pa·ke·te
packet *pakete* pa·ke·te
padlock *kandado* kan·da·do
page *páhina* pa·hee·na
pain *sakít* sa·keet
painful *masakít* ma·sa·keet
painkiller *pang-alís na sakít* pang·a·lees nang sa·keet
painter *pintór* peen·tor
painting (a work) *pintura* peen·too·ra
painting (the art) *pagpipintá* pag·pee·peen·ta
pair (couple) *pareha* pa·re·ha
Pakistan *Pakistán* pa·kees·tan
palace *palasyo* pa·las·yo
pan *pan* pan
pants (trousers) *pantalón* pan·ta·lon
panty liners *pasadór* pa·sa·dor
pantyhose *pántihos* pan·tee·hos
Papa New Guinea *Papa New Guinea* pa·pa nyoo gee·nee
papaya *papaya* pa·pa·ya
pap smear *pap ismír* pap ees·meer
paper *papél* pa·pel
paperwork *papeles* pa·pe·les
paraplegic *paraplidyik* pa·ra·plee·jeek
parcel *pakete* pa·ke·te
parents *magulang* ma·goo·lang
park *parke* par·ke
park (a car) *iparada/pumarada (parada)* ee·pa·ra·da/poo·ma·ra·da (pa·ra·da)
parliament *parlyamento* parl·ya·men·to
part (component) *bahagi* ba·ha·gee
part-time *partaym* par·taim
party (night out) *parti* par·tee
party (politics) *partido* par·tee·do
pass (ticket) Ⓝ *tiket* tee·ket
passenger *pasahero* pa·sa·he·ro
passionfruit *pásyonprut* pas·yon·proot
passport *pasaporte* pa·sa·por·te
passport number *número ng pasaporte* noo·me·ro nang pa·sa·por·te
past *nakaraán* na·ka·ra·an
pasta *pasta* pas·ta
pastry *pasteleryá* pas·te·ler·ya
path *landás* lan·das
pay Ⓝ *suweldo* soo·wel·do
payment *bayad* ba·yad
pea *gisantes* gee·san·tes
peace *katahimikan* ka·ta·hee·mee·kan
peach *pits* peets

peak (mountain) *tuktók* took·tok
peanut *manê* ma·ne'
pear *peras* pe·ras
pedal Ⓝ *pedál* pe·dal
pedestrian *taong naglálakád* ta·ong nag·la·la·kad
pen (ballpoint) *bolpen* bol·pen
pencil *lapis* la·pees
penis *ari ng lalaki* a·ree nang la·la·kee
penknife *korta-pluma* kor·ta·ploo·ma
pensioner *pensyonado/a* Ⓜ/Ⓕ pens·yo·na·do/a
people *mga tao* ma·nga ta·o
pepper (black) *pamintá* pa·meen·ta
pepper (bell) *bel peper* bel pe·per
per cent *porsiyento* por·see·yen·to
perfect *perpekto* per·pek·to
performance *palabás* pa·la·bas
perfume *pabangó* pa·ba·ngo
period pain *dismenoryá* dees·me·nor·ya
permission *permiso* per·mee·so
permit Ⓝ *permiso* per·mee·so
person *tao* ta·o
petition *petisyón* pe·tees·yon
petrol *gasolina* ga·so·lee·na
petrol station *istasyón ng gasolina* ees·tas·yon nang ga·so·lee·na
pharmacist *parmasyotiko/a* Ⓜ/Ⓕ par·ma·syo·ti·ko/a
pharmacy *botika* bo·tee·ka
phone book *ponbuk* pon·book
phone box *pon baks* pon baks
phone card *pon kard* pon kard
photo *litrato* leet·ra·to
photographer *litratista* leet·ra·tees·ta
photography *potograpiya* po·to·gra·pee·ya
phrasebook *buk ng prase* book nang pra·se
pickaxe *piko* pee·ko
pickles *atsara* at·sa·ra
pickpocket *nagnanakaw* nag·na·na·kaw
picnic *piknik* peek·neek
pie *pay* pai
piece *piraso* pee·ra·so
pig *baboy* ba·boy
pill *píldora* peel·do·ra
(the) Pill *pil* peel
pillow *unan* oo·nan
pillowcase *pundá* poon·da
pineapple *pinyá* peen·ya
pink *kulay rosas* koo·lai ro·sas
pistachio *pistasyo* pees·tas·yo
place *lugár* loo·gar
place of birth *lugár ng kapanganakan* loo·gar nang ka·pa·nga·na·kan
plane *eruplano* e·roo·pla·no
planet *planeta* pla·ne·ta

plant ⓝ *halaman* ha-*la*-man
plastic *plastik* plas-teek
plate *pinggán* peeng-*gan*
plateau *talampás* ta-lam-*pas*
platform *plataporma* pla-ta-*por*-ma
play cards *magbaraha* av mag-*ba*-ra-ha
play guitar *maggitara* av mag-gee-*ta*-ra
play (theatre) ⓝ *magpalabás*
　mag-pa-la-*bas*
plug ⓝ *plag* plag
plum *plam* plam
poached (egg) *sinuwám* see-noo-*wam*
pocket *bulsá* bool-*sa*
pocketknife *laseta* la-*se*-ta
poetry *mga tulá* ma-*nga* too-*la'*
point ⓝ *dulo* doo-lo
point ⓥ *ituró* pv ee-too-ro'
poisonous *nakalalason* na-ka-la-*la*-son
police ⓝ *pulisyá* poo-lees-*ya*
police officer (in city) *pulís* poo-*lees*
police officer (in country) *pulís* poo-*lees*
police station *istasyón ng pulisyá*
　ees-tas-*yon* nang poo-lees-*ya*
policy *pátakarán* pa-ta-ka-*ran*
politician *pulítiko* poo-*lee*-tee-ko
politics *pampulítika* pam-poo-*lee*-tee-ka
pollen *polen* po-len
pollution *polusyón* po-loos-*yon*
pool (game) *pul* pool
pool (swimming) *languyan* la-*ngoo*-yan
poor *mahirap* ma-*hee*-rap
popular *populár* po-poo-*lar*
pork *karnéng baboy* kar-*neng ba*-boy
pork sausage *longganisang baboy*
　long-ga-*nee*-sang *ba*-boy
port (sea) *daungan* da-oo-ngan
positive *positibo* po-see-*tee*-bo
possible *posible* po-*see*-ble
postage *selyo* sel-yo
postcard *poskard* pos-*kard*
postcode *poskowd* pos-*kohd*
postcard *poskard* pos-*kard*
poster *poster* pos-*ter*
post office *pos opis* pos o-pees
pot (ceramics) *palayók* pa-la-*yok*
pot (dope) *droga* dro-ga
potato *patatas* pa-*ta*-tas
pottery *gawáng palayók* ga-*wang* pa-la-*yok*
pound (money, weight) *pawnd* pownd
poverty *kahirapan* ka-hee-ra-pan
powder *pulbós* pool-bos
power *kapangyarihan* ka-pang-ya-*ree*-han
prawn *sugpô* soog-po'
prayer *dasál* da-*sal*
prayer book *libróng dasalan* lee-*brong*
　da-*sa*-lan

prefer *mas gustó* pv mas goos-*to*
pregnancy test kit *pambuntís na tes*
　pam-boon-*tees* na tes
pregnant *buntís* boon-*tees*
premenstrual tension
　tensyón bago magkaregla
　tens-*yon ba*-go mag-ka-*reg*-la
prepare *maghandá* av mag-han-*da'*
prescription *reseta* re-*se*-ta
present (gift) *regalo* re-*ga*-lo
president *presidente* pre-see-*den*-te
pressure *presyón* pres-*yon*
pretty *magandá* ma-gan-*da*
price *presyo* pres-yo
priest *parì* pa-*ree'*
prime minister *praym mínister*
　praim *mee*-nees-ter
printer (computer) *printer* preen-ter
prison *bilangguan* bee-lang-*goo*-an
prisoner *bilanggô* bee-lang-*go'*
private *pribado* pree-*ba*-do
problem *problema* pro-*ble*-ma
produce ⓥ *gumawá* av goo-ma-*wa'*
profit ⓝ *tubò* too-bo'
program *programa* pro-*gra*-ma
prohibited *bawal* ba-wal
projector *prodyektor* pro-jek-tor
promise ⓝ *mangakò* ma-*nga*-ko'
prostitute *babaeng mababà ang lipád*
　ba-*ba*-eng ma-*ba*-ba' ang lee-*pad*
protect *pangalagaan* pv
　pa-*nga*-la-*ga*-an
protected *protektado* pro-tek-*ta*-do
protest ⓝ *protesta* pro-*tes*-ta
protest ⓥ *magprotesta* av mag-pro-*tes*-ta
provisions *panustós* pa-noos-*tos*
prune ⓝ *prun* proon
pub *pab* pab
public gardens *harding pampúbliko*
　har-*deeng* pam-*poob*-lee-ko
public relations *relasyóng pampúbliko*
　re-las-*yong* pam-*poob*-lee-ko
public telephone *teléponong pampúbliko*
　te-*le*-po-nong pam-*poob*-lee-ko
public toilet *kubetang pampúbliko*
　koo-*be*-tang pam-*poob*-lee-ko
pull *hilahin* pv hee-*la*-heen
pump ⓝ *pambomba* pam-*bom*-ba
pumpkin *kalabasa* ka-la-*ba*-sa
puncture ⓝ *butas* boo-tas
pure *puro* poo-ro
purple *lila* lee-la
purse *pitaká* pee-ta-*ka'*
push ⓥ *Itulak* pv ee-*too*-lak
put *ilagáy* pv ee-la-*gai*

Q

quadriplegic *kwadraplidyik* kwa-dra-*plee*-jeek

qualifications *mga kwalipikasyón* ma-*nga* kwa-lee-pee-kas-*yon*

quality *katangian* ka-ta-*ngee*-an

quarantine *kuwarentenas* koo-wa-ren-*te*-nas

quarter *sangkapat* sang-*ka*-pat

queen *reyna* ray-na

question ⓝ *tanóng* ta-*nong*

queue ⓝ *pila* *pee*-la

quick *mabilís* ma-bee-*lees*

quiet *tahimik* ta-*hee*-meek

quit *humintô* av hoo-meen-*to'*

R

rabbit *kuneho* koo-*ne*-ho

race (sport) *karera* ka-*re*-ra

racetrack *kárerahán* ka-re-ra-han

racing bike *bisikletang pangarera* bee-seek-*le*-tang pa-nga-re-ra

racism *pagkapoót sa lahì* pag-ka-po-*ot* sa *la*-hee'

racquet *raketa* ra-*ke*-ta

radiator *radyetor* rad-*ye*-tor

radio *radyo* rad-yo

radish *labanós* la-ba-*nos*

railway station *istasyón ng tren* ees-tas-*yon* nang tren

rain ⓝ *ulán* oo-*lan*

raincoat *kapote* ka-*po*-te

raisin *pasas* *pa*-sas

rally ⓝ *rali* *ra*-lee

rape ⓝ *gahasâ* ga-ha-*sa'*

rape ⓥ *gahasain/gumahasâ (gahasâ)* ga-ha-sa-*een*/goo-ma-ha-*sa'* (ga-ha-*sa'*)

rare (uncommon) *bihirà* bee-*hee*-ra'

rare (food) *medyo hindî lutô* *med*-yo heen-*dee'* loo-*to'*

rash ⓝ *singáw* see-*ngow*

rat *dagâ* da-*ga'*

rave (dance party) *reyb* reyb

raw *hiláw* hee-low

razor *pang-ahit* pang-*a*-heet

razor blade *pang-ahit na bleyd* pang-*a*-heet na blayd

read *basahin/magbasá (basa)* ba-sa-*heen*/mag-ba-*sa* (*ba*-sa)

ready *handâ* han-*da'*

real estate agent *ahente ng mga lupain* a-*hen*-te nang ma-*nga* loo-pa-*een*

realistic *buháy na buháy* boo-*hai* na boo-*hai*

rear (location) *sa likód* sa lee-*kod*

reason (excuse) *katwiran* kat-*wee*-ran

receipt *resibo* re-*see*-bo

recently *kailán lang* ka-ee-*lan* lang

recommend *magrekomendá* av mag-re-ko-men-*da*

record ⓥ *irekord* pv ee-re-kord

recording *rekording* re-kor-deeng

recyclable *puwedeng iresaykel* poo-*we*-deng ee-re-*sai*-kel

recycle *iresaykel* pv ee-re-*sai*-kel

red *mapulá* ma-poo-*la*

red-light district *lugár ng mga babaing mababà ang lipád* loo-*gar* nang ma-*nga* ba-*ba*-eeng ma-ba-*ba'* ang lee-*pad*

referee (sport) *réperi* re-*pe*-ree

reference *reperensiyá* re-pe-ren-see-*ya*

reflexology *repleksólodyi* rep-lek-so-lo-jee

refrigerator *rep* rep

refugee *takas* *ta*-kas

refund ⓝ *perang ibinalík* pe-rang ee-bee-na-*leek*

refuse ⓥ *tanggihán* pv tang-gee-*han*

regional *pangrehiyón* pang-re-hee-*yon*

(by) registered mail/post *rehistrado* re-hees-*tra*-do

rehydration salts *mga salitreng panlaban sa panunuyót* ma-*nga* sa-lee-treng pan-*la*-ban sa pa-noo-noo-*yot*

reiki *reyki* ray-kee

relationship *relasyón* re-las-*yon*

relax *reláks* av re-*laks*

relic *alaala* a-la-*a*-la

religion *relihiyón* re-lee-hee-*yon*

religious *relihiyoso* re-lee-hee-yo-so

remote *malayò* ma-*la*-yo'

remote control *remót kontról* re-mot kon-*trol*

rent ⓥ *magrenta* av mag-*ren*-ta

repair ⓥ *magkumpuní* av mag-koom-poo-*nee*

republic *repúblika* re-*poob*-lee-ka

reservation (booking) *reserbasyón* re-ser-bas-*yon*

rest ⓥ *magpahingá* av mag-pa-hee-*nga*

restaurant *restoran* res-to-ran

résumé (CV) *résume* re-soo-me

retired *retirado* re-tee-*ra*-do

return (come back) *magbalík* av mag-ba-*leek*

return (ticket) *balikan* ba-lee-kan

review ⓝ *repaso* re-*pa*-so

rhythm *ritmo* reet-mo

rib *tadyáng* tad-*yang*

rice (cooked) *kanin* *ka*-neen*

rice (uncooked) *bigás* bee-*gas*
rice field *palayan* pa-*lai*-yan
rich (wealthy) *mayaman* ma-*ya*-man
ride ⓝ *sakáy* sa-*kai*
ride (a horse) ⓥ *mangabayo* av
ma-nga-*ba*-yo
right (correct) *tamà* ta-*ma'*
right (direction) *kanan* ka-nan
right-wing *rayt wing* rait weeng
ring (on finger) *singsíng* seeng-*seeng*
ring (of the phone) ⓝ *kumuliling*
koo-moo-lee-*leeng*
rip-off *panloko* pan-*lo*-ko
risk *panganib* pa-*nga*-neeb
river *ilog* ee-log
road *daán* da-*an*
road map *mapa ng daán* ma-pa nang da-*an*
rob *nakawin/magnakaw (nakawin)*
na-ka-ween/mag-*na*-kow (na-ka-*ween*)
rock ⓝ *batô* ba-*to*
rock music *rak* rak
rock climbing
pag-akyát sa malalaking batô
pag-ak-*yat* sa ma-la-la-*keeng* ba-to
rock group *rak grup* rak groop
rockmelon *milón* mee-lon
roll (bread) *pan de sal* pan de sal
rollerblading *roler bleyding*
ro-ler blay-deeng
romantic *romántiko* ro-man-tee-ko
room *kuwarto* koo-war-to
room number *rum namber* room nam-ber
rope *lubid* loo-beed
round ⓐ *bilóg* bee-log
roundabout *ráwndabáwt* rown-da-bowt
route *rota* ro-ta
rowing *rowing* ro-weeng
rubbish *basura* ba-soo-ra
rubella *rubelya* roo-bel-ya
rug *rag* rag
rugby *ragbi* rag-bee
ruins *mga labî* ma-*nga* la-*bee*
rule ⓝ *pátakarán* pa-ta-ka-*ran*
rum *ram* ram
run ⓥ *tumakbó* av too-mak-*bo*
running *pagtakbó* pag-tak-*bo*

S

sad *malungkót* ma-loong-*kot*
saddle *upuan* oo-poo-an
safe ⓝ *kaha de yero* ka-ha de ye-ro
safe ⓐ *ligtás* leeg-*tas*
safe sex *ligtás na pakikipag-seks*
leeg-*tas* na pa-kee-kee-pag-*seks*

saint *santo/a* ⓜ/ⓕ san-to/a
salad *salad* sa-lad
salami *salami* sa-la-mee
salary *suweldo* soo-wel-do
sale *baratilyo* ba-ra-teel-yo
sales tax *buwis sa panindá*
boo-wees sa pa-neen-*da*
salmon *salmón* sal-mon
salt *asín* a-seen
same *pareho* pa-re-ho
sand *buhangin* boo-ha-ngeen
sandal *sandalyas* san-dal-yas
sanitary napkin *pasadór* pa-sa-dor
sardine *sardinas* sar-dee-nas
Saturday *Sábado* sa-ba-do
sauce *sows* sohs
saucepan *sows pan* sohs pan
sauna *sauna* sow-na
sausage *sosis* so-sees
say *sabihin* pv sa-bee-heen
scalp *anit* a-neet
scarf *bandana* ban-da-na
school *páaralán* pa-a-ra-*lan*
science *siyénsiya* see-yen-see-ya
scientist *siyentípiko* see-yen-tee-pee-ko
scissors *gunting* goon-teeng
score ⓥ *umiskór* av oo-mees-kor
scoreboard *iskorbord* ees-kor-bord
Scotland *Eskosya* es-kos-ya
scrambled (eggs) *binatî* bee-na-tee'
sculpture *iskultura* ees-kool-too-ra
sea *dagat* da-gat
seasick *liyó* lee-yo
seaside *baybayin ng dagat*
bai-ba-yeen nang da-gat
season *panahón* pa-na-hon
seat (place) *upuan* oo-poo-an
seatbelt *sitbelt* seet-belt
second ⓐ *ikalawá* ee-ka-la-*wa*
second class *sekon klas* se-kon klas
second-hand *segunda mano*
se-goon-da ma-no
second-hand shop
tindahan ng segunda mano
teen-*da*-han nang se-*goon*-da ma-no
secretary *sekretarya* sek-re-tar-ya
see *makita/makakita (kita)*
ma-kee-ta/ma-kee-ka-ta (*kee*-ta)
self-employed *sariling trabaho* sa-*ree*-leeng
tra-ba-ho
selfish *sakím* sa-keem
self-service *selp serbis* selp ser-bees
sell *itindá/magtindá (itinda)*
ee-teen-*da*/mag-teen-*da* (ee-teen-*da*)
send *ipululú/magpadalá (ipadalá)*
ee-pa-da-*la*/mag-pa-da-*la* (ee-pa-da-*la*)

sensible *makatwiran* ma·kat·wee·ran
sensual *senswál* sens·*wal*
separate *hiwaláy* hee·wa·*lai*
September *Setyembre* set·*yem*·bre
serious *seryoso/a* ⓜ/ⓕ ser·yo·so/a
service *serbisyo* ser·bees·yo
service charge *serbis tsards* ser·bees tsarj
service station *serbis istesyon* ser·bees ees·*tes*·yon
serviette *serbilyeta* ser·beel·ye·ta
several *ilán* ee·lan
sew *tahiín/tumahì (tahì)* ta·hee·*een*/too·ma·*hee'* (ta·*hee'*)
sex *seks* seks
sexism *tungkól sa kasarián* toong·*kol* sa ka·sa·ree·an
sexy *seksi* sek·see
shade *lilim* lee·leem
shadow *anino* a·nee·no
shampoo *siyampu* see·*yam*·poo
shape ⓝ *korte* kor·te
share (a dorm) *makihati sa* av ma·kee·*ha*·tee sa
share (with) *makihati kay* av ma·kee·*ha*·tee kai
shave ⓥ *mag-ahit* av mag·*a*·heet
shaving cream *pang-ahit na krema* pang·*a*·heet na *kre*·ma
she *siyá* see·*ya*
sheep *tupa* too·pa
sheet (bed) *kumot* koo·mot
shelf *istante* ees·tan·te
shiatsu *siyatsu* see·*yat*·soo
shingles (illness) *buni* boo·nee
ship *bapór* ba·por
shirt *kamisadentro* ka·mee·sa·*den*·tro
shoe shop *tindahan ng sapatos* teen·*da*·han nang sa·*pa*·tos
shoe(s) *sapatos* sa·*pa*·tos
shoot *magsyút* mag·*syoot*
shop ⓝ *tindahan* teen·*da*·han
shop ⓥ *mamilí* av ma·mee·*lee*
shopping *pamimilí* pa·mee·mee·*lee*
shopping centre *syaping senter* sya·peeng *sen*·ter
short (height) *maliít* ma·lee·*eet*
shortage *kakulangán* ka·koo·la·*ngan*
shorts *syorts* syorts
shoulder *balikat* ba·lee·kat
shout ⓥ *isigáw/sumigáw (sigáw)* ee·see·*gow*/soo·mee·*gow* (see·*gow*)
show ⓝ *palabás* pa·la·*bas*
show ⓥ *ipakita* pv ee·pa·*kee*·ta
shower ⓝ *páliguán* pa·lee·goo·an
shrine *altár* al·*tar*
shut ⓐ *sarado* sa·ra·do
shy *mahiyain* ma·hee·*ya*·een

sick *may sakít* mai sa·*keet*
side *tagiliran* ta·gee·*lee*·ran
sign ⓝ *karátula* ka·*ra*·too·la
signature *pirma* peer·ma
silk ⓝ *sutlâ* soot·*la'*
silver *pilak* pee·lak
similar *katulad* ka·too·lad
simple *simple* seem·ple
since (May) *mulá noóng (Mayo)* moo·*la* no·ong (ma·yo)
sing ⓥ *kantá* av kan·*ta*
Singapore *Singapór* seeng·ga·por
singer *mang-aawit* mang·a·a·weet
single (person) *binatà/dalaga* m/f bee·*na*·ta'/da·*la*·ga
single room *isahang kuwarto* ee·sa·hang koo·*war*·to
singlet *kamiseta* ka·mee·se·ta
sister *kapatíd na babae* ka·pa·*teed* na ba·*ba*·e
sit *maupô* av ma·oo·po'
size (general) *sukat* soo·kat
skate ⓥ *mag-iskéyt* av mag·ees·*kayt*
skateboarding *iskéytbording* ees·kayt·*bor*·deeng
ski ⓥ *mag-iskí* av mag·ees·*kee*
skiing ⓥ *iskiing* ees·kee·eeng
skim milk *gatas na iskím* *ga*·tas na ees·*keem*
skin *balát* ba·*lat*
skirt *palda* pal·da
skull *bungô* boo·*ngo'*
sky *langit* la·ngeet
sleep ⓥ *tulog* av too·log
sleeping bag *bag na tulugán* bag na too·loo·*gan*
sleeping berth *tulugán* too·loo·*gan*
sleeping car *tulugán* too·loo·*gan*
sleeping pills *gamót pampatulog* ga·*mot* na pam·pa·too·log
sleepy *inántók* ee·*na*·an·tok
slice ⓝ *hiwà* hee·wa'
slide (film) *islávd* ees·*laid*
slow *mabagal* ma·*ba*·gal
slowly *mabagal* ma·*ba*·gal
small *maliít* ma·lee·*eet*
smaller *mas maliít* mas ma·lee·*eet*
smallest *pinakamaliít* pee·na·ka·ma·lee·*eet*
smell ⓥ *amóy* a·moy
smile ⓥ *ngitián/ngumitî (ngitián)* ngee·tee·*an*/ngoo·mee·*tee'* (ngee·tee·an)
smoke (cigarette) ⓥ *manigarilyó* av ma·nee·ga·reel·yo
snack *meryenda* mer·*yen*·da
snail *susô* soo·*so'*
snake *ahas* a·has
snorkelling *mag-isnorkel* mag·ees·*nor*·kel
snow ⓝ *niyebe* nee·ye·be

snow pea *sitsaró* seet-sa-*ro*
snowboarding *isnowbording*
ees-now-bor-deeng
soap *sabón* sa-*bon*
soap opera *sop ópera* sop o-pe-ra
soccer *saker* sa-ker
social welfare *kápakanáng panlipunan*
ka-pa-ka-*nang* pan-lee-poo-nan
socialist *sosyalista* sos-ya-*lees*-ta
socks *medyas* med-yas
soft drink *sopdrink* sop-dreenk
soft-boiled *malasado* ma-la-sa-do
soldier *sundalo* soon-da-lo
some *ilán* ee-*lan*
someone *kanyá* kan-ya
something *nitó* nee-to
sometimes *kung minsan* koong meen-san
son *anák na lalaki* a-*nak* na la-*la*-kee
song *kantá* kan-ta
soon *mámayâ* ma-ma-ya'
sore ⓐ *masakít* ma-sa-*keet*
soup *sopas* so-pas
sour cream *kremang maasim*
kre-mang ma-a-seem
soursop *guyabano* goo-ya-ba-no
south *timog* tee-mog
souvenir *súbenir* soo-bee-neer
souvenir shop *tindahan ng súbinir*
teen-*da*-han nang soo-bee-neer
soy milk *soy milk* soy meelk
soy sauce *soy sows* soy sohs
space *ispéys* ees-pays
Spain *Espanya* es-pan-ya
sparkling wine *isparkling wayn*
ees-*park*-leeng wain
speak *magsalitâ* av mag-sa-lee-ta'
special *espesyâl* es-pes-yal
specialist *espesyalista* es-pes-ya-*lees*-ta
speed (velocity) *tulin* too-leen
speed limit *takdâng tulin*
tak-*dang* too-leen
speedometer *ispidómeter*
ees-pee-*do*-mee-ter
spider *gagambá* ga-gam-ba
spinach *kulitis* koo-lee-tees
spoiled (gone off) *panís* pa-nees
spoke ⓝ *rayos ng gulóng*
ra-yos nang goo-long
spoon *kutsara* koot-sa-ra
sport *ispórt* ees-port
sports store/shop *tindahan ng pang-ispórt*
teen-*da*-han nang pang-ees-port
sportsperson *manlalarô* man-la-la-ro'
sprain ⓝ *pilay* pee-lai
spring (coil) *ispríng* ees-preeng
spring (season) *tagsibol* tag-see-bol
square (town) *bayan* ba-yan

stadium *istadyum* ees-tad-yoom
stairway *hagdanan* hag-*da*-nan
stale *panís* pa-nees
stamp ⓝ *selyo* sel-yo
stand-by ticket *istambay na tiket*
ees-*tam*-bai na *tee*-ket
star ⓝ *bituín* bee-too-een
star apple *istár epol* ees-tar e-pol
start ⓝ *simulâ* see-moo-la'
start ⓥ *magsimulâ* av mag-see-moo-la'
station *istasyón* ees-tas-yon
stationer *tindahan ng papél*
teen-*da*-han nang pa-*pel*
statue *istátuwa* ees-ta-too-wa
stay (at a hotel) *manuluyan* av
ma-noo-*loo*-yan
stay (in one place) *maghintô* av
mag-heen-to'
steak (beef) *bípistik* bee-pees-teek
steal *nakawin/magnakaw (nakawin)*
na-ka-ween/mag-na-kow (na-ka-ween)
steep *matarík* ma-ta-*reek*
step ⓝ *baitáng* bai-*tang*
stereo *istiryo* ees-teer-yo
still water *istíl water* ees-teel wa-ter
stock (food) *panlasa* pan-la-sa
stockings *medyas* med-yas
stolen *nakaw* na-kow
stomach *tiyán* tee-yan
stomachache *sakít ng tiyán*
sa-*keet* nang tee-*yan*
stone *bató* ba-to
stoned (drugged) *nakadroga* na-ka-dro-ga
stop (bus) *hintuan* heen-too-an
stop (cease) *ihintô* pv ee-heen-to'
stop (prevent) *pigilin/pumigil (pigilin)*
pee-*gee*-leen/poo-mee-geel
(pee-*gee*-leen)
storm *bagyó* bag-yo
story *istorya* ees-tor-ya
stove *kalán* ka-lan
straight *diretso* dee-*ret*-so
strange *kakaibá* ka-ka-ee-ba
stranger ⓝ *taong di-kilalá*
ta-ong dee-kee-la-la
strawberry *istróberi* ees-tro-be-ree
stream *sapà* sa-pa'
street *kalye* kal-ye
street market *palengke sa kalye*
pa-leng-ke sa kal-ye
strike ⓝ *welga* wel-ga
string *pisi* pee-see'
stroke (health) *istrók* ees-trok
stroller *istroler* ees-tro-ler
strong *malakás* ma-la-kas
stubborn *matigás ang ulo*
ma-tee-*gas* ang oo-lo

student *estudyante* es-tood-*yan*-te
studio *istudyo* ees-*tood*-yo
stupid *tangá* ta-*nga*
style *istilo* ees-*tee*-lo
subtitles *mga sábtaytel* ma-*nga* sab-*tai*-tel
suburb *suburbya* soo-*boor*-bya
subway *sabwey* *sab*-way
sugar *asukal* a-soo-*kal*
suitcase *maleta* ma-*le*-ta
sultana *pasas* pa-*sas*
summer *tag-aráw* tag-a-*row*
sun *araw* a-*row*
sunblock *pananggáng-araw* pa-*nang-gang*-a-*row*
sunburn *sunóg sa araw* soo-*nog* sa a-*row*
Sunday *Linggó* leeng-*go*
sunglasses *sanglas* *san*-glas
sunny *maaraw* ma-a-*row*
sunrise *pagsikat ng araw* pag-*see*-kat nang a-*row*
sunset *paglubóg ng araw* pag-loo-*bog* nang a-*row*
sunstroke *sobrang lantád sa araw* *sob*-rang lan-*tad* sa a-*row*
supermarket *súpermarket* soo-per-mar-ket
superstition *pamahiín* pa-ma-hee-*een*
supporter *tagásuporta* ta-ga-soo-*por*-ta
surf ⓥ *magsarp* av mag-sarp
surface mail *sarpeys meyl* *sar*-pays mayl
surfboard *sarpbord* sarp-bord
surfing *sarping* *sar*-peeng
surname *apélyido* a-pel-*yee*-do
surprise ⓝ *sorpresa* sor-*pre*-sa
sweater *suwiter* soo-*wee*-ter
Sweden *Sweden* swee-den
sweet ⓐ *matamís* ma-ta-*mees*
sweets *mindtamís* mee-na-ta-*mees*
swelling ⓝ *magá* ma-*ga*'
swim ⓥ *lumangóy* av loo-ma-*ngoy*
swimming *paglangóy* pag-la-*ngoy*
swimming pool *languyan* la-*ngoo*-yan
swimsuit *damít pampaligô* da-*meet* pam-pa-*lee*-go'
Switzerland *Switserland* *sweet*-ser-land
synagogue *sínagog* *see*-na-gog
synthetic *sintetik* seen-*te*-teek
syringe *heringgilya* he-reeng-*geel*-ya

T

table *mesa* *me*-sa
table tennis *ping pong* peeng pong
tablecloth *mantél* man-*tel*
Taiwan *Taiwán* tai-*wan*
tail ⓝ *buntót* boon-*tot*

tailor *sastré* sas-*tre*
take ⓥ *kunin* pv *koo*-neen
take a photo *kumuha ng litrato* av koo-*moo*-ha nang leet-*ra*-to
talk ⓥ *magsalitâ* av mag-sa-lee-*ta*'
tall *matás* ma-ta-*as*
tampon *tampon* *tam*-pon
tanning lotion *taning losyon* ta-neeng *los*-yon
tap *gripo* *gree*-po
tap water *tubig sa gripo* *too*-beeg sa *gree*-po
tasty *malasa* ma-*la*-sa
tax *buwís* boo-*wees*
taxi *taksi* *tak*-see
taxi stand *páradahán ng taksi* pa-ra-da-*han* nang *tak*-see
tea *tsad* tsa-*a*
teacher *titser* *teet*-ser
team *tim* teem
teaspoon *kutsarita* koot-sa-*ree*-ta
technique *teknik* tek-neek
teeth *ngipin* *ngee*-peen
telegram *telegrama* te-le-*gra*-ma
telephone ⓝ *telépono* te-*le*-po-no
telephone ⓥ *teléponohán/tumelépono (teléponohán)* te-le-po-no-*han*/ too-me-*le*-po-no (te-le-po-no-*han*)
telephone box *télepon baks* *te*-le-pon baks
telephone centre *sentro ng telépono* *sen*-tro nang te-*le*-po-no
telescope *teleskopyo* te-les-*kop*-yo
television *telebisyón* te-le-bees-*yon*
tell *sabihin* pv sa-*bee*-heen
temperature *témperatura* tem-pe-ra-*too*-ra
temple (to pray) *sambahan* sam-*ba*-han
tennis *tenis* *te*-nees
tennis court *tenis kort* *te*-nees kort
tent *tolda* *tol*-da
tent peg *pako ng tolda* *pa*-ko nang *tol*-da
terrible *terible* te-*ree*-ble
terrorism *terorismo* te-ro-*rees*-mo
terrorist *terorista* te-ro-*rees*-ta
test ⓝ *tes* tes
thank ⓥ *pasalamat* av pa-sa-*la*-mat
Thank you. *Salamat sa iyó.* sa-*la*-mat sa ee-*yo*
that (one) *iyón* ee-*yon*
theatre *teatro* te-*at*-ro
their *nilá* nee-*la*
theirs *kaniláng* ka-nee-*lang*
them *silá* see-*la*
there *doón* do-*on*
they *silá* see-*la*
thick *makapál* ma-ka-*pal*

thief *magnanakaw* mag·na·*na*·kow
thin *payát* pa·*yat*
think *mag-isíp* av mag·ee·*seep*
third *pangatló* pa·ngat·*lo*
thirsty *nauhaw* ma·oo·how
this (one) *itó* ee·*to*
thread *sinulid* see·noo·leed
throat *lalamunan* la·la·moo·nan
thrush (health) *tras* tras
thunderstorm *bagyó* bag·*yo*
Thursday *Huwebes* hoo·*we*·bes
ticket *tiket* *tee*·ket
ticket collector *konduktór* kon·dook·*tor*
ticket machine *tiket masín* *tee*·ket ma·*seen*
ticket office *bilihan ng tiket*
  bee·*lee*·han nang *tee*·ket
tide *paglaki at pagkati ng tubig*
  pag·la·*kee* at pag·*ka*·tee nang *too*·beeg
tight *masikíp* ma·see·*keep*
time ⓝ *oras* o·ras
time difference *diperénsiya sa oras*
  dee·pe·*rens*·ya sa o·ras
timetable *taymteybol* taim·*tay*·bol
tin (can) *lata* *la*·ta
tin opener *abrelata* ab·re·*la*·ta
tiny *maliít* ma·lee·*eet*
tip (gratuity) *tip* teep
tire *gulóng* goo·*long*
tired *pagód* pa·*god*
tissues *tisyu* *tees*·yoo
to *sa* sa
toast ⓝ *tost* tost
toaster *toster* *tos*·ter
tobacco *tabako* ta·*ba*·ko
tobacconist *tabákonista* ta·ba·ko·*nees*·ta
tobogganing *pagtotobogán*
  pag·to·to·bo·*gan*
today *ngayón* nga·*yon*
toe *daliri sa paá* da·lee·*ree* sa pa·*a*
tofu *tokwa* *tok*·wa
together *magkasama* mag·ka·*sa*·ma
toilet *kubeta* koo·*be*·ta
toilet paper *tóilet peyper* *to*·ee·let *pay*·per
tomato *kamatis* ka·ma·tees
tomato sauce *tomeyto sows* to·*may*·to sohs
tomorrow *bukas* boo·kas
tomorrow afternoon *bukas ng hapon*
  boo·kas nang *ha*·pon
tomorrow evening *bukas ng gabí*
  boo·kas nang ga·*bee*
tomorrow morning *bukas ng umaga*
  boo·kas nang oo·*ma*·ga
tonight *ngayong gabí* nga·*yong* ga·*bee*
too (expensive) *masyadong mahal*
  mas·*ya*·dong ma·*hal*
tooth *ngipin* *ngee*·peen

toothache *sakít ng ngipin*
  sa·*keet* nang *ngee*·peen
toothbrush *sepilyo* se·*peel*·yo
toothpaste *pangsepilyo* pang·se·*peel*·yo
toothpick *tutpik* *toot*·peek
torch (flashlight) *plaslayt* *plas*·lait
touch ⓥ *hipuin/humipò (hipuin)*
  hee·poo·een/hoo·*mee*·po (hee·poo·een)
tour ⓝ *tur* toor
tourist *turista* too·*rees*·ta
tourist office *upisina ng turismo*
  oo·pee·*see*·na nang too·*rees*·mo
towards *tungo sa* too·ngo sa
towel *tuwalya* too·*wal*·ya
tower *tore* to·re
toxic waste *aksayáng nakalalason*
  ak·sa·*yang* na·ka·la·*la*·son
toy shop *tindahan ng laruán*
  teen·*da*·han nang la·roo·*an*
track (path) *landás* lan·*das*
track (sport) *trak* trak
trade ⓥ *kálakalán* ka·la·ka·*lan*
tradesperson *mangangalakal*
  ma·nga·nga·*la*·kal
traffic *trápiko* *tra*·pee·ko
traffic light *ilaw trápiko* ee·low *tra*·pee·ko
trail ⓝ *landás* lan·*das*
train *tren* tren
train station *istasyón ng tren*
  ees·tas·*yon* nang tren
tram *trambiyá* tram·bee·*ya*
transit lounge *transit lounge*
  tran·seet lownds
translate *isalin sa* pv ee·sa·leen sa
transport *transportasyón* trans·por·tas·*yon*
travel *maglakbáy* av mag·lak·*bai*
travel agency *travel agency* *tra*·bel *ay*·jen·see
travellers cheque *trábelers tsek*
  tra·be·lers tsek
travel sickness *pagkaliyó sa biyahe*
  pag·ka·lee·*yo* sa bee·*ya*·he
tree *puno* poo·no'
trip (journey) *paglalakbáy* pag·la·lak·*bai*
trolley *troli* *tro*·lee
trousers *pantalón* pan·ta·*lon*
truck *trak* trak
trust ⓥ *magtiwalà* av mag·tee·*wa*·la'
try ⓥ *sikapin/magsikap (sikapin)*
  see·*ka*·peen/mag·*see*·kap (see·*ka*·peen)
T-shirt *ti syert* tee syert
tube (tyre) *gulóng* goo·*long*
Tuesday *Martes* *mar*·tes
tumour *tumór* too·*mor*
tuna *tulingán* too·lee·*ngan*
tune ⓝ *tono* to·no
turkey *pabo* *pa*·bo

turn ⓥ *lumikô* loo-mee-ko'
TV *TV* tee-bee
tweezers *tiyani* tee-ya-nee'
twice *makálawa* ma-ka-la-wa
twin beds *kambál na kama* kam-bal na ka-ma
twins *kambál* kam-bal
two *dalawá* da-la-wa
type ⓝ *tipò* tee-po'
typhoon *bagyó* bag-yo
typical *tipikál* tee-pee-kal
tyre *gulóng* goo-long

U

ultrasound *últrasawnd* ool-tra-sownd
umbrella *payong* pa-yong
uncomfortable *asiwâ* a-see-wa'
understand *máintindihán* av ma-een-teen-dee-han
underwear *damít panloób* da-meet pan-lo-ob
unemployed *waláng trabaho* wa-lang tra-ba-ho
unfair *hindî makátarungan* heen-dee ma-ka-ta-roo-ngan
uniform ⓝ *uniporme* oo-nee-por-me
universe *sanlibután* san-lee-boo-tan
university *unibersidád* oo-nee-ber-see-dad
unleaded *anleded* an-le-ded
unsafe *hindî ligtás* heen-dee leeg-tas
until *hanggáng sa* hang-gang sa
unusual *hindî pangkaraniwan* heen-dee pang-ka-ra-nee-wan
up *patáas* pa-ta-as
uphill *paakyát* pa-ak-yat
urgent *nagmámadalì* nag-ma-ma-da-lee'
urinary infection *impeksiyón sa daanan ng ihì* eem-pek-see-yon sa da-a-nan nang ee-hee'
us *kamí* ka-mee
USA *Estados Unidos* es-ta-dos oo-nee-dos
useful *makatutulong* ma-ka-too-too-long
uterus *bahay-batà* ba-hay ba-ta'

V

vacancy *may bakante* mai ba-kan-te
vacant *bakante* ba-kan-te
vacation *bakasyón* ba-kas-yon
vaccination *bakuna* ba-koo-na
vagina *maselang pag-aari ng babae* ma-se-lang pag-a-a-ree nang ba-ba-e
validate *ipátotoó* pv ee-pa-to-to-o
valley *libís* lee-bees
valuable ⓐ *mahalagá* ma-ha-la-ga
value (price) ⓝ *presyo* pres-yo
van *ban* ban
veal *karnéng buló* kar-neng boo-lo'
vegetable ⓝ *gulay* goo-lai
vegetarian ⓐ *bedyetaryan* bed-ye-tar-yan
vein *ugát* oo-gat
venereal disease *sakit sa babae* sa-keet sa ba-ba-e
venue *lugár* loo-gar
very *nápaka-* na-pa-ka-
video recorder *bídeyo rekorder* bee-de-yo re-kor-der
video tape *bídeyo teyp* bee-de-yo tayp
view ⓝ *tanawin* ta-na-ween
village *baryo* bar-yo
vine *baging* ba-geeng
vinegar *sukà* soo-ka'
vineyard *ubasán* oo-ba-san
virus *mikrobyo* meek-rob-yo
visa *bisa* bee-sa
visit ⓥ *bisitahin/bumisita (bisitahin)* bee-see-ta-heen/boo-mee-see-ta (bee-see-ta-heen)
vitamins *mga bitamina* ma-nga bee-ta-mee-na
vodka *bodka* bod-ka
voice ⓝ *boses* bo-ses
volcanic mudslide *agos ng putik mula sa bulkán* a-gos nang poo-teek moo-la sa bool-kan
volcano *bulkán* bool-kan
volleyball (sport) *bálibol* ba-lee-bol
volume ⓝ *lakás* la-kas
vote ⓥ *bumoto* av boo-mo-to

W

wage *suweldo* soo-wel-do
wait (for) *hintayín/maghintáy (hintáy)* heen-tai-yeen/mag-heen-tai (heen-tai)
waiter *weyter* way-ter
waiting room *weyting rum* way-teeng room
wake (someone) up *gisingin* gee-see-ngeen
walk ⓥ *lakad* la-kad
wall (outer) *padér* pa-der
want *gustó* goos-to
war *giyera* gee-ye-ra

wardrobe *mga kasuotan*
ma-*nga* ka-soo-o-tan

warm *mainit* ma-ee-neet

warn *balaan/magbalá (balaan)*
ba-*la*-an/mag-ba-ba-*la* (ba-*la*-an)

wash (oneself) *maligô* av ma-*lee*-go'

wash (something) *labhan/maglabá (labhan)* lab-han/mag-la-ba (lab-*han*)

wash cloth (flannel) *pamunas*
pa-*moo*-nas

washing machine *wasing masín*
wa-seeng ma-*seen*

watch ⓝ *reló* re-lo

watch ⓥ *pagmasdán/magmasid (masdan)* pag-mas-*dan*/mag-ma-seed (mas-*dan*)

water *tubig* too-beeg

water bottle *bote ng tubig*
bo-te nang *too*-beeg

(hot) water bottle *bote ng mainit na tubig* bo-te nang ma-ee-neet na *too*-beeg

water buffalo *kalabáw* ka-la-*bow*

waterfall *talón* ta-*lon*

watermelon *pakwán* pak-*wan*

waterproof *di tinátagusán ng tubig*
dee tee-na-ta-goo-*san* nang *too*-beeg

water-skiing *mag-water iskiing*
mag-*wa*-ter ees-*kee*-eeng

wave (water) *alon* a-lon

way *wey* way

we *kamí* ka-*mee*

weak *mahiná* ma-hee-na'

wealthy *mayaman* ma-ya-man

wear *isuót/magsuót (isuót)*
ee-soo-ot/mag-soo-ot (ee-soo-ot)

weather *panahón* pa-na-hon

wedding *kasál* ka-*sal*

wedding cake *weding keyk*
we-deeng kayk

wedding present *regalo sa kasál*
re-*ga*-lo sa ka-*sal*

Wednesday *Miyérkoles*
mee-*yer*-ko-les

week *linggó* leeng-go

weekend *Sábado at Linggó*
sa-ba-do at leeng-go

weigh ⓥ *timbangín* pv teem-ba-*ngeen*

weight ⓝ *timbáng* teem-*bang*

weights *panimbáng* pa-neem-*bang*

welcome *tanggapín/tumanggáp (tanggapín)* tang-ga-*peen*/too-mang-gap (tang-ga-*peen*)

welfare *kápakanán* ka-pa-ka-nan

well *mabuti* ma-*boo*-tee

west ⓐ *kanluran* kan-*loo*-ran

wet *basâ* ba-sa'

whale shark *butanding* boo-tan-deeng

what *anó* a-no

wheel *gulóng* goo-*long*

wheelchair *silyang de-gulóng*
seel-yang de-goo-*long*

when *kailán* ka-ee-*lan*

where *saán* sa-an

which *alín* a-*leen*

whisky *wiski* wees-kee

white *maputî* ma-poo-tee'

who *sino* see-no

wholemeal bread *tinapay na holmil*
tee-na-pai na *hol*-meel

why *bakit* ba-keet

wide *maluwáng* ma-loo-*wang*

wife *asawa* a-sa-wa

win ⓥ *manalo* av ma-*na*-lo

wind ⓝ *hangin* ha-ngeen

window *bintanà* been-*ta*-na'

windscreen *winskrin* weens-kreen

windsurfing *winsarping*
ween-sar-peeng

wine *alak* a-lak

wings *mga pakpák* ma-*nga* pak-*pak*

winner *panalo* pa-*na*-lo

winter *taglamíg* tag-la-*meeg*

wire ⓝ *alambre* a-*lam*-bre

wish ⓥ *nais* na-ees

with *may* mai

within *sa loób ng* sa lo-*ob* nang

without *walâ* wa-*la*'

wok *wok* wok

woman *babae* ba-ba-e

wonderful *magaling* ma-ga-*leeng*

wood *kahoy* ka-hoy

wool *lana* la-na

word *salitâ* sa-lee-ta'

work ⓝ *trabaho* tra-ba-ho

work ⓥ *magtrabaho* av
mag-tra-ba-ho

work experience *karanasán sa trabaho* ka-ra-na-san sa tra-ba-ho

workout ⓝ *mag-ehersisyo*
mag-e-her-sees-yo

work permit *permiso sa trabaho*
per-mee-so sa tra-ba-ho

workshop *págawaan* pa-ga-wa-an

world *mundó* moon-do

worms *mga bulati* ma-*nga* boo-la-tee

worried *balisâ* ba-lee-sa'

worship ⓥ *sambahín/sumambá (sambahín)* see-nam-ba-heen/ soo-mam-ba (sam-ba-heen)

wrist *pulsó* pool-so

write *sumulat* soo-moo-lat

writer *sumúsulat* soo-moo-soo-lat

wrong *malî* ma-lee'

Y

year *taón* ta·on
yellow *diláw* dee·low
yes *oo* o·o
yesterday *kahapon* ka·ha·pon
(not) yet *(hindi) pa* (heen·dee) pa
yoga *yoga* yo·ga
yogurt *yogurt* yo·goort
you inf pl *kayó* ka·yo
you inf sg *ikáw* ee·kaw
you pol pl *kayó* ka·yo
you pol sg *kayó* ka·yo
young *batà* ba·ta'
your inf pl *ninyó* neen·yo
your inf sg *mo* mo

your pol sg *ninyó* neen·yo
your pol pl *ninyó* neen·yo
yours inf pl *inyóng* een·yong
yours inf sg *iyó* ee·yo
yours pol pl *iyó* ee·yo
yours pol sg *inyóng* een·yong
youth hostel *pangkabataang hostel*
   pang·ka·ba·*ta*·ang *hos*·tel

Z

zip/zipper *siper* see·per
zodiac *sodyak* sod·yak
zoo *su* soo
zucchini *sukini* soo·kee·nee

Filipino alphabetical order is used in this dictionary. Unless otherwise specified, the verbs listed have three forms organised in the following way: root verb followed by the patient voice (pv), then actor voice (av) verbs in brackets. For example the verb entry for *lutò* 'cook' is *lutò (ilutò/maglutò)*. If only one form of the verb is given then this is the most commonly used form and is marked either as a patient or actor voice verb. See the **phrasebuilder** for explanations on verbs. You'll also find words marked as adjective ⓐ, noun ⓝ, verb ⓥ, preposition ⓟ, singular sg, plural pl, masculine ⓜ and feminine ⓕ where necessary.

A

abenida a·be·*nee*·da *avenue*
abogado a·bo·*ga*·do *lawyer*
abogasyá a·bo·gas·*ya law (study, professsion)*
aborsyón a·bors·yon *abortion*
abrelata ab·re·*la*·ta *can opener • tin opener*
Abril ab·*reel April*
abukado a·boo·*ka*·do *avocado*
akáwnt a·*kownt account*
akin a·keen *me • my*
aklatan ak·*la*·tan *library*
akó a·ko *I*
akomodasyón a·ko·mo·das·yon *accommodation*
aksayáng nakalalason ak·sa·*yang* na·ka·la·*la*·son *toxic waste*
aksayáng nukliyár ak·sa·*yang* nook·lee·*yar nuclear waste*
aksidente ak·see·*den*·te *accident*
aktibista ak·tee·*bees*·ta *activist*
akupangtiyúr a·koo·pang·tee·yoor *acupuncture*
adaptor a·*dap*·tor *adaptor*
adiksyón a·*deeks*·yon *addiction*
— **sa droga** sa *dro*·ga *drug addiction*
administrasyón ad·mee·nees·tras·yon *administration*
adrés a·*dres direction*
adwana ad·*wa*·na *customs*
agahan a·*ga*·han *breakfast*
agos ng putik mula sa bulkán a·gos nang poo·teek moo·la sa bool·*kan volcanic mudslide*
Agosto a·*gos*·to *August*

agrikultura ag·ree·kool·*too*·ra *agriculture*
ahas a·has *snake*
ahensiyá ng mga lupaín a·hen·see·*ya* nang ma·*nga* loo·pa·*een estate agency*
ahente ng mga lupain a·*hen*·te nang ma·*nga* loo·pa·*een real estate agent*
AIDS ayds *AIDS*
alaala a·la·*a*·la *relic*
alagaan pv a·la·*ga*·an *look after*
álagaán ng batà a·la·ga·an nang *ba*·ta' *crèche*
alahas a·*la*·has *jewellery*
alak a·lak *wine*
alám pv a·*lam know*
alambre a·*lam*·bre *wire*
alarm klak a·*larm* klak *alarm clock*
albularyo al·boo·*lar*·yo *herbalist*
Alemanya a·le·*man*·ya *Germany*
alerhiya a·ler·*hee*·ya *allergy*
alín a·*leen which*
alinmán ay hindî a·*leen*·man ai heen·*dee'* *either*
alon a·lon *wave (water)*
altár al·*tar altar • shrine*
amá a·*ma father*
ambulansiya am·boo·*lan*·see·ya *ambulance*
amin a·meen *our*
amóy a·*moy smell* ⓝ
ampetamin am·pe·ta·*meen amphetamines*
anák a·*nak child*
— **na babae** a·nak na ba·*ba*·e *girl • daughter*
— **na lalaki** a·nak na la·*la*·kee *boy • son*
anarkista a·nar·*kees*·ta *anarchist*
anemya a·*nem*·ya *anaemia*
anino a·*nee*·no *shadow*

anit *a-*neet *scalp*
anleded an-*le-*ded *unleaded*
anó a-*no what*
antibayótiko an-tee-ba-yo-tee-ko *antibiotics*
antigo an-*tee-*go *antique*
antinúkliyar an-tee-nook-lee-yar *antinuclear*
antiséptiko an-tee-*sep-*tee-ko *antiseptic*
anumán á-noo-*man any*
anúnsiyo a-*noon-*see-yo *advertisement*
aparadór a-pa-ra-*dor cupboard*
apartment a-*part-*ment *apartment • flat*
apelyído a-pel-*yee-*do *family name • surname*
apendiks a-*pen-*deeks *appendix (body)*
apó a-*po grandchild*
apóy a-*poy fire*
Áprica ap-ree-ka *Africa*
aprikota ap-ree-*ko-*ta *apricot*
araw a-*row day • sun*
— **ng Paskó** nang pas-*ko Christmas Day*
araw-araw a-*row*-a-*row daily*
arkeholóhikal ar-ke-ho-*lo-*hee-kal *archaeological*
arkilahán ng kotse
 ar-kee-la-*han* nang *kot-*se *car hire*
arkilá (arkilahín/umarkilá) ar-kee-*la*
 (ar-kee-la-*heen/*oo-mar-kee-*la*) *hire*
arkitekto/a ⓜ/ⓕ ar-kee-*tek-*to/a *architect*
arkitektura ar-kee-tek-*too-*ra *architecture*
aresto (arestuhin/umaresto) a-res-*to*
 (a-res-too-*hin/*a-res-to) *arrest* ⓥ
ari ng lalaki a-ree nang la-*la-*kee *penis*
arina a-*ree-*na *flour*
aromáterapi a-ro-ma-*te-*ra-pee *aromatherapy*
arte ar-te *art*
artista ar-*tees-*ta *artist • actor*
asawa a-*sa-*wa *spouse • husband • wife*
asín a-*seen salt*
asiwâ a-see-*wa' uncomfortable*
aso a-so *dog*
asong taga-akay ng bulág a-song
 ta-ga-a-kai nang boo-*lag guide dog*
aspáragus as-*pa-*ra-goos *asparagus*
áspirin as-pee-reen *aspirin*
asukal a-*soo-*kal *sugar*
asúl a-*sool blue*
Asya as-ya *Asia*
at at *and*
atake sa pusò a-*ta-*ke sa poo-*so' heart attack*
atáy a-*tai liver*
atis a-tees *custard apple*
atletiks at-*le-*teeks *athletics*
ÁTM ay-tee-em
 automated teller machine (ATM)
atmóspera at-*mos-*pe-ra *atmosphere*
atsara at-*sa-*ra *pickles*
Australya ows-*tral-*ya *Australia*

babae ba-*ba-*e *woman • female*
babaing mababà ang lipád ba-*ba-*eeng
 ma-ba-ba' ang lee-*pad prostitute*
babay ba-bai *goodbye*
baboy ba-boy *pig*
backpack bak-pak *backpack*
baka ba-ka *cow*
bakâ ba-*ka' maybe*
bakante ba-*kan-*te *vacant* ⓐ *• vacancy* ⓝ
bakasyón ba-kas-*yon holidays • vacation*
bakit ba-keet *why*
baklâ bak-*la' gay • homosexual*
bakod ba-kod *fence*
bakuna ba-*koo-*na *vaccination*
badyet bad-yet *budget*
bag bag *bag*
— **na tulugán** na too-loo-*gan*
 sleeping bag
bagà ba-*ga' lung*
bagahe ba-*ga-*he *baggage • luggage*
baging ba-geeng *vine*
bago ba-*go before* ⓟ *• new* ⓐ
Bagong Taón ba-gong ta-on *New Year's Day*
bagót ba-got *bored*
bagyó bag-yo *storm • thunderstorm • typhoon*
bahâ ba-*ha' flood*
bahagi ba-*ha-*gee *part (component)*
bahay ba-hai *house*
bahay-bisita ba-hai-bee-see-ta *guesthouse*
baitáng bai-*tang step* ⓝ
balaan (balaan/magbalá)
 ba-*la-*an (ba-*la-*an/mag-ba-ba-*la*) *warn*
balanse ng akáwnt ba-*lan-*se nang a-*kownt*
 balance (account)
balát ba-*lat skin*
baléy ba-lay *ballet*
bálibol ba-lee-bol *volleyball (sport)*
balikan ba-lee-kan *return (ticket)*
balikat ba-lee-kat *shoulder*
balisá ba-lee-*sa worried*
balità ba-*lee-*ta' *news*
bálkoni bal-ko-nee *balcony*
banda ban-da *band (music)*
bandana ban-*da-*na *scarf*
bandera ban-*de-*ra *flag* ⓝ
band-eyd band-ayd *Band-Aid*
banggaan bang-*ga-*an *crash*
bangín ba-*ngeen cliff*
bangko bang-ko *bank* ⓝ
baníg ba-neeg *mat*
bank akáwnt bank a-*kownt bank account*
bansâ ban-*sa' country*
bantóg ban-*tog famous*

banyagà ban-*ya*-ga' *foreign*
banyera ban-*ye*-ra *bath*
banyo ban-*yo bathroom*
bapór ba-*por boat • ship*
bar bar *bar*
barado ba-*ra*-do *blocked*
baraha ba-*ra*-ha *(playing) cards*
baratilyo ba-ra-*teel*-yo *sale*
barbero bar-*be*-ro *barber*
baríl ba-*reel gun*
baryá bar-*ya coins • loose change*
baryo bar-*yo village*
basâ ba-*sa' wet* ⓐ
basa (basahin/magbasá)
    basa (basaheen/mag-ba-*sa) read*
basket *bas*-ket *basket*
básketbol *bas*-ket-bol *basketball*
baso ba-*so (drinking) glass*
basura ba-*soo*-ra *rubbish • garbage*
básurahán ba-soo-ra-*han garbage can*
batà ba-*ta' child • young* ⓐ
batang babae ba-tang ba-*ba*-e *girl*
batang lalaki ba-tang la-*la*-kee *boy*
batás ba-*tas law • legislation*
bateryá ba-ter-*ya battery*
bató ba-*to rock • stone • kidney*
bawa't ba-*wat every*
bawang ba-*wang garlic*
bayad ba-*yad fare • payment*
bayan ba-*yan town square*
baybayin bai-ba-*yeen coast*
    — ng dagat nang da-*gat seaside*
bedyetaryan bed-ye-tar-yan
    vegetarian
bekè be-*ke' mumps*
bel peper bel *pe*-per *capsicum*
Bélhika bel-*hee*-ka *Belgium*
bendahe ben-*da*-he *bandage* ⓝ
bentiladór ben-tee-la-*dor fan (machine)*
berde ber-de *green*
bert kontról bert kon-*trol birth control*
bert sertípiket bert ser-*tee*-pee-ket
    birth certificate
bertdey *bert*-day *birthday*
beybi *bay*-bee *baby*
bibi bee-*bee duck*
bibíg bee-*beeg mouth*
Bíbliya *beeb*-lee-ya *Bible*
bídeyo rekorder bee-de-yo re-*kor*-der
    video recorder
bídeyo teyp bee-de-yo tayp *video tape*
bigás bee-*gas rice (uncooked)*
bigyan (ibigay/magbigáy) beeg-yan
    (ee-bee-*gai*/mag-bee-*gai) give*
bihag bee-*hag hostage*
bihirà bee-*hee*-ra' *rare (uncommon)*

bihisán bee-hee-*san changing room (in shop)*
bilanggô bee-lang-*go' prisoner*
bilangguan bee-lang-goo-an *prison*
bilangin pv bee-*la*-ngeen *count* ⓥ
bilí pv bee-*lee buy*
bilihan ng tiket bee-*lee*-han nang *tee*-ket
    ticket office
bilóg bee-*log round*
bimpo *beem*-po *face cloth*
bin bean *bean*
binatà bee-na-*ta' single (male)*
binatì bee-na-*tee' scrambled*
bingí bee-*ngee deaf*
Binibini bee-nee-*bee*-nee *Ms • Miss*
bintanà been-*ta*-na' *window*
bintî been-*tee' leg*
binyág been-*yag baptism*
bisikleta bee-seek-*le*-ta *bicycle • bike*
bisikletang pambundók bee-seek-*le*-tang
    pam-boon-*dok mountain bike*
bisikletang pangarera bee-seek-*le*-tang
    pa-nga-*re*-ra *racing bike*
bisitahin (bisitahin/bumisita)
    bee-*see*-ta-heen (bee-*see*-ta-heen/
    boo-mee-*see*-ta) *visit*
biskwít bees-*kweet biscuit • cookie*
bisnis klas bees-nees klas *business class*
Bisperás ng Bagong Taón bees-pe-ras
    nang ba-gong ta-*on New Year's Eve*
Bisperás ng Paskó bees-pe-ras nang pas-ko
    Christmas Eve
bituín bee-too-*een star*
biyaheng pangnegosyo
    bee-*ya*-heng pang-ne-*gos*-yo *business trip*
biyanáng babae bee-ya-nang ba-*ba*-e
    mother-in-law
biyanáng lalaki bee-ya-nang la-*la*-kee
    father-in-law
Biyernes bee-*yer*-nes *Friday*
    — Santo san-to *Good Friday*
blangket *blang*-ket *blanket*
bodka *bod*-ka *vodka*
bola (sport) bo-la *ball*
bolpen bol-pen *pen (ballpoint)*
bombilya bom-*beel*-ya *light bulb*
bording haus bor-deeng hows
    boarding house
bording pas bor-deeng pas *boarding pass*
boses bo-ses *voice* ⓝ
bota bo-ta *boot (footwear)*
botang panlakad nang mahabà bo-tang
    pan-*la*-kad nang ma-ha-ba' *hiking boots*

bote *bo*·te *bottle* ⓝ
— **ng (mainit na) tubig** nang (ma·*ee*·neet na) *too*·beeg *(hot) water bottle*
botika bo·*tee*·ka *pharmacy • chemist (shop)*
bra bra *bra*
brandi bran·dee *brandy*
bras ng buhók bras nang boo·*hok* *hairbrush*
brasel ispráwt *bra*·sel ees·*prowt* *Brussels sprout*
brokoli bro·*ko*·lee *broccoli*
brongkitis brong·*kee*·tees *bronchitis*
bubuwít boo·boo·*weet* *mouse*
bubuyog boo·boo·*yog* *bee*
buk ng prase book nang *pra*·se *phrasebook*
bukáng liwaywáy boo·*kang* lee·wai·*wai* *dawn*
bukás boo·*kas* *open* ⓐ
bukas *boo*·kas *tomorrow*
— **ng gabí** nang ga·*bee* *tomorrow evening*
— **ng hapon** nang *ha*·pon *tomorrow afternoon*
— **ng umaga** nang oo·*ma*·ga *tomorrow morning*
bukung-bukong boo·koong·*boo*·kong *ankle*
Budista boo·*dees*·ta *Buddhist*
buhangin boo·*ha*·ngeen *sand*
buhay *boo*·hai *life*
buhay na buháy boo·hai na boo·*hai* *realistic*
buhók boo·*hok* *hair*
bulág boo·*lag* *blind*
bulak *boo*·lak *cotton balls*
bulaklák boo·lak·*lak* *flower*
bulati boo·*la*·tee *intestinal worm(s)*
bulkán bool·*kan* *volcano*
bulsá bool·*sa* *pocket*
bulutong-tubig boo·loo·tong·*too*·beeg *chicken pox*
bumabá av boo·ma·*ba'* *get off (a train)*
bumoto av boo·*mo*·to *vote* ⓥ
bundók boon·*dok* *mountain*
bungô *boo*·ngo' *skull*
buni *boo*·nee *shingles (illness)*
buntís boon·*tees* *pregnant*
buntót boon·*tot* *tail* ⓝ
buról boo·*rol* *hill*
bus boos *bus*
butas *boo*·tas *puncture* ⓝ
butanding boo·*tan*·ding *whale shark*
butikí boo·tee·*kee'* *lizard*
butó boo·*to* *bone*
butones boo·*to*·nes *button*
buwán boo·*wan* *month • moon*
buwís boo·*wees* *income tax*
— **sa erport** sa er·*port* *airport tax*
— **sa panindá** sa pa·neen·*da* *sales tax*

C

CD see·dee *CD*
CV see·bee *CV • résumé*

K

ka ka *you*
kaakit-akit ka·*a*·keet·*a*·keet *charming*
kabayo ka·*ba*·yo *horse*
kaber tsards *ka*·ber tsarj *cover charge*
kabuté ka·boo·*te* *mushroom*
kakaibá ka·ka·ee·*ba* *different* ⓐ • *stranger* ⓝ
kakauntí ka·ka·oon·*tee'* *less*
kakilákilabot ka·kee·*la*·kee·*la*·bot *awful*
kakteyl *kak*·tayl *cocktail*
kakulangán ka·koo·la·*ngan* *shortage*
kada *ka*·da *each • per*
kadena ka·*de*·na *chain* ⓝ
— **ng bisikleta** nang bee·seek·*le*·ta *bike chain*
kagamitán ka·ga·mee·*tan* *equipment*
— **para sa kama** *pa*·ra sa *ka*·ma *bedding*
kagamitáng pangdaybing ka·ga·mee·*tang* pang·*dai*·beeng *diving equipment*
kagandahang-loób ka·gan·*da*·hang lo·*ob* *hospitality*
kagát ka·*gat* *bite (dog/insect)* ⓝ
kaha *ka*·ha *cash register*
— **de yero** de ye·ro *safe* ⓝ
kahapon ka·*ha*·pon *yesterday*
kahél ka·*hel* *orange (fruit)*
kaher/a ⓜ/ⓕ ka·*he*·ro/a *cashier*
kahirapan ka·hee·*ra*·pan *poverty*
kahón ka·*hon* *box* ⓝ
kahoy *ka*·hoy *wood*
kaibigan ka·ee·*bee*·gan *friend*
kailán ka·ee·*lan* *when*
— **lang** lang *recently*
kailangan ka·ee·*la*·ngan *necessary* ⓐ
kailangan pv ka·ee·*la*·ngan *need* ⓥ
kainán ka·ee·*nan* *dining car*
kain (kainin/kumain) ka·*een* (ka·ee·neen/koo·*ma*·een) *eat*
kalabasa ka·la·*ba*·sa *pumpkin*
kalabáw ka·la·*bow* *water buffalo*
kalahatì ka·la·*ha*·tee' *half*
kálakalán ka·la·ka·*lan* *trade*
kalán ka·*lan* *stove*
kalendaryo ka·len·*dar*·yo *calendar*
kalesa ka·*le*·sa *carriage (horse-drawn)*
kalikasan ka·lee·*ka*·san *nature*
kalimutan pv ka·lee·*moo*·tan *forget*
kalinisan ka·lee·*nee*·san *cleaning*

kaliwâ ka·lee·wa' *left (direction)*
kalkuletor kal·koo·le·tor *calculator*
kalusugan ka·loo·soo·gan *health*
kalye kal·ye *street*
kama ka·ma *bed*
kamakalawá ka·ma·ka·la·wa *(the) day before yesterday*
kamakatló ka·ma·kat·lo *three days ago*
kamatis ka·ma·tees *tomato*
kamáy ka·mai *hand*
kambál kam·bal *twins*
— **na kama** na ka·ma *twin beds*
kambíng kam·beeng *goat*
kámbiyo kam·bee·yo *clutch (car)*
kámera ka·me·ra *camera*
kamí ka·mee *we*
kamisadentro ka·mee·sa·den·tro *shirt*
kamiseta ka·mee·se·ta *singlet*
kampeonato kam·pe·yo·na·to *championships*
kampíngan kam·pee·ngan *campsite • camping ground*
Kánada ka·na·da *Canada*
kanan ka·nan *right (direction)*
kandado kan·da·do *padlock • lock* ⓝ
— **ng bisikleta** nang bee·seek·le·ta *bike lock*
kandado (kandaduhan/magkandado) kan·da·do (kan·da·doo·han/ mag·kan·da·do) *lock* ⓥ
kandilà kan·dee·la *candle*
kanilá ka·nee·la *their*
kanin ka·neen *rice (cooked)*
kanluran kan·loo·ran *west*
kanselahín (ikanselá/magkanselá) kan·se·la·heen (ee·kan·se·la/ mag·kan·se·la) *cancel*
kanser kan·ser *cancer*
kantá kan·ta *song*
kantá av kan·ta *sing*
kanto kan·to *corner*
kanyá kan·ya *her • his • someone*
kapa ka·pa *coat*
kápakanán ka·pa·ka·nan *welfare*
kápakanáng panlipunan ka·pa·ka·nang pan·lee·poo·nan *social welfare*
kapaligirán ka·pa·lee·gee·ran *environment*
kapangánakan ka·pa·nga·na·kan *birthday*
kapangyarihan ka·pang·ya·ree·han *power*
kapatíd ka·pa·teed *sibling*
— **na babae** na ba·ba·e *sister*
— **na lalaki** na la·la·kee *brother*
kapé ka·pe *coffee*
kapihan ka·pee·han *café*
kapote ka·po·te *raincoat*

káraban ka·ra·ban *caravan*
karanasán ka·ra·na·san *experience*
— **sa trabaho** sa tra·ba·ho *work experience*
karapatáng pantao ka·ra·pa·tang pan·ta·o *human rights*
karapatáng sibíl ka·ra·pa·tang see·beel *civil rights*
karátula ka·ra·too·la *sign* ⓝ
karayom ka·ra·yom *needle (sewing)*
karera ka·re·ra *races (sport)*
kárerahán ka·re·ra·han *racetrack*
kari ka·ree *curry*
karitela ka·ree·te·la *carriage (horse-drawn)*
karné kar·ne *meat • beef*
karnéng bulô kar·neng boo·lo' *veal*
karnéng baboy kar·neng ba·boy *pork*
karot ka·rot *carrot*
karpintero kar·peen·te·ro *carpenter • builder*
kartón kar·ton *carton*
kasál ka·sal *marriage* ⓝ • *wedding* ⓝ • *married* ⓐ
kasalanan ka·sa·la·nan *(someone's) fault*
kasali ka·sa·lee *included*
kasama ka·sa·ma *companion*
kasero/a ⓜ/ⓕ ka·se·ra *landlord • landlady*
kasét ka·set *cassette*
kasino ka·si·no *casino*
kasóy ka·soy *cashew*
kastanyas kas·tan·yas *chestnut*
kastilyo kas·teel·yo *castle*
kásunduang pakákasál ka·soon·doo·ang pa·ka·ka·sal *engagement (to be married)*
katabí ng ka·ta·bee nang *next to*
katad ka·tad *leather*
katahímikan ka·ta·hee·mee·kan *peace*
katangian ka·ta·ngee·an *quality*
katapát ka·ta·pat *opposite*
katapusán ka·ta·poo·san *end* ⓝ • *finish* ⓝ
katás ka·tas *juice*
katawán ka·ta·wan *body*
katedrál ka·ted·ral *cathedral*
kathâ kat·ha' *fiction*
katí ka·tee *itch* ⓝ
katól ka·tol *mosquito coil*
Katóliko ka·to·lee·ko *Catholic*
Katólisismo ka·to·lee·sees·mo *Catholicism*
katrabaho ka·tra·ba·ho *colleague*
katulad ka·too·lad *similar*
katunayan ka·too·na·yan *certificate*
— **ng pagmamay-ari ng kotse** nang pag·ma·mai·a·ree nang kot·se *car owner's title*
katwiran kat·wee·ran *reason* ⓝ
kauntî ka·oon·tee' *little (not much)*
kawalì ka·wa·lee' *frying pan*

kawaní ka·wa·*nee* employee
  — **sa upisina** sa oo·*pee·see·*na office worker
kawili-wili ka·wee·lee·*wee·*lee interesting
kayó ka·*yo* pl
kebol kar *ke·*bol kar cable car
kendi *ken·*dee lollies • candy
keso *ke·*so cheese
ketsap *ket·*sap ketchup
keyk kayk cake
kidnap *keed·*nap kidnap
kídnaping *keed·*na·peeng kidnapping
kilo *kee·*lo kilogram • kilo
kilometro kee·*lo·me·*tro kilometre
kinabukasan kee·na·boo·*ka·*san future ⓝ
kinder *keen·*der kindergarten
kiropraktor kee·ro·*prak·*tor
  chiropractor
kita (makita/makakita)
  *kee·*ta (ma·*kee·*ta/ma·kee·*kee·*ta) see
kíwiprut *kee·*wee·proot kiwifruit
klase *kla·*se class (category)
klasikál kla·see·*kál* classical
kliyente klee·*yen·*te client
ko ko *I* • me • *my*
kokéyn ko·*kayn* cocaine
kokwa *kok·*wa cocoa
koléhiyo ko·*le·*hee·yo college
kolék kol ko·*lek* kol collect call
koliplawer ko·lee·*pla·*wer cauliflower
komedya ko·*med·*ya comedy
komisyón ko·mees·*yon* commission
kompanyá kom·pan·*ya* company (firm)
kompas *kom·*pas compass
kompirénsiya kom·pee·ren·*see·*ya conference
komportable kom·por·*tab·*le comfortable
kompyuter komp·*yoo·*ter computer
  — **geym** gaym computer game
komunikasyón ko·moo·nee·kas·*yon*
  communications (profession)
komunista ko·moo·*nees·*ta communist
komunyón ko·moon·*yon* communion
kondísyoner kon·*dees·*yo·ner conditioner
kondisyón sa pusò
  kon·dees·*yon* sa poo·*so'* heart condition
kondom *kon·*dom condom
konduktór kon·*dook·*tor ticket collector
kondyángtibaytis kon·*jang·*tee·bai·tees
  conjunctivitis
koneksiyón ko·nek·see·*yon* connection
konserbatibo kon·ser·ba·*tee·*bo
  conservative ⓡ
konsiyerto kon·see·*yer·*to concert
konsulado kon·soo·*la·*do consulate
kontak lens *kon·*tak lens contact lenses
kontrasepsiyón kon·tra·sep·see·*yon*
  contraceptives

kontrata kon·*tra·*ta contract
koreó ko·*re·*o mail (postal system)
kornpleks *korn·*pleks cornflakes
korta-pluma kor·ta·*ploo·*ma penknife
korte *kor·*te court (legal) • shape
koryente kor·*yen·*te current (electricity)
kostumbre kos·*toom·*bre custom
kosyer *kos·*yer kosher
koton *ko·*ton cotton (fabric)
  — **bad bad** bad bad cotton buds
kotse *kot·*se car
kredit *kre·*deet credit
  — **kard** kard credit card
krema *kre·*ma cream
kremang maasim *kre·*mang ma·*a·*seem
  sour cream
Kristiyano krees·tee·*ya·*no Christian
krus kroos cross (religious)
kubeta koo·*be·*ta toilet
kubetang pampúbliko koo·*be·*tang
  pam·*poob·*lee·ko public toilet
kuhanán ng bagahe koo·ha·*nan* nang
  ba·*ga·*he baggage claim
kulambô koo·lam·*bo'* mosquito net
kulay koo·*lai* colour
  — **abó** a·*bo* grey • gray
  — **lupà** *loo·*pa brown
  — **rosas** *ro·*sas pink
kulitis koo·*lee·*tees spinach
kumbento koom·*ben·*to convent
kumita av koo·*mee·*ta earn
kumot koo·*mot* sheet (bed)
  — **sa kama** sa *ka·*ma bed linen
kumpisál koom·pee·*sal* confession
kumuha ng litrato av koo·*moo·*ha nang
  leet·*ra·*to take a photo
kumuliling av koo·moo·lee·*leeng* ring (of
  the phone)
kumulô koo·moo·*lo'* boiled
kundiman koon·dee·*man* indigenous
  Filipino music adapted to Western style
kuneho koo·*ne·*ho rabbit
kung koong if
  — **minsan** meen·*san* sometimes
kunin (kinuha/kumuha) koo·*neen*
  (kee·*noo·*ha/koo·*moo·*ha) get • take
kusina koo·*see·*na' kitchen
kuto koo·*to* lice
kutsara koot·*sa·*ra spoon
  — **at tinidór** at tee·nee·*dor* cutlery
kutsarita koot·sa·*ree·*ta teaspoon
kutsilyo koot·*seel·*yo knife
kutsón koot·*son* mattress
kuwarentenas koo·wa·ren·*te·*nas
  quarantine
kuwarto koo·*war·*to room

kuwartong pandalawahan koo-*war*-tong pan-da-la-*wa*-han *double room*

kuweba koo-*we*-ba *cave*

kuwintás koo-ween-*tas* *necklace*

kwadraplidyik kwa-dra-*plee*-jeek *quadriplegic*

kuwartong tulugán koo-*war*-tong too-loo-*gan* *bedroom*

D

daán da-*an* *road* • *route*
 — **sa paglalakád nang mahabà** sa pag-la-la-*kad* nang ma-ha-ba' *hiking route*

daanan da-*a*-nan *path* • *aisle (on plane)*
 — **ng bisikleta** nang bee-*seek*-le-ta *bike path*
 — **ng tao** nang *ta*-o *footpath*

dagâ da-*ga'* *rat*

dagat *da*-gat *sea* • *ocean*

dahil *da*-heel *because*

dahon *da*-hon *leaf*

dalaga da-*la*-ga *single (female)*

dalandán da-lan-*dan* *mandarin*

dalawá da-la-*wa* *two*

dalawáng linggó da-la-*wang* leeng-*go* *fortnight*

dalá (dalhín/magdalá) da-*la* (dal-heen/mag-da-*la*) *bring* • *carry*

daliri da-*lee*-ree' *finger*
 — **sa paá** sa pa-*a* *toe*

dami *da*-mee *dummy* • *pacifier*

(ang) dami (ang) *da*-mee *a lot*

damít da-*meet* *clothing* • *dress*
 — **pampaligò** pam-pa-lee-*go'* *swimsuit*
 — **panloób** pan-lo-*ob* *underwear*

damó da-*mo* *grass* • *herb*

dasál da-*sal* *prayer*

dátiles *da*-tee-les *date (fruit)*

datingan da-*tee*-ngan *arrivals*

daungan da-oo-ngan *port (sea)*

dayap da-*yap* *lime (fruit)*

dáyari da-*ya*-ree *diary*

daybing *dai*-beeng *diving*

days dais *dice*

delikado de-lee-*ka*-do *fragile*

demokrasya de-mo-*kras*-ya *democracy*

demonstrasyón de-mons-tras-*yon* *demonstration*

Denmark *den*-mark *Denmark*

dentista den-*tees*-ta *dentist*

department istór de-*part*-ment ees-*tor* *department store*

departyur geyt de-*part*-yoor gayt *departure gate*

depósito de-*po*-see-to *deposit (bank)*

deyódorant de-*yo*-do-rant *deodorant*

déyt (dinéyt/magdéyt) dayt (dee-*nayt*/mag-*dayt*) *date (a person)*

dibdíb deeb-*deeb* *chest (body)*

diborsiyado/a ⓜ/ⓕ dee-bor-see-*ya*-do *divorced*

digrí dee-*gree* *degrees (temperature)*

di-kasali dee-ka-*sa*-lee *excluded*

diksiyunaryo deek-see-yoo-nar-yo *dictionary*

diláw dee-*law* *yellow*

diler ng droga *dee*-ler nang *dro*-ga *drug dealer*

di-maáari dee-ma-a-*a*-ree *impossible*

din deen *also*

diperénsiya sa oras dee-pe-*rens*-ya sa *o*-ras *time difference*

dirék-dayal dee-*rek*-da-yal *direct-dial*

direktór dee-rek-*tor* *director*

diretso dee-*ret*-so *straight* • *direct*

disenyo dee-*sen*-yo *design*

disk deesk *disk (CD-ROM)*

diskaríl dees-ka-*reel* *derailleur*

disko *dees*-ko *disco*

diskriminasyón dees-kree-mee-nas-*yon* *discrimination*

diskuwento dees-koo-*wen*-to *discount*

dismenoryá dees-me-nor-*ya* *period pain*

Disyembre dees-*yem*-bre *December*

disyerto dees-*yer*-to *desert*

di tinátagusán ng tubig dee tee-na-ta-goo-*san* nang *too*-beeg *waterproof*

dito *dee*-to *here*

diyabetis dee-ya-*be*-tees *diabetes*

diyam *jam* *jam*

diyaryo dee-*yar*-yo *newspaper*

diyeta dee-*ye*-ta *diet* ⓝ

diyornalista jor-na-*lees*-ta *journalist*

diyós dee-*yos* *god (general)*

doble *dob*-le *double*

dobol bed *do*-bol bed *double bed*

doktór dok-*tor* *doctor*

dokumentaryo do-koo-men-*tar*-yo *documentary*

dolyár dol-*yar* *dollar*

doón do-*on* *there*

dosena do-*se*-na *dozen*

dram dram *drum*

drama *dra*-ma *drama*

droga *dro*-ga *drug* • *pot (dope)*

dugô doo-*go'* *blood*

dulo *doo*-lo *point* ⓝ

dumating ⓐⓥ doo-ma-*teeng* *arrive* • *come*

duyan doo-*yan* *hammock*

DVD dee-bee-dee *DVD*

dyads hukóm jads *judge* ⓝ
dyaging ja·geeng *jogging*
dyaket ja·ket *jacket*
dyamper lids jam·per leeds *jumper leads*
dyet lag jet lag *jet lag*
dyim jeem *gym (place)*
dyimnastiks jeem·nas·teeks *gymnastics*
dyins jeens *jeans*
dyip jeep *jeep*

E

ekónomi klas e·ko·no·mee klas *economy class*
eksakto ek·sak·to *exactly*
eksema ek·se·ma *eczema*
eksprés eks·pres *express* ⓐ
— **meyl** mayl *express (mail)*
ékstasi eks·ta·see *ecstacy (drug)*
ekstensyón eks·tens·yon *extension (visa)*
edád e·dad *age* ⓝ
éditor e·dee·tor *editor*
edukasyón e·doo·kas·yon *education*
elebeytor e·le·bay·tor *elevator • lift*
eleksiyón e·lek·see·yon *election*
eléktrikal istór e·lek·tree·kal ees·tor *electrical store*
eléktrisidád e·lek·tree·see·dad *electricity*
embahadór em·ba·ha·dor *ambassador*
émbasi em·ba·see *embassy*
emérdyensi e·mer·jen·see *emergency*
émeyl e·mayl *email* ⓝ
emosyonál e·mos·yo·nal *emotional*
enerhiyáng nukliyár e·ner·hee·yang nook·lee·yar *nuclear energy*
Enero e·ne·ro *January*
epilepsi e·pee·lep·see *epilepsy*
erkon er·kon *airconditioning*
ermeyl er·mayl *airmail*
erobiks e·ro·beeks *aerobics*
erport er·port *airport*
eruplano e·roo·pla·no *aeroplane • airplane • airline*
eskaleytor es·ka·lay·tor *escalator*
Eskosya es·kos·ya *Scotland*
eskrima es·kree·ma *fencing (sport)*
Espanya es·pan·ya *Spain*
espesyál es·pes·yal *special*
espesyalista es·pes·ya·lees·ta *specialist*
estado es·ta·do *marital status*
Estados Unidos es·ta·dos oo·nee·dos *USA*
estudyante es·tood·yan·te *student*
Europa yoo·ro·pa *Europe*

F

Filipino pee·lee·pee·no *Filipino (language)*
Filipino/a ⓜ/ⓕ pee·lee·pee·no/a *Filipino*
— **Balik Bayan** ba·leek bai·yan *Filipino expatriate*
first aid pers ayd *first-aid kit*
first class pers klas *first class*
football foot·bal *football*
— **ng Amerikano** nang a·me·ree·ka·no *American football*
foul powl *foul (sport)*
full-time pool·taim *full-time*

G

gabí ga·bee *evening • night*
gagambá ga·gam·ba *spider*
gahasà ga·ha·sa' *rape* ⓝ
gahasà (gahasain/gumahasà) ga·ha·sa' (ga·ha·sa·een/goo·ma·ha·sa') *rape*
galeriyang pang-arte ga·le·ree·yang pang·ar·te *art gallery*
galít ga·leet *angry*
gamót ga·mot *medicine• pill*
— **na pampatulog** na pam·pa·too·log *sleeping pills*
— **sa ubó** sa oo·bo *cough medicine*
garahe ga·ra·he *garage*
garántisado ga·ran·tee·sa·do *guaranteed*
garapón ga·ra·pon *jar*
garbansos gar·ban·sos *chickpea*
garden gar·den *garden*
gas gas *gas (for cooking)*
gasa ga·sa *gauze*
gasolina ga·so·lee·na *gas (petrol)*
gatas ga·tas *milk*
— **na iskím** na ees·keem *skim milk*
gawaing bahay ga·wa·eeng ba·hai *housework*
gawáng palayók ga·wang pa·la·yok *pottery*
gawín (gawín/gumawà) ga·ween (ga·ween/goo·ma·wa) *do • make*
geyt gayt *gate (airport, etc)*
gilagid gee·la·geed *gums*
Ginang gee·nang *Mrs*
giniling gee·nee·leeng *mince*
ginokolohista gee·no·ko·lo·hees·ta *gynaecologist*
Ginoó gee·no·o *Mr*
gintô geen·to' *gold*
gisantes gee·san·tes *pea*
gisingin gee·see·ngeen *wake (someone) up*
gitara gee·ta·ra *guitar*

giya *gee*·ya *guide (person)*
— **tungkól sa libangan** toong·*kol* sa lee·*ba*·ngan *entertainment guide*
giyang libró *gee*·yang lee·*bro* *guidebook*
giyera gee·*ye*·ra *war*
glándiyular piber glan·dee·yoo·lar *pee*·ber *glandular fever*
gobyerno gob·*yer*·no *government*
gogel ma·*nga* go·gel *goggles*
gol gol *goal*
gramo *gra*·mo *gram*
gripo *gree*·po *tap • faucet*
groseryá gro·ser·*ya* *grocery • delicatessen*
grupo ng dugô *groo*·po nang doo·*go'* *blood group*
gubat *goo*·bat *forest*
gulay *goo*·lai *vegetable*
— **na butó** na boo·*to* *legume*
gulóng goo·*long* *wheel • tyre • tube (tyre)*
gumagamit ng droga goo·ma·*ga*·meet nang *dro*·ga *drug user*
gumawâ av goo·ma·*wa'* *produce* Ⓥ
guniguni goo·nee·goo·*nee* *hallucination*
gunting goon·*teeng* *scissors*
gupit goo·*peet* *haircut*
gusalì goo·*sa*·lee *building*
gustó (gustó/magustuhán) goos·*to* (goos·*to*/ma·goos·too·*han*) *like • want*
guwantes goo·*wan*·tes *glove(s)*
guwapo/a Ⓜ/Ⓕ goo·*wa*·po/a *handsome • good-looking* Ⓜ • Ⓕ
guyabano goo·ya·*ba*·no *soursop*

H

hagdanan hag·*da*·nan *stairway*
halagá ng pagpasok ha·la·*ga* nang pag·*pa*·sok *admission (price)*
halakhák (halakhakán/humalakhák) ha·lak·*hak* (ha·lak·ha·*kan*/hoo·ma·lak·*hak*) *laugh* Ⓥ
halál ha·*lal* *halal*
halaman ha·*la*·man *plant* Ⓝ
hálidey ha·lee·day *holiday*
halík ha·*leek* *kiss* Ⓝ
halikán pv ha·lee·*kan* *kiss* Ⓥ
halimbawà ha·leem·*ba*·wa *example*
halò ha·*lo'* *ingredient*
haluán pv ha·lo'·*an* *mix* Ⓥ
halos ha·los *almost*
hamón ha·*mon* *ham*
hanapin (hanapin/maghanap) ha·*na*·peen (ha·*na*·peen/mag·ha·*nap*) *find • look for*
hanbag han·bag *handbag*
handâ han·*da'* *ready*

hangganan hang·*ga*·nan *border*
hanggáng sa (Biyernes) hang·*gang* sa (bee·yer·nes) *until (Friday)*
hangin ha·ngeen *wind • air*
hapon ha·pon *afternoon*
Hapón ha·*pon* *Japan*
hapunan ha·*poo*·nan *dinner*
hardinero har·dee·ne·ro *gardener*
harding botánika har·*deeng* bo·*ta*·nee·ka *botanic garden*
hardíng pampúbliko har·*deeng* pam·poob·lee·ko *public gardens*
harì ha·*ree'* *king*
hatinggabí ha·teeng·ga·*bee* *midnight*
hawakán ha·wa·*kan* *handlebars*
hayop ha·*yop* *animal*
haywey hai·way *highway • main road*
helmet hel·met *helmet*
hepataytis he·pa·*tai*·tees *hepatitis*
hering he·reeng *herring*
heringgilya he·reeng·*geel*·ya *needle (syringe)*
héroín he·ro·ween *heroin*
héyselnat hay·sel·nat *hazelnut*
higít pa hee·*geet* pa *more*
hikà hee·*ka'* *asthma*
hikaw hee·kow *earrings*
hilagà hee·*la*·ga' *north*
hilahin pv hee·*la*·heen *pull*
hiláw hee·low *raw*
hiló hee·*lo* *dizzy*
himpilan ng militár heem·*pee*·lan nang mee·lee·*tar* *military base*
hindî heen·*dee'* *not*
— **kailanmán** ka·ee·lan·*man* *never*
— **ligtás** leeg·*tas* *unsafe*
— **makátarungan** ma·ka·ta·roo·ngan *unfair*
— **pa** pa *not yet*
— **pangkaraniwan** pang·ka·ra·nee·wan *unusual*
Hindu heen·doo *Hindu*
hintáy (hintayín/maghintáy) heen·*tai* (heen·tai·*yeen*/mag·heen·*tai*) *wait (for)*
hintuan heen·*too*·an *stop (bus)* Ⓝ
— **ng bus** nang boos *bus stop*
hipuin (hipuin/humipò) hee·*poo*·een (hee·*poo*·een/hoo·mee·po) *touch • feel* Ⓥ
hiram (ipahiram/humirám) hee·ram (ee·pa·*hee*·ram/hoo·mee·ram) *borrow*
hiring eyd hee·reeng ayd *hearing aid*
HIV ayts·ai·bee *HIV*
hiwà hee·wa' *fillet • slice* Ⓝ
hiwain pv hee·wa·een *cut* Ⓥ
hiwaláy hee·wa·lai *separate*
hiyumánitis hee·yoo·ma·*nee*·tees *humanities*

homeópati ho·me·yo·pa·tee *homeopathy*
hóroskop ho·ros·kop *horoscope*
Hudyó hood·yo *Jewish*
hulaan (hulaan/humulà) hoo·la·an
(hoo·la·an/hoo·moo·la) *guess* ⓥ
hulí hoo·lee *late*
hulugán ng sulat
hoo·loo·gan nang soo·lat *mailbox*
Hulyo hool·yo *July*
humigâ av hoo·mee·ga' *lie (not stand)*
humingá av hoo·mee·nga *breathe*
humingî av hoo·mee·ngee'
ask (for something)
humintô av hoo·meen·to' *quit*
Hunyo hoon·yo *June*
hustó hoos·to *enough*
Huwebes hoo·we·bes *Thursday*

I

ibá ee·ba *other • another*
ibáng bansâ ee·bang ban·sa' *overseas*
ibon ee·bon *bird*
búk (ibúk/magbúk) *book* (ee·book/
mag·book) *book (make a booking)*
ibukás pv ee·boo·kas *open* ⓥ
ID ai·dee *identification*
ikalawá ee·ka·la·wa *second* ⓐ
ikasál pv ee·ka·sal *marry*
ikáw ee·kaw *you inf sg*
iksibisyón eek·see·bees·yon *exhibition*
igos ee·gos *fig*
ihatíd pv ee·ha·teed *deliver*
ihintô pv ee·heen·to' *stop • cease*
ilagáy pv ee·la·gai *put*
ilán ee·lan *few • several • some*
ilaw ee·low *light*
    — sa unahán sa oo·na·han *headlights*
    — trápiko tra·pee·ko *traffic light*
ilog ee·log *river*
ilóng ee·long *nose*
imbitahín pv eem·bee·ta·heen *invite* ⓥ
imigrasyón ee·mee·gras·yon *immigration*
impeksiyón eem·pek·see·yon *infection*
    — sa daanan ng ihì
    sa da·a·nan nang ee·hee' *urinary infection*
impormasyón eem·por·mas·yon *information*
importante eem·por·tan·te *important*
iná ee·na *mother • mom • mum*
ináantók ee·na·an·tok *sleepy*
inapó ee·na·po *descendant*
Índiya een·dee·ya *India*
indústriya een·doos·tree·ya *industry*
indyiniring een·jee·nee·reeng *engineering*
Inglatera eeng·gla·te·ra *England*

Inglés eeng·gles *English*
inhinyero een·heen·ye·ro *engineer*
iniksiyón ee·neek·see·yon *injection*
iniksiyunán (iniksiyunán/
    mag-iniksiyun) ee·neek·see·yoo·nan
    (ee·neek·see·yoo·nan/
    mag·ee·neek·see·yon) *inject*
init ee·neet *heat*
inosente ee·no·sen·te *innocent*
insekto een·sek·to *bug* ⓝ
ínterbyu een·ter·byoo *interview* ⓝ
intermisyon een·ter·mees·yon *intermission*
internasyonál een·ter·nas·yo·nal
international
ínternet een·ter·net *Internet*
    — kapé ka·pe *Internet café*
inumin ee·noo·meen *drink* ⓝ
inóm (inumín/uminóm) ee·nom
    (ee·noo·meen/oo·mee·nom) *drink* ⓥ
ipadalá (ipadalá/magpadalá) ee·pa·da·la
    (ee·pa·da·da·la/mag·pa·da·la) *send*
ipakita pv ee·pa·kee·ta *show* ⓥ
ipamigáy pv ee·pa·mee·gai
    deal (cards) ⓥ
ipátotoó pv ee·pa·to·to·o *validate*
ipis ee·pees *cockroach*
irekord ee·re·kord *record*
iresaykel pv ee·re·sai·kel *recycle*
Irlándiya eer·lan·dee·ya *Ireland*
isá ee·sa *one*
isahang kuwarto ee·sa·hang koo·war·to
single room
isalin sa Inglés/Pilipino pv ee·sa·leen sa
    eeng·les/pee·lee·pee·no *translate to
    English/Filipino*
isáng paá ng medyas
    ee·sang pa·a nang med·yas *a sock*
isará (isará/magsará)
    ee·sa·ra (ee·sa·ra/mag·sa·ra) *close*
isdâ ees·da' *fish* ⓝ
sigáw (isigáw/sumigáw) see·gow
    (ee·see·gow/soo·mee·gow) *shout*
iskoba ees·ko·ba *brush* ⓝ
iskultura ees·kool·too·ra *sculpture*
isla ees·la *island*
isláyd ees·laid *slide (film)*
isnowbording ees·now·bor·deeng
snowboarding
ispidómiter ees·pee·do·mee·ter
speedometer
ispórt ees·port *sport*
Ísrael ees·ra·el *Israel*
istambay na tiket ees·tam·bai na tee·ket
stand by ticket
istante ees·tan·te *shelf*
(four-)istár (por-)ees·tar (four-)star

istasyón ees·tas·*yon* station
— **ng bus** nang boos *bus station*
— **ng gasolina** nang ga·so·*lee*·na *petrol station*
— **ng metro** nang *met*·ro *metro station*
— **ng pulisyá** nang poo·lees·*ya police station*
— **ng tren** nang tren *train station • railway station*
istátuwa ees·*ta*·too·wa *statue*
istíl water ees·*teel* wa·ter *still water*
istilo ees·*tee*·lo *style*
istiryo ees·*teer*·yo *stereo*
istóriko ees·to·ree·ko *historical*
istorya ees·*tor*·ya *history • story*
istróberi ees·tro·be·ree *strawberry*
istrók ees·*trok* *stroke (health)*
istroler ees·tro·ler *stroller*
istudyo ees·*tood*·yo *studio*
isuót (isuót/magsuót) ees·soo·ot (ee·soo·ot/mag·soo·ot) *wear*
IT *ai*·*tee* IT
Italya ee·*tal*·ya *Italy*
itayô (itayô/magtayô) ee·ta·*yo'* (ee·ta·*yo'*/mag·ta·*yo'*) *build*
itinda (itindá/magtindá) ee·teen·*da* (ee·teen·*da*/mag·teen·*da*) *sell*
itlóg eet·*log* *egg*
itó ee·*to* *this (one)*
itulak pv ee·*too*·lak *push* ⓥ
iturò pv ee·too·ro' *point* ⓥ
IUD *ai*·yoo·dee *IUD*
iyó ee·*yo* *your*
iyón ee·*i* *that (one) • it*

L

laba *la*·ba *lava*
laban *la*·ban *fight* ⓝ
labanós la·ba·*nos* *radish*
labasan la·*ba*·san *exit* ⓝ
lakad *la*·kad *walk* ⓝ
lakás *la*·kas *strength*
laker ng bagahe *la*·ker nang ba·*ga*·he *luggage locker*
labhan (labhán/maglabá) lab·*han* (lab·*han*/mag·la·*ba*) *wash (something)*
labi *la*·bee *foyer*
labì *la*·bee' *lips*
labî *la*·bee *ruins*
lagakan ng mga balabal la·*ga*·kan nang ma·*nga* ba·la·bal *cloakroom*
lagnát lag·*nat* *fever*
lahát la·*hat* *all • everyone • everything*
lálabhan *la*·lab·han *laundry (clothes)*

lalaki la·*la*·kee *male • man*
lalamunan la·la·*moo*·nan *throat*
lamíg la·*meeg* *cold* ⓝ
lamók la·*mok* *mosquito*
lampasán pv lam·*pas*·an *pass* ⓥ
lampín lam·*peen* *nappy • diaper*
lana *la*·na *wool*
landás lan·*das* *path • track • trail*
— **sa bundók** sa boon·*dok* *mountain path*
lang lang *only*
langgám lang·*gam* *ant*
langís la·*ngees* *oil*
— **ng oliba** nang o·*lee*·ba *olive oil*
langit *la*·ngeet *sky*
languyan la·*ngoo*·yan *pool (swimming)*
lapis *la*·pees *pencil*
laptap *lap*·tap *laptop*
largabista lar·ga·*bees*·ta *binoculars*
larô la·*ro'* *game (sport)*
larong kriket *la*·rong *kree*·ket *cricket (sport)*
laseta la·*se*·ta *pocket knife*
lasíng la·*seeng* *drunk*
lata *la*·ta *can • tin*
lawà *la*·wa' *lake*
layp dyaket laip *ja*·ket *life jacket*
layt miter lait *mee*·ter *light meter*
layter *lai*·ter *cigarette lighter*
legál le·*gal* *legal*
lens lens *lens*
lentil *len*·teel *lentil*
lepwing *lep*·weeng *left-wing*
letsugas let·*soo*·gas *lettuce*
leys lays *lace*
libing lee·*beeng* *funeral*
libís lee·*bees* *valley*
libre *lee*·bre *available • complimentary (free)*
libró lee·*bro* *book* ⓝ
libróng dasalan lee·*brong* da·*sa*·lan *prayer book*
ligtás leeg·*tas* *safe*
— **na pakikipag-seks** na pa·kee·kee·pag·*seks* *safe sex*
likód lee·*kod* *back (body)*
lila *lee*·la *purple*
lilim lee·*leem* *shade*
limón lee·*mon* *lemon*
limonada lee·mo·*na*·da *lemonade*
lindól leen·*dol* *earthquake*
linen *lee*·nen *linen (material)*
Linggó leeng·*go* *Sunday*
linggó leeng·*go* *week*
linis (linisin/maglinis) lee·*nees* (lee·*nee*·seen/mag·*lee*·nees) *clean* ⓥ
lip bam leep bam *lip balm*

lípistik *lee-pees-teek* lipstick
lisénsiya *lee-sen-see-ya* licence
— sa pagmamaneho
sa pag-ma-ma-ne-ho drivers licence
litratista *leet-ra-tees-ta* photographer
litrato *leet-ra-to* photo
liyó *lee-yo* seasick
lokal *lo-kal* local ⓐ
lolo/a ⓜ/ⓕ *lo-lo/a*
grandfather/grandmother
londri *lon-dree* laundry • launderette
longganisang baboy
long-ga-nee-sang ba-boy pork sausage
lubid *loo-beed* rope
lubrikante *loo-bree-kan-te* lubricant
lugár *loo-gar* place • venue
— ng kapanganakan nang
ka-pa-nga-na-kan place of birth
— ng mga babaing mababà ang lipád
*nang ma-nga ba-ba-eeng ma-ba-ba' ang
lee-pad* red-light district
lukúlukó *loo-koo-loo-ko* crazy
lumabás av *loo-ma-bas* go out
lumangóy av *loo-ngoy* swim ⓥ
lumipád av *loo-mee-pad* fly ⓥ
lundág (lundagín/lumundág)
loon-dag (loon-dag-een/loo-moon-dag)
jump ⓥ
Lunes *loo-nes* Monday
lupà *loo-pa'* land ⓝ
lutò (ilutò/maglutò) *loo-to* (ee-loo-to/
mag-loo-to') cook ⓥ

M

maáarì *ma-a-a-ree* can (be able)
maaga *ma-a-ga* early
maaraw *ma-a-row* sunny
mababà *ma-ba-ba'* low
mabagal *ma-ba-gal* slow • slowly
mabaít *ma-ba-eet* kind • nice
mabigát *ma-bee-gat* heavy
mabilís *ma-bee-lees* fast • quick
mabuti *ma-boo-tee* good • nice • fine • well
makálawa *ma-ka-la-wa* twice
makalipas *ma-ka-lee-pas* after
makapál *ma-ka-pal* thick
makatutulong *ma-ka-too-too-long* useful
makatwiran *ma-kat-wee-ran* sensible
makihati kay av *ma-kee-ha-tee kai*
share (with)
makihati sa av *ma-kee-ha-tee sa* share ⓥ
mákina *ma-kee-na* engine • machine
makiníg (sa) av *ma-kee-neeg (sa)*
listen (to)

makipagkilala av
ma-kee-pag-kee-la-la chat up
madalás *ma-da-las* often
madalí *ma-da-lee'* easy
madilím *ma-dee-leem* dark
madre *ma-dre* nun
magá *ma-ga'* swelling
magaán *ma-ga-an* light (not heavy)
mag-ahit *ma-g-a-heet* shave ⓥ
magalíng *ma-ga-leeng*
brilliant • great • wonderful
magandá *ma-gan-da* beautiful • pretty
mágasin *ma-ga-seen* magazine
magbalík *mag-ba-leek* return (come back)
magbaraha av *mag-ba-ra-ha* play cards
magbayad av *mag-ba-yad* pay ⓥ
magbisikleta av *mag-bee-seek-le-ta* cycle
magkakarné *mag-ka-kar-ne* butcher ⓝ
magkamping av *mag-kam-peeng* camp ⓥ
magkano *mag-ka-no* how much
magkasama av *mag-ka-sa-ma* together
magkita av *mag-kee-ta* meet
magkumpuní av *mag-koom-poo-nee* repair
magdamág *mag-da-mag* overnight
magdesisyón av *mag-de-sees-yon* decide
mag-ehersisyo av *mag-e-her-sees-yo*
work out (exercise)
maggitara av *mag-gee-ta-ra* play guitar
maghandá av *mag-han-da'* prepare
maghintô av *mag-heen-to'*
stay (in one place)
mag-iisdâ *mag-ee-ees-da'* fish monger
magíng av *ma-geeng* be • become
mag-isíp av *mag-ee-seep* think
mag-iskéyt av *mag-ees-kayt* skate ⓥ
mag-isnorkel *mag-ees-nor-kel* snorkelling
maglakád nang mahabà av
mag-la-kad nang ma-ha-ba' hike ⓥ
maglakbáy av *mag-lak-bai* travel
magmahál sa av *mag-ma-hal sa* care for ⓥ
magnanakaw *mag-na-na-kow* thief
magpahingá av *mag-pa-hee-nga* rest
magpakailanmán
mag-pa-ka-ee-lan-man forever
magpalabás av *mag-pa-la-bas* play (theatre) ⓝ
magprotesta av *mag-pro-tes-ta* protest ⓥ
magreklamo av *mag-rek-la-mo* complain
magrenta av *mag-ren-ta* rent ⓥ
magsalitâ av *mag-sa-lee-ta'* talk • speak
magsasaká *mag-sa-sa-ka* farmer
magsayá av *mag-sa-ya* enjoy (oneself)
magsimulâ av *mag-see-moo-la'* start ⓥ
magsyút av *mag-syoot* shoot ⓥ
magtalo av *mag-ta-lo* argue
magtindá ng bulaklák *mag-tee-teen-da*
nang boo-lak-lak florist

magtiwalà av mag·tee·*wa*·la' *trust* ⓥ

magtrabaho av mag·tra·*ba*·ho *work* ⓥ

magulang ma·*goo*·lang *parents*

magutom ma·*goo*·tom *hungry*

magyelo av mag·*ye*·lo *freeze (up)*

mahabà ma·*ha*·ba' *long*

mahál ma·*hal* *expensive · dear (endearment)*

mahál (mahál/magmahál)
ma·*hal* (ma·*hal*/mag·ma·*hal*) *love* ⓥ

mahalagá ma·ha·la·*ga* valuable*

mahinà ma·*hee*·na' *weak*

mahirap ma·*hee*·rap
difficult · poor (not wealthy)

mahiyain ma·hee·*ya*·een *shy*

maingay ma·*ee*·ngai *noisy*

mainit ma·*ee*·neet *warm · hot*
— na tubig na too·beeg *hot water*

máintindihán av ma·een·teen·dee·*han*
understand

maís ma·*ees* corn*

maitím ma·*ee*·teem *dark · black*

malakás ma·la·*kas* strong · loud*

malakí ma·la·*kee* big · huge · large*

malalim ma·*la*·leem *deep*

malamig ma·la·*meeg*
cold · cool (temperature)

malapit ma·*la*·peet *close by · near · nearby*

malasa ma·*la*·sa *tasty*

malasado ma·la·*sa*·do *soft-boiled*

malayà ma·*la*·ya' *free (not bound)*

malayò ma·*la*·yo' *far · remote*

Malaysia ma·*lays*·ya *Malaysia*

maleta ma·*le*·ta *suitcase*

malî ma·*lee*' *wrong*

maligayang batì ma·lee·*ga*·yang ba·*tee*'
congratulations

maligò av ma·lee·go' *wash (oneself)*

maliít ma·lee·*eet*
little · small · tiny · short (height)

malinis ma·*lee*·nees *clean* ⓐ

malungkót ma·loong·*kot* sad*

maluwág ma·loo·*wag* loose*

maluwáng ma·loo·*wang* wide*

mamatáy av ma·ma·*tai* die*

mámayâ *ma*·ma·ya' later · soon*

mamilí av ma·mee·*lee* shop ⓥ · go shopping*

mámogram *ma*·mo·gram *mammogram*

manalo av ma·*na*·lo *win* ⓥ

manê ma·*ne*' *peanut*

mánedyer *ma*·ned·yer *manager*

maneho (manehohin/magmaneho)
ma·*ne*·ho (ma·ne·ho·heen/mag·ma·*ne*·ho)
drive ⓥ

mang-aawit mang·a·a·*weet* singer*

mangabayo av ma·nga·*ba*·yo *ride (a horse)* ⓥ

mangakò ma·*nga*·ko' *promise* ⓝ

mangangalakal ma·nga·nga·*la*·kal
tradesperson

manggá mang·*ga* *mango*

manggagawa sa pábrika
mang·ga·ga·wa sa *pab*·ree·ka
factory worker

mánghahangà mang·ha·ha·*nga*' *fan (sport)*

manghuhulà mang·hoo·hoo·*la*' *fortune teller*

mangkók mang·*kok* bowl*

mangungulot ma·ngoo·*ngoo*·lot
hairdresser

manigarilyó av ma·nee·ga·reel·*yo*
smoke (a cigarette) ⓥ

manika ma·*nee*·ka *doll*

manlalarò man·la·la·ro' *sportsperson*

manloloko man·lo·*lo*·ko *cheater* ⓝ

manók ma·*nok* chicken*

mansanas man·*sa*·nas *apple*

mantekilya man·te·*keel*·ya
butter · margarine

mantél man·*tel* tablecloth*

mantikà man·tee·ka *oil (cooking)*

manuluyan av ma·noo·loo·yan
stay (at a hotel)

manwál na trabahadór
man·*wal* na tra·ba·ha·*dor* *manual worker*

mapa *ma*·pa *map*
— ng daán nang da·*an* *road map*

mapaklá ma·pak·*la* bitter*

mapulá ma·poo·*la* red*

maputî ma·poo·*tee*' white*

marami ma·*ra*·mee *many*

marihuwana ma·ree·hoo·*wa*·na
marijuana

márinig pv *ma*·ree·neeg *hear*

mármaleyd *mar*·ma·layd *marmalade*

Marso *mar*·so *March*

marsyal art *mars*·yal art *martial arts*

Martes *mar*·tes *Tuesday*

martilyo mar·*teel*·yo *hammer*

marumí ma·roo·*mee* dirty*

masakít ma·sa·*keet*
sore ⓐ · *painful*

masayá ma·*sa*·ya *happy*

masahe ma·*sa*·he *massage*

masahista ma·sa·*hees*·ta
masseur · masseuse

masamâ ma·sa·ma' bad*

masamáng sikmurà
ma·sa·*mang* seek·moo·ra' *indigestion*

masayá ma·*sa*·ya *happy* ⓐ · *fun* ⓐ

masdan (pagmasdán/magmasíd) mas·*dan*
(pag·mas·*dan*/mag·ma·*seed*) *watch* ⓥ

masel *ma*·sel *muscle*

maselang pag-aari ng babae ma·*se*·lang
pag·a·a·ree nang ba·ba·e *vagina*

mas gustó pv mas goos·to *prefer*
masikíp ma·see·*keep tight*
mas magalíng mas ma·ga·*leeng better*
mas malakí mas ma·la·kee *bigger*
mas malíit mas ma·lee·eet *smaller*
masuwerte ma·soo·wer·te *lucky*
masyado(ng mahál) mas·ya·do(ng ma·hal)
   too (expensive)
matá ma·ta *eye(s)*
mataás ma·ta·as *tall* • *high*
   — na páaralán na pa·a·ra·lan *high school*
matabâ ma·ta·ba' *fat* ⓐ
matamís ma·ta·mees *dessert* • *sweet* ⓐ
matandâ ma·tan·da' *old*
matapang ma·ta·pang *brave*
matarík ma·ta·reek *steep*
matigás ma·tee·gas *hard (not soft)*
matigás ang ulo ma·tee·gas ang oo·lo
   stubborn
matuto av ma·too·to *learn*
mauhaw ma·oo·how *thirsty*
maulap ma·oo·lap *foggy* • *cloudy*
maupô ma·oo·po' *sit*
may mai *with*
may kásunduang pakákasál
   mai ka·soon·doo·ang pa·ka·ka·sal
   engaged (to be married)
may katiwalián mai ka·tee·wa·lee·an
   corrupt ⓐ
máykroweyb *mai·*kro·wayb
   microwave (oven)
may disabilidád
   mai dees·a·bee·lee·dad *disabled*
may erkon mai er·kon *air-conditioned*
may giyang tur
   mai gee·yang toor *guided tour*
may sakít mai sa·keet *sick*
may sipón av mai see·pon *have a cold*
may sirà mai see·ra' *faulty*
mayaman ma·ya·man *rich* • *wealthy*
may-arì mai·a·ree *owner*
maybahay mai·ba·hai *homemaker*
maygreyn *mai·*grayn *migraine*
Mayo *ma·*yo *May*
mayonesa ma·yo·ne·sa *mayonnaise*
mayroón av mai·ro·on *have*
maysakít mai·sa·keet *ill*
maysala mai·sa·la *guilty*
medikasyón me·dee·kas·yon
   medicine (medication)
medisina me·dee·see·na
   medicine (study, profession)
meditasyón me·dee·tas·yon *meditation*
medyas *med·*yas socks • *stockings*
mekániko me·ka·nee·ko *mechanic*
mensahe men·sa·he *message*

menú me·noo *menu*
meryenda mer·yen·da *snack* ⓝ
mesa *me·*sa *table*
metál me·tal *metal* ⓐ
metro *met·*ro *metre*
metro tren *met·*ro tren *metro (train)*
meyk ap mayk ap *make-up*
meyor *me·*yor *mayor*
mga batà ma·nga ba·ta *children*
mga bitamina ma·nga bee·ta·mee·na
   vitamins
mga bundók ma·nga boon·dok
   mountain range
mga kwalipikasyón ma·nga
   kwa·lee·pee·kas·yon *qualifications*
mga detalye ma·nga de·tal·ye *details*
mga manggagawa ma·nga mang·ga·ga·wa
   human resources
mga salitreng panlaban sa panunuyót
   ma·nga sa·lee·treng pan·la·ban sa
   pa·noo·noo·yot *rehydration salts*
mga tao ma·nga ta·o *people*
mga tulâ ma·nga too·la' *poetry*
midya *meed·*ya *media*
mikrobyo meek·rob·yo *virus*
milimetro mee·lee·met·ro *millimetre*
milítar mee·lee·tar *military*
milón mee·lon *melon* • *cantaloupe* •
   rockmelon
milyón meel·yon *million*
minátamís mee·na·ta·mees *sweets*
míneral water mee·ne·ral wo·ter
   mineral water
minsan meen·san *once*
minuto mee·noo·to *minute*
misa *mee·*sa *mass (Catholic)*
miyembro mee·yem·bro *member*
Miyérkoles mee·yer·ko·les *Wednesday*
mo mo *you* • *your*
mobayl pon *mo·*bail pon *mobile phone*
moda *mo·*da *fashion*
modem *mo·*dem *modem*
moderno mo·der·no *modern*
monasteryo mo·nas·ter·yo *monastery*
monghe mong·he *monk*
monumento mo·noo·men·to *monument*
mosk mosk *mosque*
motél mo·tel *motel*
mótorbowt *mo·*tor·boht *motorboat*
motorsiklo mo·tor·seek·lo *motorcycle*
mótorway *mo·*tor·way *motorway* • *tollway*
mukhâ mook·ha' *face* ⓝ
mulâ moo·la' *from*
mulá noóng (Mayo)
   moo·la no·ong (ma·yo) *since (May)*
multá mool·ta *fine (penalty)*

mundó moon·do *Earth • world*
mura *moo·ra cheap*
murà *moo·ra' light (of colour)*
museo moo·se·o *museum*
músika moo·see·ka *music*
musikero moo·see·ke·ro *musician*
musli *moos·lee muesli*
Muslím moos·leem *Muslim*
mustasa moos·ta·sa *mustard*
muwebles moo·web·les *furniture*

N

nakabábagót na·ka·ba·ba·got *boring*
nakakandado na·ka·kan·da·do *locked*
nakadroga na·ka·dro·ga *stoned (drugged)*
nakalalason na·ka·la·la·son *poisonous*
nakalistá na·ka·lees·ta *itemised*
nakaraán na·ka·ra·an *last • previous • past*
nakasakáy na·ka·sa·kai *aboard*
nakatátawá na·ka·ta·ta·wa *funny*
nakaw *na·kow stolen*
nakawin (nakawin/magnakaw)
  na·ka·ween (na·ka·ween/mag·na·kow)
  steal • rob
nag-íisá nag·ee·ee·sa *alone*
nagmámadalî nag·ma·ma·da·lee'
  in a hurry • urgent
nagmámahál nag·ma·ma·hal *lover*
nagpapakita nag·pa·pa·kee·ta *indicator*
nagpapasalamat nag·pa·pa·sa·la·mat
  grateful
nagyelo nag·ye·lo *frozen*
nahihiyâ na·hee·hee·ya' *embarrassed*
nais *na·ees wish* ⓥ
naiwang bagahe na·ee·wang ba·ga·he
  left luggage
nalaglág na·lag·lag *fall (down)*
namuóng hamóg na·moo·ong ha·mog *frost*
nanganganib na urì na·nga·nga·neeb na
  oo·ree' *endangered species*
nápaka na·pa·ka *very*
nápakagalíng na·pa·ka·ga·leeng *excellent*
napakatandá na na·pa·ka·tan·da na *ancient*
napkin *nap·keen napkin*
nars *nars nurse*
nasa edád na·sa e·dad *adult* ⓐ
nasa ibáng bansá na·sa ee·bang ban·sa'
  abroad
nasa oras na·sa o·ras *on time*
nasa unahán na·sa oo·na·han *ahead*
nasaktán na·sak·tan *injured*
nasirà av na·see·ra' *break down*
nasugatan na·soo·ga·tan *injury*
nasyonalidád nas·yo·na·lee·dad *nationality*

natuyoropatí na·too·yo·ro·pa·tee
  naturopathy
nawalâ na·wa·la' *lost*
naytklab nait·klab *nightclub*
néktarin nek·ta·reen *nectarine*
negatibo ne·ga·tee·bo *negative*
negosyante ne·gos·yan·te *business person*
negosyanteng babae
  ne·gos·yan·teng ba·ba·e *business woman*
negosyanteng lalaki
  ne·gos·yan·teng la·la·kee *business man*
negosyo ne·gos·yo *business*
net net *net*
New Zealand nyoo see·land *New Zealand*
nilagâ nee·la·ga' *hard-boiled*
ninang nee·nang *godmother*
ninong nee·nong *godfather*
nitó nee·to *something*
niyebe nee·ye·be *snow* ⓝ
niyóg nee·yog *coconut*
nobya nob·ya *girlfriend • fiancée*
Nobyembre nob·yem·bre *November*
nobyo nob·yo *boyfriend• fiancé*
Norway nor·way *Norway*
número noo·me·ro *number*
  — ng lisensiya nang lee·sen·see·ya
  license plate number
  — ng pasaporte nang pa·sa·por·te
  passport number
  — ng plaka nang pla·ka *numberplate*
nuwés noo·wes *nut • groundnut*

Ng

ngayón nga·yon
  now • present (time) • today
ngayong gabí nga·yong ga·bee *tonight*
ngipin ngee·peen *tooth • teeth*
ngitián (ngitián/ngumitî)
  ngee·tee·an (ngee·tee·an/ngoo·mee·tee')
  smile ⓥ

O

o o *or*
obaryo o·bar·yo *ovary*
óberkot o·ber·kot *overcoat*
oksiheno ok·see·he·no *oxygen*
Oktubre ok·too·bre *October*
Olanda o·lan·da *Netherlands*
oliba o·lee·ba *olive*
Olimpik Geyms o·leem·peek gayms
  Olympic Games
oo o·o *yes*

ópera *o*-pe-ra *opera*
— haus hows *opera house*
operasyón *o*-pe-ras-*yon* *operation (medical)*
opereytor *o*-pe-ray-tor *operator*
opinyón *o*-peen-*yon* *opinion*
óptiko *op*-tee-ko *optometrist*
oras *o*-ras *hour • time*
— ng bukasan nang boo-*ka*-san *opening hours*
orasán *o*-ra-*san* *clock*
order *or*-der *order* ⓝ
order (order/magorder) *or*-der (*or*-der/mag-*or*-der) *order* ⓥ
ordinaryo *or*-dee-*nar*-yo *ordinary*
orens *o*-rens *orange (colour)*
orens juice *o*-rens joos *orange juice*
orgasmo *or*-gas-mo *orgasm*
orihinál *o*-ree-hee-*nal* *original*
órkestra *or*-kes-tra *orchestra*
oson leyer *o*-son *le*-yer *ozone layer*
ospitál *os*-pee-tal *hospital*
otél *o*-tel *hotel*
owts ohts *oats*

P

paá pa-*a* *foot*
paakyát pa-ak-*yat* *uphill*
paano pa-*a*-no *how*
páaralán pa-*a*-ra-lan *school*
pab pab *pub • bar*
pababá pa-ba-*ba* *downhill*
pabangó pa-ba-*ngo* *perfume*
pabo *pa*-bo *turkey*
pábrika *pab*-ree-ka *factory*
pakainin pv pa-ka-ee-neen *feed* ⓥ
pakiramdám pa-kee-ram-*dam* *feelings*
Pakistan pa-kee-*stan* *Pakistan*
pakete pa-*ke*-te *packet • parcel*
pako ng tolda *pa*-ko nang *tol*-da *tent peg*
paks paks *fax machine*
pakulutan pa-koo-*loo*-tan *beauty salon*
páhina *pa*-hee-na *page*
padér pa-*der* *wall (outer)*
pag-aalaga ng batà
pag-a-a-*la*-ga na ba-*ta'* *childminding*
pag-akyát sa malalaking bató
pag-ak-*yat* sa ma-la-la-*keeng* ba-*to* *rock climbing*
pag-alís pag-a-*lees* *departure*
pagamutan pa-ga-*moo*-tan *hospital*
págawaan pa-*ga*-wa-an *workshop*
pagbasa pag-*ba*-sa *reading*
pagbibisikleta pag-bee-bee-seek-*le*-ta *cycling*
pagkaantala pag-ka-an-*ta*-la *delay* ⓝ

pagkakalóg ng utak
pag-ka-ka-log nang oo-*tak* *concussion*
pagkakámali pag-ka-*ka*-ma-lee' *mistake* ⓝ
pagkakápantáy-pantáy
pag-ka-*ka*-pan-*tai*-pan-*tai* *equality*
pagkakátaón pag-ka-*ka*-ta-on *chance*
pagkakunan pag-ka-*koo*-nan *miscarriage*
pagkain pag-*ka*-een *food • meal*
— ng beybi nang *bay*-bee *baby food*
pagkaliyó pag-ka-lee-*yo* *nausea*
— sa biyahe sa bee-*ya*-he *travel sickness*
pagkamámamayán pag-ka-*ma*-ma-ma-*yan* *citizenship*
pagkapoót sa lahì pag-ka-po-ot sa la-*hee'* *racism*
pagkaubos ng gubat pag-ka-*oo*-bos nang *goo*-bat *deforestation*
pagdiriwang pag-dee-*ree*-wang *celebration*
paggagarden pag-ga-*gar*-den *gardening*
paglabás sa gabí
pag-la-*bas* sa ga-*bee* *night out*
paglakí at pagkati ng tubig pag-la-*kee* at pag-*ka*-tee nang *too*-beeg *tide*
paglalakád nang mahabà
pag-la-la-*kad* nang ma-ha-ba' *hiking*
paglalakbáy pag-la-lak-*bai* *trip • journey*
paglangóy pag-la-*ngoy* *swimming (sport)*
paglubóg ng araw
pag-loo-*bog* nang *a*-row *sunset*
paglulutò pag-loo-loo-to' *cooking*
pagmamahál pag-ma-ma-*hal* *love* ⓝ
pagód pa-*god* *tired*
pagpatáy sa tao pag-pa-*tai* sa *ta*-o *murder* ⓝ
pagpipintá pag-pee-peen-*ta* *painting (the art)*
pagsabog pag-*sa*-bog *eruption (volcanic)*
pagsasamantalá pag-sa-sa-man-ta-*la* *exploitation*
pagsikat ng araw pag-*see*-kat nang *a*-row *sunrise*
pagsusuká pag-soo-soo-*ka* *morning sickness*
pagsusuri sa dugô
pag-soo-soo-ree sa doo-*go'* *blood test*
pagtakbó pag-tak-*bo* *running*
pagtatáe pag-ta-ta-*e* *diarrhoea • gastroenteritis*
pakwán pak-*wan* *watermelon*
pálabahan pa-la-*ba*-han *laundry (room)*
palabás pa-la-*bas* *performance • show • gig*
palagì pa-la-*gee'* *always*
palapág pa-la-*pag* *floor (storey)*
palasyo pa-*las*-yo *palace*
palayan pa-*lai*-yan *rice field*
palayaw pa-la-*yow* *nickname*
palayók pa-la-*yok* *pot (ceramics)*
palda *pal*-da *skirt*

palengke pa-*leng*-ke market • flea market
— **sa kalye** sa *kal*-ye street market
páliguán *pa*-lee-goo-an shower ⓝ
palít pa-*leet* exchange ⓝ
palít (ipalít/magpalít) pa-*leet* (ee-pa-*leet*/mag-pa-*leet*) exchange • cash (a cheque) • change (money) ⓥ
palitan pa-*lee*-tan exchange rate
— **ng pera** nang *pe*-ra currency exchange
paltík pal-*teek* crop
paltós pal-*tos* blister ⓝ
pamahíin pa-ma-*hee*-een superstition
pamamagâ pa-ma-ma-*ga'* inflammation
pamamaríl pa-ma-ma-*reel* hunting (with guns)
pangangasó pa-nga-nga-*so* hunting (with dogs)
pamasak sa tenga pa-*ma*-sak sa *te*-nga earplugs
pambomba pam-*bom*-ba pump ⓝ
pambukás ng bote pam-*boo*-kas nang *bo*-te bottle opener
pambuntís na tes pam-boon-*tees* na tes pregnancy test kit
pamilya pa-*meel*-ya family
pamimilí pa-mee-mee-*lee* shopping
pamimítas ng prutas pa-mee-mee-*tas* nang *proo*-tas fruit picking
pamintá pa-*meen*-ta pepper
pampainit pam-pa-*ee*-neet heater • heating
pampalambót pam-pa-lam-*bot* moisturiser
pampalusaw pam-pa-*loo*-sow laxative
pampaták sa matá pam-pa-*tak* sa ma-*ta* eye drops
pampulítika pam-poo-*lee*-tee-ka politics
pamumundók pa-moo-moon-*dok* mountaineering
pamunas pa-*moo*-nas wash cloth • flannel
pan pan pan
pan de sal pan de sal bread rolls
panaginip pa-na-*gee*-neep dream ⓝ
panahón pa-na-*hon* weather • season
panalo pa-*na*-lo winner
pananggáng-araw pa-nang-*gang*-a-row sunblock
panbelt *pan*-belt fanbelt
pandikít pan-dee-*keet* glue
panederyá pa-ne-der-*ya* bakery
pangâ pa-*nga* jaw
pang-ahit pang-*a*-heet razor
— **na bleyd** na blayd razor blade
— **na krema** na *kre*-ma shaving cream
pangalagaan pv pa-nga-la-ga-an protect
pangalan pa-*nga*-lan name • Christian name • first name
pangalawá pa-nga-la-*wa* second (ordinal)

pang-alís sa sakít pang-a-*lees* nang sa-*keet* painkiller
pangangabayo pa-nga-nga-*ba*-yo horse riding
panganib pa-*nga*-neeb risk ⓝ
pangatló pa-ngat-*lo* third ⓝ
panggatong pang-*ga*-tong firewood
panggugô pang-goo-*go* shampoo
panggupit ng kukó pang-*goo*-peet nang koo-*ko* nail clippers
pangingisdâ pa-ngee-ngees-*da'* fishing
pangkabataang hostel pang-ka-ba-*ta*-ang *hos*-tel youth hostel
pangkasalukuyang pangyayari pang-ka-sa-loo-*koo*-yang pang-ya-*ya*-ree current affairs
pangmatapos mag-ahit pang-ma-*ta*-pos mag-a-*heet* aftershave
pang-mayaman pang-ma-*ya*-man luxury
pangrehiyón pang-re-hee-*yon* regional
pangsepilyo pang-se-*peel*-yo toothpaste
pangungulila pa-ngoo-ngoo-*lee*-la miss (feel absence of)
panimbáng pa-neem-*bang* weights
paní pa-*nees* off • rancid • spoiled • stale
panlasa pan-*la*-sa stock (food)
panliligalig pan-lee-lee-*ga*-leeg harassment
panlinis sa kontak lens pan-*lee*-nees sa *kon*-tak lens contact lens solution
panloko pan-*lo*-ko rip-off
panloób na tubo pan-lo-*ob* na *too*-bo inner tube
pansindí pan-seen-*dee* lighter
pantalón pan-ta-*lon* pants • trousers
pantáy-pantáy na oportunidád pan-*tai*-pan-*tai* na o-por-too-nee-*dad* equal opportunity
pántihos *pan*-tee-hos pantyhose
pantóg pan-*tog* bladder
panustós pa-noos-*tos* provisions
— **na pagkain** na pag-*ka*-een food supplies
panyô pan-*yo'* handkerchief
papaya pa-*pa*-ya papaya
Papa New Guinea pa-pa nyoo *gee*-nee Papa New Guinea
papél pa-*pel* paper
papeles pa-*pe*-les paperwork
paputók pa-poo-*tok* cracker (fireworks)
parada (iparada/pumarada) pa-*ra*-da (ee-pa-*ra*-da/poo-ma-*ra*-da) park (a car)
páradahán ng sasakyán pa-ra-da-*han* nang sa-sak-*yan* car park
páradahán ng taksi pa-ra-da-*han* nang tak-*see* taxi stand

paraplidyik pa·ra·*plee*·jeek *paraplegic* ⓐ
pareha pa·*re*·ha *both · pair* ⓝ · *same*
pari pa·*ree*′ *priest*
parke *par*·ke *park* ⓝ
parkeng nasyonál *par*·keng nas·yo·*nal* *national park*
parlyamento parl·ya·*men*·to *parliament*
parmasyótiko/a ⓜ/ⓕ par·mas·yo·*tee*·ko/a *chemist (person) · pharmacist*
paros pa·*ros* *mussel*
partaym *par*·taim *part-time*
parti *par*·tee *party (night out)*
partido par·*tee*·do *party (politics)*
paruparó pa·roo·pa·*ro* *butterfly*
pasâ pa·*sa*′ *bruise* ⓝ
pasadór pa·sa·*dor* *panty liner(s) · sanitary napkin(s)*
pasahero pa·sa·*he*·ro *passenger*
pasalamat pv pa·sa·*la*·mat *thank*
pasaporte pa·sa·*por*·te *passport*
pasas pa·*sas* *raisin · sultana*
pasimano pa·see·*ma*·no *ledge*
pasipayer pa·see·*pa*·yer *pacifier · dummy*
Paskó pas·*ko* *Christmas*
pasò pa·*so*′ *burn* ⓝ
pasok (papasukin/magpapasok) pa·*sok* (pa·pa·*soo*·keen/mag·pa·*pa*·sok) *admit (into a place)*
pasta pas·ta *pasta*
pasteleryá pas·te·ler·*ya* *pastry*
pasukán pa·soo·*kan* *entry*
pásyonprut pas·yon·*proot* *passionfruit*
pataás pa·ta·*as* *up*
pátakarán pa·ta·ka·*ran* *policy · rule*
patatas pa·*ta*·tas *potato*
patawarin pv pa·ta·*wa*·reen *forgive*
patáy pa·*tai* *dead*
pawnd pownd *pound (money/weight)*
payát pa·*yat* *thin*
payo pa·*yo* *advice*
payong pa·yong *umbrella*
Pebrero peb·*re*·ro *February*
pedál pe·*dal* *pedal*
peligroso pe·lee·*gro*·so *dangerous*
pelikula pe·*lee*·koo·la *film (cinema) · movie*
pensyonado/a ⓜ/ⓕ pens·yo·*na*·do/a *pensioner*
pera pe·*ra* *cash · money*
perang ibinalík pe·rang ee·bee·na·*leek* *refund* ⓝ
perang papél pe·rang pa·*pel* *banknote*
peras pe·*ras* *pear*
peri pe·*ree* *ferry* ⓝ
permiso per·*mee*·so *permission · permit*
— **sa trabaho** sa tra·*ba*·ho *work permit*
pero pe·*ro* *but · however*

perpekto per·*pek*·to *perfect*
petisyón pe·tees·*yon* *petition*
petsa pet·sa *date (day)*
— **ng kapanganakan** nang ka·pa·nga·na·*kan* *date of birth*
péysmeyker pays·may·ker *pacemaker*
piknik peek·neek *picnic*
pigilin (pigilin/pumigil) pee·*gee*·leen (pee·*gee*·leen/poo·mee·geel) *stop · prevent*
piko pee·ko *pickaxe*
pil peel *peel (the) pill*
pila pee·la *queue* ⓝ
pilak pee·lak *silver* ⓝ
pilay pee·lai *sprain* ⓝ
píldora peel·*do*·ra *pill*
pili pee·*lee*′ *almond*
pilì (piliin/pumili) pee·*lee* (pee·lee·*een*/ poo·mee·*lee*′) *choose*
pilm peelm *film (for camera)*
piltrado peel·*tra*·do *filtered*
pinakaimportante pee·na·ka·eem·por·*tan*·te *main*
pinakamagalíng pee·na·ka·ma·ga·*leeng* *best*
pinakamalakí pee·na·ka·ma·la·*kee* *biggest*
pinakamalapit pee·na·ka·ma·*la*·peet *nearest*
pinakamalíìt pee·na·ka·ma·lee·*eet* *smallest*
pinaglílingkurán pee·nag·*lee*·leeng·koo·*ran* *employer*
pinagyeluhin pv pee·nag·ye·lo·heen *freeze (something)*
pinainitan pee·na·ee·*nee*·tan *heated*
pinasok (pasukin/pumasok) pee·na·sok (pa·*soo*·keen/poo·ma·sok) *enter*
ping pong peeng pong *table tennis*
pinggán peeng·*gan* *plate*
pinirito pee·nee·*ree*·to *fried*
Pinlándiya peen·*lan*·dee·ya *Finland*
pintô peen·*to*′ *door*
pintór peen·*tor* *painter*
pintura peen·*too*·ra *painting (a work)*
pinyá peen·*ya* *pineapple*
pipi pee·pee *mute*
pipino pee·*pee*·no *cucumber*
piraso pee·ra·so *piece*
pirma *peer*·ma *signature*
pisì pee·*see*′ *string*
pistasyo pees·*tas*·yo *pistachio*
pitakà pee·*ta*·ka′ *purse*
pits peets *peach*
piyesta pee·*yes*·ta *festival*
plag plag *plug*
plam plam *plum*
planeta pla·*ne*·ta *planet*
plantsa *plant*·sa *iron (for clothes)*
plaslayt plas·lait *flashlight · torch*
plastik plas·*teek* *plastic*

plat plat *flat* ⓐ

plataporma pla·ta·*por*·ma *platform*

playt plait *flight*

plopi disk *plo*·pee deesk *disk (floppy)*

plu ploo *flu*

polen *po*·len *pollen*

polusyón po·loos·*yon* *pollution*

polyeto pol·*ye*·to *brochure*

pon baks pon baks *phone box*

pon kard pon kard *phone card*

ponbuk *pon*·book *phone book*

pool pool *(game)*

populár po·poo·*lar* *popular*

porsiyento por·see·*yen*·to *per cent*

portpolyo port·*pol*·yo *briefcase*

pos opis pos o·pees *post office*

posible po·*see*·ble *possible*

positibo po·see·*tee*·bo *positive*

poskard *pos*·kard *postcard*

poskowd *pos*·kohd *post code*

nósporo *pos*·po·ro *matches (for lighting)*

poster *pos*·ter *poster*

potograpiya po·to·gra·*pee*·ya *photography*

pranela pra·*ne*·la *flannel • wash cloth*

Pránsiya *pran*·see·ya *France*

preno *pre*·no *brakes*

presidente pre·see·*den*·te *president*

preso *pre*·so *jail*

presyo *pres*·yo *price • value*

presyón pres·*yon* *pressure*

— ng dugô nang doo·*go*' *blood pressure*

presyuhán pres·yoo·*han* *cost* ⓝ

pribado pree·*ba*·do *private*

printer *preen*·ter *printer (computer)*

prito (iprito/pumirito) *pree*·to (ee·*pree*·to/poo·mee·*ree*·to) *fry*

prodyektor pro·*jek*·tor *projector*

programa pro·*gra*·ma *program*

protektado pro·tek·*ta*·do *protected*

protesta pro·*tes*·ta *protest* ⓝ

prun proon *prune (dried fruit)*

prutas *proo*·tas *fruit*

pugón poo·*gon* *oven*

pulbós pool·*bos* *powder*

— ng beybi nang *bay*·bee *baby powder*

pulgás pool·*gas* *flea*

pulís poo·*lees* *police officer*

pulisyá poo·lees·*ya* *police* ⓝ

pulítiko/a ⓜ/ⓕ poo·*lee*·tee·ko/a *politician*

pulót-gatâ poo·*lot*·ga·*ta*' *honeymoon*

pulót-pukyutan poo·*lot*·pook·yoo·tan *honey*

pulsó pool·*so* *wrist*

pulubi poo·*loo*·bee *beggar*

pundá poon·*da* *pillowcase*

puno poo·*no*' *tree*

punô poo·*no*' *full*

---

punó na poo·*no* na *booked out*

puntód poon·*tod* *grave* ⓝ

punuín pv poo·noo·*een* *fill*

púpuntahán poo·poon·ta·*han* *destination*

puro *poo*·ro *pure*

pusà poo·*sa*' *cat*

pusò poo·*so*' *heart*

pustá poos·*ta* *bet* ⓝ

putahe poo·*ta*·he *dish*

putik poo·*teek* *mud*

puwede ba av poo·*we*·de ba *can (have permission)*

puwedeng iresaykel poo·*we*·deng ee·re·*sai*·kel *recyclable*

puwerto poo·*wer*·to *harbour*

puwit poo·*weet* *bottom (body)*

R

rak rak *rock (music)*

— grup groop *rock group*

raketa ra·*ke*·ta *racquet*

radyetor rad·*ye*·tor *radiator*

radyo *rad*·yo *radio*

rag rag *rug*

ragbi *rag*·bee *rugby*

rali *ra*·lee *rally (protest)* ⓝ

ram ram *rum*

rásberi *ras*·be·ree *raspberry*

ráwndabáwt *rown*·da·bowt *roundabout*

rayt wing rait weeng *right-wing*

regalo re·*ga*·lo *gift • present*

— sa kasál sa ka·*sal* *wedding present*

regla *reg*·la *menstruation*

rehistrado re·hees·*tra*·do *(by) registered (mail/post)*

rehistrasyón ng kotse re·hees·tras·*yon* nang *kot*·se *car registration*

reklamo rek·*la*·mo *complaint*

rekomendá (Irekomendá/ magrekomendá) re·ko·men·*da* (ee·re·ko·men·*da*/mag·re·ko·men·*da*) *recommend*

rekording re·*kor*·deeng *recording*

reláks av re·*laks* *relax*

relasyón re·las·*yon* *relationship*

relasyóng pampúbliko re·las·*yong* pam·*poob*·lee·ko *public relations*

relihiyón re·lee·hee·*yon* *religion*

relihiyoso re·lee·hee·*yo*·so *religious*

reló re·*lo* *watch (clock)*

remót kontról re·*mot* kon·*trol* *remote control*

rep rep *fridge*

repridyeretor re·*preed*·ye·re·tor *refrigerator*

repaso re·*pa*·so *review* ⓝ

reperensiyá re·pe·ren·see·ya reference
réperi re·pe·ree referee (sport)
repleksólodyi rep·lek·so·lo·jee reflexology
repolyo re·pol·yo cabbage
república re·poob·lee·ka republic
reserbasyón re·ser·bas·yon
booking • reservation
reseta re·se·ta prescription
resibo re·see·bo receipt
restoran res·to·ran restaurant
résume re·soo·me résumé • CV
retirado re·tee·ra·do retired
reyki ray·kee reiki
reyna ray·na queen
rin reen also
ritmo reet·mo rhythm
romántiko ro·man·tee·ko romantic
rota ro·ta route
rowing ro·weeng rowing
rubelya roo·bel·ya rubella
rum number room nam·ber room number

S

sa sa at • in • to
— harapán ng ha·ra·pan nang in front of
— ibabâ ee·ba·ba' below • down
— ibabaw ee·ba·bow on
— ilalim ee·la·leem bottom (position)
— itaás ng ee·ta·as nang above
— kabilâ ka·bee·la' across
— labás la·bas outside
— likód lee·kod rear (seat)
— likurán lee·koo·ran behind
— loób lo·ob indoor • inside
— loób ng lo·ob nang within
— pagitan pa·gee·tan between
— tabí ta·bee beside
sa probínsiya sa pro·been·see·ya countryside
sa súsunód na (buwán) sa soo·soo·nod na
(boo·wan) next (month)
saán sa·an where
Sábado sa·ba·do Saturday
— at Linggó at leeng·go weekend
sabihin PV sa·bee·heen tell • say
sabón sa·bon soap
sabong sa·bong cock fight • cockfighting
sábtaytel sab·tai·tel subtitles
sabwey sab·way subway
sakahán sa·ka·han farm
sakáy sa·kai ride ⓝ
sakáy (isakáy/sumakáy) sa·kai (ee·sa·kai/
soo·ma·kai board (a plane)
saker sa·ker soccer
sakím sa·keem selfish

sakít sa·keet pain • disease
— ng ngipin nang ngee·peen toothache
— ng tiyán nang tee·yan stomachache
— ng ulo nang oo·lo headache
— sa babae sa ba·ba·e venereal disease
saktan (saktan/masaktan)
sak·tan (sak·tan/ma·sak·tan)
hurt (someone)
sadyáng pagpatáy sa tao
sad·yang pag·pa·tai sa ta·o murder ⓝ
saging sa·geeng banana
sagót sa·got answer ⓝ
sahíg sa·heeg floor ⓝ
salad sa·lad salad
Salamat sa iyó. sa·la·mat sa ee·yo Thank you.
salami sa·la·mee salami
salamín sa·la·meen mirror
salitâ sa·lee·ta' word
salmón sal·mon salmon
samakalawá sa·ma·ka·la·wa
(the) day after tomorrow
sambahan sam·ba·han temple
sambahín (sambahín/sumambá)
sam·ba·heen (see·nam·ba·heen/
soo·mam·ba) worship ⓥ
sampayan sam·pa·yan clothesline
sandaán san·da·an hundred
sandalyas san·dal·yas sandals
sangkalan sang·ka·lan chopping board
sangkapat sang·ka·pat quarter ⓐ
sanglas san·glas sunglasses
sanlibután san·lee·boo·tan universe
santo/a ⓜ/ⓕ san·to/a saint
sapà sa·pa' stream
sapatos sa·pa·tos shoe(s)
sarado sa·ra·do closed • shut
sardinas sar·dee·nas sardine
sariling trabaho sa·ree·leeng tra·ba·ho
self-employed
sariwà sa·ree·wa fresh
sarpbord sarp·bord surfboard
sarpeys meyl sar·pays mayl surface mail
sarping sar·peeng surfing
sastré sas·tre tailor
sauna sow·na sauna
sayawan sa·ya·wan dancing
sayder sai·der cider
sekon klas se·kon klas second class
sekretarya sek·re·tar·ya secretary
seks seks sex
seksi sek·see sexy
segunda mano se·goon·da ma·no
second-hand
seguro se·goo·ro insurance
seloso/a ⓜ/ⓕ se·lo·so/a jealous
selyo sel·yo stamp • postage

Semana Santa se·*ma*·na san·ta Easter • Holy Week
sementeryo se·men·*ter*·yo cemetery
senswál sens·*wal* sensual
sentimetro sen·tee·*me*·tro centimetre
séntimo sen·*tee*·mo cent
sentro sen·tro centre
  — **ng siyudád** nang see·yoo·*dad* city centre
  — **ng telépono** nang te·*le*·po·no telephone centre
sepilyo se·*peel*·yo toothbrush
serámiko se·*ra*·mee·ko ceramics
serbesa ser·*be*·sa beer
serbilyeta ser·beel·*ye*·ta serviette
serbis istesyon ser·bees ees·*tes*·yon service station
serbis tsards ser·bees tsarj service charge
serbisyo ser·*bees*·yo service
serbisyong militár ser·*bees*·yong mee·lee·*tar* military service
seryoso/a ⓜ/ⓕ ser·yo·so/a serious
Setyembre set·*yem*·bre September
shep shep chef
sibuyas see·*boo*·yas onion
sikapin (sikapin/magsikap) see·*ka*·peen (see·*ka*·peen/mag·*see*·kap) try ⓥ
siklista seek·*lees*·ta cyclist
siksikan seek·*see*·kan crowded
sigarilyo see·ga·*reel*·yo cigarette
silá si·*la* them • they
silangan see·*la*·ngan east
sili see·lee chilli
  — **sohs** sohs chilli sauce
silyang de-gulóng seel·yang de·goo·*long* wheelchair
silyang pambatà seel·yang pam·*ba*·ta' highchair
simbahan seem·*ba*·han church
simple *seem*·ple simple
simulâ see·moo·*la'* start ⓝ
sínagog see·na·gog synagogue
sinehán see·ne·*han* cinema
Singapór seeng·ga·*por* Singapore
singáw see·*ngow* rash ⓝ
  — **dahil sa lampín** da·heel sa lam·*peen* nappy rash
singsíng seeng·*seeng* ring (on finger)
sining *see*·neeng crafts
sinisero see·nee·*se*·ro ashtray
sino *see*·no who
sintetik seen·*te*·teek synthetic
sinulad see·*noo*·lad cotton • thread
sinungaling see·noo·*nga*·leeng liar
sinuwám see·noo·*wam* poached

sipà see·pa' kick ⓝ
siper see·*per* zip • zipper
sipón see·*pon* hay fever • runny nose
sirâ see·*ra'* broken • out of order
sirain ⓟⓥ see·*ra*·een break ⓥ
siriyál see·ree·*yal* cereal
sirko *seer*·ko circus
sis sa obaryo sees sa o·*bar*·yo ovarian cyst
sistaytis sees·*tai*·tees cystitis
sistema ng klase sees·*te*·ma nang *kla*·se class system
sitbelt *seet*·belt seatbelt
sitsaró seet·sa·*ro* snow pea
siyá see·*ya* he • him • her • she
siyampu see·*yam*·poo shampoo
siyatsu see·*yat*·soo shiatsu
siyénsiya see·*yen*·see·ya science
siyentípiko see·yen·*tee*·pee·ko scientist
siyudád see·yoo·*dad* city
sobra *sob*·ra excess/(baggage)
sobrang dosis *sob*·rang do·sees overdose
sobrang lantád sa araw *sob*·rang lan·*tad* sa *a*·row sunstroke
sobre *so*·bre envelope
sodyak *sod*·yak zodiac
sombrero som·*bre*·ro hat
sop ópera sop o·pe·ra soap opera
sopas *so*·pas soup
sopdrink *sop*·dreenk soft drink
sorbetes sor·*be*·tes ice cream
sorpresa sor·*pre*·sa surprise
sosis *so*·sees sausage
sosyalista sos·ya·*lees*·ta socialist
sows sohs sauce
sows pan sohs pan saucepan
soy milk soy meelk soy milk
soy sows soy sohs soy sauce
su soo zoo
súbenir soo·bee·*neer* souvenir
suburbya soo·*boor*·bya suburb
sukà *soo*·ka' vinegar
sukat *soo*·kat size (general)
sukini soo·*kee*·nee courgette • zucchini
sukláy sook·*lai* comb
sugpô soog·*po'* prawn
suhà *soo*·ha' grapefruit
suhol *soo*·hol bribe ⓝ
suklî sook·*lee'* change (coins) ⓝ
sulat *soo*·lat letter • mail
sumayáw ⓐⓥ soo·ma·*yow* dance ⓥ
sumulat soo·*moo*·lat write
sumunód ⓐⓥ soo·moo·*nod* follow
sumúsulat soo·moo·soo·lat writer
sundalo soon·*da*·lo soldier
sunóg soo·*nog* burnt
  — **sa araw** sa *a*·row sunburn

súpermarket *soo-per-mar-ket*
  supermarket
susì *soo-see'* key
suso *soo-so* breast (body)
susô *soo-so'* snail
sutlâ *soot-la'* silk
suweldo *soo-wel-do* salary • wage
suwerte *soo-wer-te* luck
Sweden *swee-den* Sweden
Switserland *sweet-ser-land* Switzerland

T

taás *ta-as* altitude
tabako *ta-ba-ko* cigar • tobacco
tabákonista *ta-ba-ko-nees-ta* tobacconist
tabíng-dagat *ta-beeng-da-gat* beach
takas *ta-kas* refugee
takdáng bigát ng bagahe
  tak-*dang* bee-*gat* nang ba-*ga*-he
  baggage allowance
takdáng tulin tak-*dang* too-leen *speed limit*
tadyáng tad-*yang* rib
tag ng bagahe tag nang ba-*ga*-he
  luggage tag
tagalutò ta-ga-*loo*-to' cook ⓥ
tagapag-alaga ng beybi ta-ga-pag-a-*la*-ga
  nang *bay*-bee babysitter
tagapagsalin sa wikà
  taga-pag-*sa*-leen sa *wee*-ka' interpreter
tag-aráw tag-a-*raw* summer
tagásuporta ta-*ga*-soo-*por*-ta supporter
tagiliran ta-gee-*lee*-ran side
taglagás tag-la-*gas* autumn • fall
taglamíg tag-la-*meeg* winter
tagsibol tag-*see*-bol spring (season)
tahanan ta-*ha*-nan home
tahî (tahíin/tumahî)
  ta-*hee'* (ta-hee-*een*/too-ma-*hee'*) sew
tahimik ta-*hee*-meek quiet
Taiwán *tai*-wan Taiwan
taksi tak-*see* taxi
talabá ta-la-*ba* oyster
talampás ta-lam-*pas* plateau
talón ta-*lon* waterfall
talóng ta-*long* aubergine • eggplant
tamà *ta*-ma' correct (right)
tamád ta-*mad* lazy
tambutso tam-*boot*-so exhaust (car)
tampon *tam*-pon tampon
tanawin ta-*na*-ween view ⓝ
tandáng tan-*dang* cock
tangá ta-*nga* idiot • stupid
tangké ng gaás tang-*ke* nang gas
  gas cartridge

tanggapín (tanggapín/tumanggáp)
  tang-ga-*peen* (tang-ga-*peen*/
  too-*mang*-gap) welcome ⓥ
tanggihán pv tang-gee-*han* refuse
tanghalì tang-*ha*-lee' noon
tanghalian tang-*ha*-lee-an *lunch*
tanghaling tapát tang-*ha*-leeng ta-*pat*
  midday • noon
taning losyon ta-neeng *los*-yon
  tanning lotion
tanóng ta-*nong* question ⓝ
tanong (tanong/magtanóng) ta-*nong*
  (ta-*nong*/mag-ta-*nong*) ask (a question)
tao *ta*-o person
taón ta-*on* year
taong di-kilalá ta-ong dee-kee-la-*la*
  stranger ⓝ
taong naglálakád ta-ong nag-*la*-la-*kad*
  pedestrian
tapusin pv ta-*poo*-seen finish ⓥ
tasa *ta*-sa cup
tatay *ta*-tai dad
tawag (tawagang/tumawa) *ta*-wag
  (too-*ma*-wag/ta-*wag*-an) call ⓥ
taymteybol taim-*te*-bol timetable • itinerary
teatro te-*at*-ro theatre
teknîk tek-*neek* technique
tela *te*-la fabric
telebisyón te-le-bees-*yon* television
telegrama te-le-*gra*-ma telegram
télepon baks *te*-le-pon baks telephone box
telépono te-*le*-po-no telephone ⓝ
teléponohán (teléponohán/tumelépono)
  te-le-po-*no*-han (te-le-po-*no*-han/
  too-me-*le*-po-no) telephone ⓥ
teléponong pampúbliko te-*le*-po-nong
  pam-*poob*-lee-ko public telephone
teleskopyo te-les-*kop*-yo telescope
témperatura tem-pe-ra-*too*-ra temperature
tenga *te*-nga ear
tenis *te*-nees tennis
  — kort kort court
tensyón bago magkaregla tens-*yon* ba-go
  mag-ka-*reg*-la premenstrual tension
terible te-*ree*-ble terrible
terorismo te-ro-*rees*-mo terrorism
terorista te-ro-*rees*-ta terrorist
tes tes test
testing na nukliyár *tes*-teeng na
  nook-lee-*yar* nuclear testing
ti syert tee syert T-shirt
tibî tee-*bee* constipation
tiket *tee*-ket ticket
  — masín ma-*seen* ticket machine
tigdás teeg-*das* measles
tim teem team

timbâ teem-*ba'* bucket
timbáng teem-*bang* weight
timbangín pv teem-ba-*ngeen* weigh
timog tee-*mog* south
tinapay tee-*na*-pai bread
— **na holmil** na *hol*-meel wholemeal bread
tindahan teen-*da*-han shop • kiosk
— **ng alak** nang *a*-lak liquor store
— **ng bisikleta** nang bee-seek-*le*-ta bike shop
— **ng damít** nang da-*meet* clothing store
— **ng inumin** nang ee-*noo*-meen bottle shop
— **ng isdâ** nang ees-*da'* fish shop
— **ng kámera** nang *ka*-me-ra camera shop
— **ng keso** nang *ke*-so cheese shop
— **ng keyk** nang kayk cake shop
— **ng laruán** nang la-roo-*an* toy shop
— **ng libró** nang lee-*bro* book shop
— **ng magkakarné** nang mag-ka-kar-*ne* butcher's shop
— **ng músika** nang moo-see-ka music shop
— **ng páhayagán** nang *pa*-ha-ya-gan newsagency • newstand
— **ng pang-ispórt** nang pang-ees-*port* sports store
— **ng pangkamping** nang pang-*kam*-peeng camping store
— **ng papél** nang pa-*pel* stationer
— **ng sapatos** nang sa-*pa*-tos shoe shop
— **ng segunda mano** nang se-*goon*-da *ma*-no second-hand shop
— **ng sorbetes** nang sor-*be*-tes ice-cream parlour
— **ng súbinir** nang soo-bee-neer souvenir shop
tindahang sari-sarì teen-*da*-hang sa-ree-*sa*-ree' convenience store
tindera/o Ⓜ/Ⓕ teen-*de*-ra/o greengrocer
tingnán pv teeng-*nan* check • look • look for
tinikling tee-*nee*-kleeng traditional Filipino dancing
tinidór tee-nee-*dor* fork
tip tip tip (gratuity)
tipanan tee-*pa*-nan appointment • date
tipikál tee-pee-*kal* typical
tipô *tee*-po' type Ⓝ
tirahan tee-*ra*-han address Ⓝ
tisyu tees-yoo tissues
titser *teet*-ser teacher • instructor • lecturer
tiyá tee-*ya* aunt
tiyakín (tiyakín/tumiyak) tee-ya-*keen* (tee-ya-*keen*/too-*mee*-yak) confirm (a booking)
tiyán tee-*yan* stomach

tiyanì tee-ya-*nee'* tweezers
tokwa *tok*-wa tofu
togè *to*-ge' beansprouts
tóilet peyper *to*-ee-let *pay*-per toilet paper
tolda *tol*-da tent
tomboy *tom*-boy lesbian • tomboy
tomeyto sows to-*may*-to sohs tomato sauce
tono *to*-no tune Ⓝ
tore *to*-re tower
torta *tor*-ta omelette
tost tost toast Ⓝ
toster *tos*-ter toaster
trabahadór tra-ba-ha-*dor* labourer
trabaho tra-*ba*-ho job • work
— **sa bar** sa bar bar work
trabahong kaswal tra-*ba*-hong *kas*-wal casual work
trábelers tsek *tra*-be-lers tsek travellers cheque
trak trak track (sport)
trangkaso trang-*ka*-so influenza
trambiyá tram-bee-*ya* tram
transit lounge *tran*-seet lownds transit lounge
transportasyón trans-por-tas-*yon* transport
trápiker ng droga *tra*-pee-ker nang *dro*-ga drug trafficking
trápiko *tra*-pee-ko traffic
tras tras thrush (health)
travel agency *tra*-bel *ay*-jen-see travel agency
tren tren train
tribusón tree-boo-*son* corkscrew
troli *tro*-lee trolley
tsaá tsa-*a* tea
tsampán tsam-*pan* champagne
tseke *tse*-ke check • cheque (banking)
tsit tseet bill • check • cheque
tsek-in tsek-*een* check-in (desk)
tsekpoynt tsek-*point* checkpoint
tseri *tse*-ree cherry
tserlíp *tser*-leep chairlift (skiing)
Tsina *tsee*-na China
tsokolate tso-ko-*la*-te chocolate
tsop istík tsop ees-*teek* chopsticks
tubig *too*-beeg water
— **sa gripo** sa *gree*-po tap water
tubô *too*-bo' profit Ⓝ
tuhod *too*-hod knee
tuktók took-*tok* peak (mountain)
tuláy too-*lai* bridge Ⓝ
tulin *too*-leen speed Ⓝ
tulingán too-lee-*ngan* tuna
tulog *too*-log sleep Ⓝ
tulong *too*-long help Ⓝ
tulugán too-loo-*gan* sleeping berth • sleeping car

tulong (tulungan/tumulong)
too-loong (too-*loo*-ngan/too-*moo*-long)
help ⓥ
tumakbó av too-mak-*bo* run ⓥ
tumirá av too-mee-*ra* live (somewhere)
tumór too-*mor* tumour
tumubò av too-*moo*-bo' grow
tungkól sa toong-*kol* sa about
tungkól sa kasarián
toong-*kol* sa ka-sa-ree-*an* sexism
tungo sa *too*-ngo sa towards
tupa *too*-pa lamb • sheep
tur toor tour ⓝ
turista too-*rees*-ta tourist
tutpik *toot*-peek toothpick
tuwalya too-*wal*-ya towel
tuyô *too*-yo' dry ⓐ • dried
tuyóng prutas too-*yong* proo-tas dried fruit
tuyuín (pinatuyó/magpatuyó)
too-yoo-een (pee-na-too-*yo*/
mag-pa-too-*yo*) dry (clothes, food) ⓥ

U

ubas *oo*-bas grapes
ubasán oo-ba-*san* vineyard
ubó oo-*bo* cough ⓝ
ugát oo-*gat* vein
ulán oo-*lan* rain ⓝ
ulap *oo*-lap cloud
ulî oo-*lee'* again
ulo *oo*-lo head ⓝ
últrasawnd *ool*-tra-sownd ultrasound
umaga oo-*ma*-ga morning
umakyát av oo-mak-*yat* climb ⓥ
umalís av oo-ma-*lees* go • depart • leave
umangkás av oo-mang-*kas* hitchhike
umayon av oo-*ma*-yon agree
umbók oom-*bok* lump
umiskór av oo-mees-*kor* score ⓥ
umubó av oo-moo-*bo* cough ⓥ
una *oo*-na first
unan *oo*-nan pillow
unibersidád oo-nee-ber-see-*dad*
university
uniporme oo-nee-*por*-me uniform

upisina oo-pee-*see*-na office
— **ng naiwang bagahe** nang na-*ee*-wang
ba-*ga*-he left luggage office
— **ng nawaláng ari-arian**
nang na-wa-*lang* a-ree-a-ree-*an*
lost property office
— **ng turismo** nang too-*rees*-mo
tourist office
upuan oo-*poo*-an chair • seat • saddle
— **ng batà** nang *ba*-ta' child seat
utang *oo*-tang owe

W

walâ wa-*la'* no • none • nothing • without
waláng bakante wa-*lang* ba-*kan*-te
no vacancy
waláng lamán wa-*lang* la-*man* empty ⓐ
waláng manínigarilyó wa-*lang*
ma-nee-nee-ga-reel-*yo* nonsmoking
waláng tahanan wa-*lang* ta-*ha*-nan homeless
waláng trabaho wa-*lang* tra-*ba*-ho
unemployed
wanwey wan-way one-way (ticket)
wasing masín wa-seeng ma-*seen*
washing machine
welga wel-ga strike ⓝ
weyter way-ter waiter
weyting rum way-teeng room waiting room
wikà wee-ka' language
wínsarping ween-sar-peeng windsurfing
winskrin weens-kreen windscreen
wok wok wok

Y

yakapin (yakapin/yumakap) ya-*ka*-peen
(ya-*ka*-peen/yoo-*ma*-kap) hug ⓥ
yaring-kamáy ya-reeng-ka-*mai*
handmade ⓐ • handicrafts ⓝ
yelo *ye*-lo ice
yoga *yo*-ga yoga
yoghurt *yo*-goort yogurt
yuro *yoo*-ro euro
yutanasya yoo-ta-*nas*-ya euthanasia

A

abbreviations	10
accident	58, 183
accommodation	65, 93, 201
addresses	64, 65
addressing people	108
adjectives (grammar)	17
adverbs (grammar)	17
age	112
airport	51
alcohol	168, 169
allergies	174, 190, 195
alphabet	14
alternative treatments (health)	195
ambulance	183
amounts	40, 172
animals	157
arranging to meet	133
arrivals	51
art	143
asking someone out	135
aspect (grammar)	31
assault	185
assistance	99
automated teller machine	45, 89, 90

B

babies	101, 102, 104
baggage	see *luggage*
bags	see *luggage*
bag (shopping)	76
banking	89
bargaining	77
basic phrases	105, 117, 118, 119, 120
basketball	148
beach	155
bedding	154
beliefs	141
be (verb)	18
bicycle	59, 201

Bikolano (language)	120
bill (cheque)	71, 161
boat	47, 53
body diagram	194
body language	143
body parts	194
booking (accommodation)	65, 66
booking (tickets)	48, 49, 66
books	80
border crossing	61
breast-feeding	102
Buddhist	174
bus	47, 51
business	95
buying food	171

C

calendar	42
camera	82
camping	65, 72, 155
car	56
car diagram	58
cardinal numbers	37
car keys	58
car hire	56
cash advance	45, 89
catamaran	47
Cebuano (language)	117
cell phone	87
changing money	68, 89
charity	202
checking in	46, 66
checking out	71
children (age)	112
children's menu	160
cinema	123
clothes	78, 79
cockfighting	148
coffee	167
coins	50
common interests	121
communications	83

community issues 200
complaints (accommodation) 70
complaints (shopping) 77
compliments (food) 164, 165
computers 88, 96
concessions (discounts) 93
conditions (medical) 190
conferences (business) 95
consonant sounds 12
consulates 185
contact details 92, 96, 116
contact lenses 188
contraceptives 191, 193
cooking utensils 172
credit cards 45, 67, 76, 90, 184
culinary reader 175
cultural differences 141, 142, 199
cultural tips 104, 105, 108, 116, 165
currency 46
customs (airport) 62
customs (local) 199
cycling 59-60, 201

D

dancing 122, 131, 133, 136
dates (calendar) 43
days of the week 42
day trips 93
deaf travellers 100
debit cards 45, 76
declaring things (customs) 62
delays (travel) 47
demonstratives (grammar) 18
dentist 187, 198-8
departures 51
dialects 117-120, 202
dictionary (English–Filipino) 199
dictionary (Filipino-English) 227
dictionary (shopping) 80
directions 63
disabled travellers 99-100
discount .... see concessions
diving 149, 155
doctor 183, 187, 189
doing business 95
drinking 168, 170
drinking water .... see water (drinkable)
drinks (nonalcoholoc) 160, 167
drugs (illegal) 134, 186, 189

drugs (medication) 186
duty-free 51, 62, 81

E

eating out 159
electronic goods 81
elevator 68, 99
email 87, 96
embassies 185
emergencies 183
emergency department 187
entertainment guides 80, 132
environment 129, 200
etiquette tips .... see cultural tips
exchange rates 46, 90

F

Fair Trade 201
family 114
fares (transport) 48-9, 55
farewells 116
fauna 157
fax 83, 96
feelings 125
female doctor 187
ferry 47, 53
film (cinema) 123
film (photography) 82
fines 185, 186
fire 183
flora 157
focus (grammar) 19
food 159-82, 202
food (shopping) 171
foreign exchange office 45, 89
formality (speech) 105, 108
fractions 39
fuel (car) 57
future (time) 44

G

galleries 143
gas (petrol) 57
gay travel 113, 132, 183
glasses (spectacles) 188
going out 131

goodbyes 88, 106, 118, 119, 120
grammar 15
greetings 106, 118, 119, 120
guarantee (shopping) 76
guesthouse 65
guide dog 100
guided treks 153
guidebooks 80, 91
guides 91, 94, 153, 202

H

hairdressing 79
halal (food) 173
have (verb) 21
health (children) 188, 190
health (general) 187
health (women) 191
hiking 153
Hiligaynon (language) ...... see Ilonggo
Hindu 174
hobbies 121
holidays 110
homestays 65
horse racing 151
horse riding 152
hospital 187, 190
hotel 65, 201
hote room diagram 67

I

illness 190
Ilokano (language) 120
Ilonggo (language) 118
immigration 62
injuries 147
insurance 97, 185, 188
interests 121
Internet 87, 96
introductions (people) 107
invitations 96, 116, 132, 135, 136

J

jeepney 47, 60
Jewish 174
jobs 97

K

Kapampangan
  (language) .... see Pampangan
key 69
kosher (food) 173

L

languages (of the Philippines) ... 117, 202
language difficulties 35
language map 8, 177
laundry 68, 72
lawyer 185
leaving 140
left-luggage office 50
lesbian .... see gay travel
lifeboat 54
life jackets 53, 54
lift (elevator) 68, 99
local transport 60
location (grammar) 22
looking for a job 97
lost (items) 50, 184
lost (people) 154, 184
love 139
luggage 50, 71, 184

M

mail 83-4
making conversation 108
map (Filipino language) 8
map (other languages) 117
maps 63, 91, 153
measures 40, 172
mechanic 58
medication 187, 189, 192
meeting people 105
mega-taxi 47
menu 160, 162, 175-182
messages (leaving & collecting) ... 68, 69
mobile phone 87
money 45, 184
months 42
mosquitoes 69
motel 65
motorbike hire 56

movies	123
museum	143
music	81, 122
Muslim	174

N

nationalities	111
negation (grammar)	22
newspapers	80
nonalcoholic drinks	167
nonsmoking	49, 160
nouns (grammar)	23
numbers	37

O

occupations	112
oil (car)	57
opinions	125, 126
optometrist	187
ordering food (special requests)	173
ordinal numbers	39
organic produce	173, 202
outdoors	153-8

P

Pampangan (language)	119
Pangasinan (language)	120
particles (grammar)	20, 23
parts of the body	194
party (entertainment)	132
party (political)	126, 127
passport	61, 62, 82, 90, 184
past (time)	43
pastimes	121
payments (methods of)	76
personal pronouns (grammar)	25
petrol	57, 59
pharmacist	187, 196
phone	68, 84, 85, 86, 184, 185
photography	82
pick-up lines	136
Pilipino	9
PIN	90
plane	51
plants	157

playing sport	146
police	183, 184
politeness	105, 108
politics	127
possession (grammar)	26
postage	76
poste restante	84
post office	83
preparations (food)	165
prepositions (grammar)	28
prescription (medical)	186, 196
present (time)	43
problems (accomodation)	70
problems (car & motorbike)	58
problems (restaurants)	174
problems (romance)	140
pronunciation	11, 36
public phone	84
public transport	47, 200

Q

quarantine	62
questions (grammar)	29

R

rape	185
reading (books)	80
reading (Filipino)	14
receipts	46, 76
recommendations (accommodation)	65
recommendations (food)	161
recommendations (restaurants)	159
recycling	200
refunds	46, 77
regional variations	13
rejections (romance)	137
religion	141
renting (accommodation)	73
repairs (car & motorbike)	58
repairs (bicycle)	59
repairs (general)	78
requests (accommodation)	68
requests (grammar)	30
reservations (restaurant)	160
responding to invitations	133
responsible travel	199-202

restaurant 161
restaurant diagram 163
résumé 98
romance 135

S

safe (securing valuables) 68
safe sex 189
safe travel 183-6
script (Filipino) 129
seasons 43
seating 47, 48
self-catering 171-172
senior travellers 99
service station (petrol) 57
sex 138
shopping (food) 171-2, 202
shopping (general) 75, 201
sightseeing 91, 202
signs (accommodation) 73
signs (road) 55
signs (safety) 155
signs (quirky) 94
SIM cards 87
smoking 49, 160
snorkelling 149
social issues 127, 200
Spanish numbers 38
special diets 162, 173, 174
speed limit 57
sport 145
staying with locals 74
street diagram 64
street food 166
student discounts 93
studying 112
supplies (camping & hiking) 153
sustainable travel 199-202
symptoms (medical) 190
syringe 188

T

table setting diagram 163
Tagalog 9
taxi 54, 71, 170
telephone .... see phone
telling the time 41-2

temperature (fever) 189
tense (grammar) 31
thanking people 96, 105
theatre 123
theft 50, 183, 184 186
tickets 48, 49
time 41
toilets 70, 155, 170, 184
tours 93, 94, 202
tourism 91
train 47, 53
transport 47, 93, 200
travellers cheques 45, 67,76, 89, 184
tricycle 54

U

utensils (cooking) 172

V

vaccinations 188
vegan 173, 174
vegetarian 173, 174
verbs (grammar) 19, 32
video 81
visa 61, 186
Visayan (language) 117
volunteering 199
vowel sounds 11

W

Waray (language) 117
water (drinkable) 69, 72, 154, 197
weather 156
weights (amounts) 40, 172
well-wishing 115
wheelchairs 99, 100
women's health 191, 193
women travellers 183
word order (grammar) 33
word stress 13
work 97
writing Filipino 14

Y

youth hostel 65

When's the next flight to (San José)?	Kailán ang súsunód na flight sa (San José)?	ka·ee·*lan* ang *soo*·soo·nod na plait sa (*san* ho·*se*)
What's the next station?	Anó ang súsunód na istasyón?	a·*no* ang *soo*·soo·nod na ees·tas·*yon*
Where do I buy a ticket?	Saán ako bibilí ng tiket?	sa·*an* a·*ko* bee·bee·*lee* nang *tee*·ket
How much (to Tuba)?	Magkano (hanggáng sa Tuba)?	mag·*ka*·no (hang·*gang* sa *too*·ba)
Can you show me (on the map)?	Maáari bang ipakita mo sa akin (sa mapa)?	ma·a·*a*·ree bang ee·pa·*kee*·ta mo sa *a*·keen (sa *ma*·pa)
I'd like to hire a car.	Gustó kong umarkilá ng kotse.	goos·*to* kong oo·mar·kee·*la* nang *kot*·se
Do I need to book?	Dapat ba akóng mag-buk?	*da*·pat ba a·*kong* mag·*book*
Could you please help?	Puwede ka bang tumulong?	poo·*we*·de ka bang too·*moo*·long
How much is it?	Magkano?	mag·*ka*·no
That's too expensive.	Masyadong mahál.	mas·*ya*·dong ma·*hal*
Can you write down the price?	Pakisulat mo ang presyo?	pa·kee·*soo*·lat mo ang *pres*·yo